The Enlightened Pharisee

Donald Keenan

The Enlightened *Pharisee*

a novel

Pleasant Word
A Division of WinePress Group

Pleasant Word (a division of WinePress Publishing, PO Box 428, Enumclaw, WA 98022) functions only as book publisher. As such, the ultimate design, content, editorial accuracy, and views expressed or implied in this work are those of the author.

Hard Cover:
ISBN 13: 978-1-4141-1227-5
ISBN 10: 1-4141-1227-0

Soft Cover:
ISBN 13: 978-1-4141-1226-8
ISBN 10: 1-4141-1226-2

Library of Congress Catalog Card Number: 2008902961

Contents

Preface

THE FIRST TIME I walked into an adult Bible study class I was amazed to discover that most of the others there were as ignorant of the contents of the world's best-selling book as I was. We did not need to confess to our lack of knowledge; the questions we asked betrayed us. What was still more revealing about our group was our intense desire to learn. All of us realized something vital was missing in our lives, and we were desperate to find it—to grasp it.

Time passed, and bit by bit we all learned something about the story the Bible had to tell, but that little knowledge brought still more questions demanding answers. With the explanation of Bible passages came the need for background information. Who were the Pharisees? What was life like for the very first Christians? How far did Paul walk on his journeys?

Eventually the answers to these and other questions came and with them the suggestion of a story waiting to be told. When we were very young, many of us were read Bible stories that we enjoyed, but that interest soon disappeared when we were introduced to more exciting ways to spend the years of our youth. Now that we are more mature, we are beginning to realize what we have missed. The time has come for another Bible story—the one we didn't read in our teenage years.

Such a story can be found in the lives of others who lived long before us. Many of them shared our lack of knowledge and desperate search for the truth. They were the first century Christians. *The Enlightened Pharisee* is a novel about those early Christians. More than two hundred footnotes will help the reader separate fact from fiction and hopefully foster an interest in further Bible study.

Prologue

MANY CENTURIES BEFORE the events of this story began, Nebuchadnezzar, the Babylonian warrior-king, led his storm troopers into Jerusalem, destroyed Solomon's Temple and force-marched thousands of the most intelligent and capable of the Jews hundreds of miles to Babylon. The destruction of the Temple was a catastrophic loss for the exiles; the presence of God disappeared for them when the walls of the sanctuary came down.

But the Jews did not despair. Deprived of the Temple, they knew they must have a place where they could search for God through a study of the Torah, and they developed such a place: the synagogue. There they could meet, worship, and study. Those most intimately connected to the synagogue belonged to a closely-knit group dedicated to rigidly following the Law. As time passed, this group developed into a political-religious party known as *Pharisees*.

The strict adherence of the Pharisees to the Law demanded that certain words in it be defined. The duty of the Pharisaic scribes was to supply the necessary definitions. They met to study the Law, discuss it among themselves, and agree on what certain terms meant. This was a mammoth, never-ending task. As an example of what was entailed in this project, consider the commandment

God gave his people through Moses that forbade them to do any work on the Sabbath. The Pharisees realized that if work was not to be permitted their people must know every activity that could be considered work. After much deliberation, they determined writing to be one such activity, but then writing had to be defined. Eventually the scribes concluded that the use of more than two letters of the alphabet constituted writing. This definition evolved into a rule that forbade placing more than two characters on papyrus on the Sabbath. Disobeying the rule would be committing a sin. So on and on the scribes developed rule after rule they thought necessary to live a life pleasing to God.

The scribes who did this work were considered to be special among the Pharisees. Very often the scribal position was passed down from father to son. A family of Pharisees living in Alexandria had followed this custom through many generations. Silas, a fifteen-year-old boy of this family, had pledged to carry on the tradition of interpreting the Law by studying under his grandfather at the famous library at Alexandria, when suddenly his life took a different course and the story begins.

Chapter 1

Alexandria

"OH, FATHER, PLEASE don't do this to me! In just a few days I will have my fifteenth birthday and then everything I've been working for will be mine if we don't leave Alexandria. But if we move to Jerusalem I will lose it all." Silas paused to brush away a tear and then continued. "I can't believe it. In spite of the love I know we share, you have shattered the dream of my youth. I can't understand why you are now making it impossible for me to reach the goal I was told you set for me the day I was born."

Both Silas and his father became silent. Ten years earlier when Silas returned from his grandparents' home, he had run to Thomas and said, "Father I want to be just like Grandfather when I grow up. I want to go to the library every day and read and study like he does."

"Silas, that's wonderful! I had been hoping that you would want to be like your grandfather and I will do everything possible to make your dream come true. As I've told you often before, you are a very special boy. Your grandfather is a *research scribe,* and a very famous one at that. I will help you become just as great as he is."

On another visit Silas asked his grandfather, "Why does my father keep telling me I am a very special boy?"

"Silas, there are three reasons for what your father says to you so often," Matthew said. "The first and most important one is that, like your father and me, you are a Pharisee. There are not many of us in the entire world, but we know precisely what the Law says we can and cannot do, and that makes us special. Because we obey all our rules and regulations, we live perfect lives. We are truly the best of God's chosen people. The second reason is that you belong to a special family. For more than one hundred years the men of our family have devoted their lives to the study of the Law so they could determine the exact meaning for others less gifted. The third reason is that you live in Alexandria. It is known as the cultural, literary, and scientific capital of the world. When you are a little older, you will understand what these words mean, and that they explain why our city is the best place to study the Law."

"Grandfather, I understand most of what you say. I will study and work so I can become a special Pharisee and do all the good things that you do."

When seven-year-old Silas entered synagogue school, he had no doubt that he was indeed a very special individual. He began his formal education full of pride because of the knowledge that he had been born a Pharisee and was superior to most, if not all, of the boys in his class. Silas was sure that he was envied by the other scholars, especially those who were not Pharisees but hoped to be allowed to take their vows some day and become novitiates. A most pleasant stage of life began for Silas on that first day at the synagogue. It was the beginning of a perfect existence in a perfect city.

Silas waited patiently for his thirteenth birthday. Finally the day came, but it was a quiet, sober one when Matthew stood, approached his grandson, and looking very serious said, "Silas, the time has come for you to take the next step up the career ladder toward reaching your goal. I challenge you today to formally accept the responsibility to carry on the family tradition to study the Law and lead the disciplined life that this requires. Then, if you accept, when you graduate from the synagogue school at age fifteen, you will join me at the library. Here you will begin the advanced study necessary to become a research scribe."

"Grandfather, thank you. I accept the challenge and I promise to study long hours and make you proud of me. What has been only a dream for me has today become a solemn pledge as well. I know now that my life has a definite purpose. It is to study the Law and search for, find, and tell others the truth."

Almost two years later when all Jews were looking forward to celebrating the Passover season, Silas's father said, "Silas, it's such a beautiful day, let's go for a walk. The morning sun has already chased the fog away. There isn't a cloud left in the sky and the wind off the sea will keep the temperature comfortably cool. Let's wander down to the shore."

"I'm ready. Let's go. I don't know why you thought it was necessary to tempt me to go with you by describing the beauty of the day. You should know by now that there is nothing I would rather do than stroll along the waterfront. It always reminds me of the perfect life I'm living. Any little worry I might have seems to dissolve in the salt air whenever I'm down by the water."

No matter how often Silas came to the edge of the Great Sea, he would always marvel at the sight of the tiered tower of the Pharos Lighthouse. He recalled one day when he was just a small boy and he asked his father, "Does the Pharos Lighthouse stretch all the way up to heaven?"

"Well it doesn't go up quite that high, but it does reach far enough into the sky that ships far, far out on the water can see this famous wonder of the world. Then they know that Alexandria is hidden in the distance."

Alexandria! Yes, Alexandria! Whenever Silas had heard that word in recent years he could only think about the wonderful city where he would live for the rest of his life, devoting himself to the study of the Law.

"I live in the most beautiful spot in the world," Silas said with his first glimpse of the seascape. "Look, Father, the harbor is bustling with activity, but it's a quiet activity because the sea is so calm today. The ships coming and going just seem to be drifting along in the gentle breeze. The crews actually look relaxed, as they seem to enjoy the light wind that's giving them an easy time. I would much rather see a day like this, than one when the ships are being battered by huge waves.

"I do not want to think about days like that. They remind me of the one I just suffered through, arguing with a misguided liberal friend who thought that ceremonial washing before the Passover meal was foolishness. My progressive-minded friends upset me with their new ideas. I'm glad we've come to the harbor where the peaceful surroundings will help me forget about my friends with their disturbing fanciful whims.

"Look, Father, out there on the deep water. Can you see that ship just now slipping into view over the horizon? It is probably from some faraway country. And look there above us, closer to shore, those soundless gulls are gliding by full of grace and beauty, possibly admiring the food within easy reach below them. This is exactly the kind of day I always hope for when we come down to the harbor."

Thomas did not respond. Silas did not mind his father's silence, it just added to the serenity of the shore. Then Thomas suddenly began to speak. "I brought you to your special place today for a long look at the harbor because you may never see it again. You will leave Alexandria with your mother and me within the next day or two to move to Jerusalem. We will start off just as soon as we can make the necessary final arrangements!"

Silas's jaw dropped. He could only wonder why his father would want to leave the city that had been their family home since long ago when his ancestor had arrived in Alexandria from Jerusalem to study the Law. He and his descendants had become very prominent Pharisees in the city.

His father was well educated and well prepared for a career at Alexandria. He was fluent in Hebrew and Aramaic, in addition to Greek. He was a scribe like Silas's grandfather, and was a devout Pharisee.

His decision just didn't make sense to Silas, but Silas continued his respectful silence. Just when he began to wonder if he had heard the last word on the subject, Thomas started to speak again, this time in a much softer tone of voice. "Silas, let me explain my position. Because there appears to be one lawyer for every street in the Jewish quarter of Alexandria, I can barely scrape out a living here by writing letters for the illiterate among us. I realize that I could carry on like this for the rest of my days, but I believe the prospects in Jerusalem will be much better.

"Of course, Silas, I have considered your future too. I want to give you the life you deserve. You already have a good education, and I am sure that you are mature enough to adjust to living in a new city. I believe there will even be opportunities in Jerusalem for the advanced study you desire."

Silas could not understand why his father had not mentioned the promise he had made to his grandfather. Surely he did not believe it could be carried to completion anywhere but in Alexandria. He could not accept as the truth the reason his father had given for depriving him of the chance to fulfill the pledge he had made to continue the family tradition. The visionary, faraway expression on his father's face told Silas that he had not been told the true reason for his decision to leave Alexandria.

Before long Thomas began to speak once more, "Silas, I know that Jerusalem is not the place you would choose to make your home, but listen to what else I have to say. I have not told you the complete story. For some time now I have experienced an irresistible and unexplainable urge to go to Jerusalem. It is something that I do not understand. There seems to be a compelling, supernatural force pulling me there, just as if the destiny of our family is waiting to be fulfilled in that city.

"The pressure became so strong that a few weeks ago I realized I had no choice but to leave Alexandria. Since then I have wondered many times if I am making the wrong decision. Sometimes I feel I should stay in the city I know so well and love so much rather than move to a city that I have never even visited.

"I know there is a strong argument for remaining where I am. Alexandria has become a great melting pot of people from all over the world, and like most cities of our time, it has a large Greek-speaking Jewish population. There are almost as many Jews living in Alexandria as in Jerusalem, and it is second only to Jerusalem as the focal point of Judaism. We live at peace in the delta district, unmolested by the authorities and with religious freedom. It seems like an ideal place for any Pharisee to live and work.

"But, Silas, I cannot resist any longer this strange force pulling me to Jerusalem, and I cannot help but believe that this force concerns you even more than it does me and it supersedes your family obligation. Sometimes I feel that the pull on you may even come from beyond Jerusalem. It is almost as if I have received a vision of a great future for you far away from both Alexandria and Jerusalem. At any rate, I have made the decision, and there can be no turning back."

Silas was still shocked both by his father's irrational decision and the unbelievable reason he gave for making it. When Silas recovered sufficiently he began to speak once more, "Father, it grieves me that I will probably not be able to fulfill my pledge to Grandfather. Nevertheless, because of my deep religious belief and because I am loyal to you, I have no alternative but to submit to your will—even though I fear it will mean the end to the dream we shared."

"Silas, I understand how you feel, but I do not believe that your future will turn out to be as hopeless as you now think it will. I have done everything possible in the past to help you achieve your goal, and I will continue to do that in the future no matter where we live." After a brief, awkward silence Thomas said, "Now let's make one last tour of our beloved city."

So Silas went on with his father, shocked and bewildered by the strange story he had just heard. Surely his father did not believe that he had received a message from God. The prophets had been silent for four hundred years. The one thing he did know was that it was the saddest day of his young life. He feared that he would soon walk the streets of his beloved city for the last time.

Silas reluctantly followed his father away from the waterfront. It was the ninth hour when they began their walk back toward the city. That was the time appointed for the afternoon prayers, so they stopped where they were to recite those prescribed by the traditional law.

Most uncircumcised pagans passed by respectfully, but a few stared at them with curiosity. Of course, Silas would not have anything to do with sinners like them. As a Pharisee he was concerned only with the souls of his own kind and not the souls of infidels. When the prayers were over, they continued on and soon reached the huge city gate where they entered the wide main avenue of Alexandria.

As they walked along, Silas, still speechless, was lost in disturbed thought about his future. He was numb from the shock that his father's announcement had sent through him. This time he paid very little attention to the streets he knew so well, streets that intersected the main avenue at right angles. The orderly design of this grid pattern made it much easier for visitors to find their way around Alexandria, and the pattern often reminded Silas of the Pharisaic belief. Just as the precise structure of the streets kept people from getting lost in the city, the multitude of the Pharisees' rules and regulations kept his people from getting lost in sin.

From time to time they switched sides of the street, but no matter which side they chose to walk on Silas was spared the sun's heat by a covering supported by a majestic colonnade. Silas's grandfather had equated this protection from the hot sun to the protection the Pharisaic belief gave God's chosen people.

Passing by many magnificent buildings that Silas had trouble believing he might never see again, he and his father soon reached the main north-south street. Alexandria's world-famous library was located at this intersection.

Silas could barely force himself to look at the building where he had expected to spend the rest of his working life. The library was the clearinghouse for the most enlightened ideas of the great thinkers of the times. Its collection of thousands of volumes was the work of leading figures in science, art, and literature from around the world.

At this library Silas's grandfather spent countless hours helping to copy, revise, collate, and edit many works of the classical Greek writers as well as to study the Law. He had once told Silas that 490,000 papyrus scrolls had been catalogued. There should have been more listed, but Julius Caesar had destroyed many scrolls during his invasion of Egypt sixty years or so before Silas was born.

Regardless of that, the library housed what was by far the largest collection of scrolls in the world. As the library passed out of sight, Silas realized that his youthful dream was fading away with it.

Of all the stories his grandfather had told him about the library, the one he liked most was about the seventy Jewish scholars who had translated the Hebrew Scriptures into the Greek language. He realized that this great work, which was known as the *Septuagint*, was important because most of the Jews in Alexandria had no knowledge of the Hebrew language but were fluent in Greek.

Finally the time came to leave the main part of the city and return to the Jewish quarter. Soon one more familiar sight came into view: the synagogue that had been a very important part of Silas's young life. He was comforted by the knowledge that the synagogue wherever it was in the world was the domain of the Pharisees and that he would find more than one of them in Jerusalem.

For the first time he realized there would be something else for him and his parents in Jerusalem, something he longed to see—the Temple. Silas knew that although the Temple was under the control of the Sadducees, the rival political-religious party to the Pharisees, it was there for all Jews. In this most holy building, and nowhere else, Jews had direct access to God, and then only by the high priest's intercession when he went behind the curtain that separated his people from God.

As Silas turned to take one last look at the synagogue, he saw a tear running down his father's face. Then the silent final tour of Alexandria was finished and it was time to return home where Silas's mother Deborah would be preparing the evening meal.

Early the next morning Thomas spoke to his son, "Silas, you must call on your grandfather because he has asked to meet with you before you say your last good-bye, which is now only a few days away."

"Of course I will go, but I fear that we will not have the pleasant time we usually share."

Along the way to his grandfather's house Silas recalled a previous meeting. On the day after his thirteenth birthday party his grandfather had said, "Silas, I was bitterly disappointed many years ago when your father decided not to become a research scribe but to become a lawyer instead. Your decision yesterday removed the last traces of my disappointment and redeemed your father. I am very pleased that you have made the proper choice for your life. Now, today, I give you my blessing and with that I will tell you that the future course our proud family takes depends completely on you.

"As you know, your ancestors contributed a great deal to the Jewish people over the past one hundred years by preserving, interpreting, and teaching the Word of God, and by living an exemplary life. Because of the obligation you assumed yesterday, you must do everything possible to ensure that your successors will dedicate their lives to the same purpose. I'm looking forward to the day when you will join me at the great library of Alexandria and begin to carry on the family tradition. It will be a wonderful time for both of us."

Silas had become very nervous by the time he reached his grandfather's home. He feared that Grandfather might be angry because of his father's decision to leave Alexandria. When his grandfather greeted him at the door, however, Silas's fear was replaced by admiration for the man he adored.

His grandfather stood at the entrance tall and erect, dressed for another busy day at the library. His beard had been trimmed and perfumed. His embroidered upper garment was made of the finest white fabric and, as always, looked as if it had just come from the fuller's. Very large tassels on his robe would draw attention to his grandfather's status as he walked the streets of Alexandria full of the pride of his station in life.

Under the robe, his inner garment reached down to just above the floor. His seal was suspended on a chain around his neck. He preferred to wear it that way rather than as a ring so his hands had more freedom for writing. Silas's grandfather obeyed all the rules and regulations of the party and made sure his dress attested to this.

His leather phylacteries, one on the wrist and one on the forehead, contained his favorite passages of the Scriptures. The best part of Matthew's appearance was the welcoming smile on his face.

"Silas," he said, "I am very disappointed with my son's plan to leave Egypt, but I will not stand in his way, and I understand that you must go with him. This, however, does not relieve you of the promise you made to me some time ago. You will still have the responsibility for preserving the special relationship our family has enjoyed with our God over the past one hundred or more years.

"When you leave Alexandria you will no longer have the resources of our fine library to help you interpret the Law of Moses, but I will make arrangements for you to continue your studies in Jerusalem with Gamaliel, the most learned rabbi in that city.

"In three years you will be of age. At that time you must leave your parents and return here to resume your life's work. Going away will not be as distressing now that you know your stay in Jerusalem will be temporary."

"Thank you, Grandfather, for giving me a second chance to reach my goal and fulfill my pledge." Silas said, and he smiled.

"Now, Silas, I must leave for the library and the work that waits for me there, but I want you to know that to make it easier for your family in Jerusalem, I have contacted an old friend and have asked him to help you in every way possible. Nicodemus is a prominent Pharisee, and I'm sure that you will benefit by a relationship with him. I wrote to him some time ago when I first learned of your father's interest in Jerusalem. I hope to hear from him before you leave."

"Thank you, Grandfather. No one could possibly replace you as my mentor, but having your friend as a counselor makes me feel less apprehensive about moving to Jerusalem, as does your telling me that I only have to spend three years there."

Silas stood watching his grandfather walk proudly away. For years Silas had dreamed of dressing like him and ostentatiously parading the streets of Alexandria just as he had always done. Then, yesterday, he thought that this would never be. Now after this encouraging visit, it once more seemed possible, but until he became a mature Pharisee he would have to be content with a simple, pure white, ankle-length robe that was appropriate for his age.

Something else was bothering Silas, and it had nothing to do with his personal appearance. He was worried about his father's wellbeing. Since the disclosure of his plan to leave Alexandria, his father seemed to be deeply troubled, as if he was worried that by following what he called an irresistible urge, he had made the wrong decision. Silas feared that he might agonize so much about his decision that it would seriously affect his health.

Chapter 2

Exodus

WHEN SILAS RETURNED home, his father was waiting for him, anxious to hear all about the meeting he had just had with his grandfather. As he walked through the door his father asked, "Well, how was it?"

"Father, I feel so much better because of my visit with Grandfather. He convinced me that leaving Alexandria will not be as damaging to my career as I thought it would be. He is making arrangements for me to continue my studies in Jerusalem under Gamaliel, who he says is the most learned rabbi in the city. Of course, this will not be the same as studying with Grandfather, but it will have to do, and it will give me the opportunity to work toward my goal and keep my promise."

"Silas, I am relieved by what you have said. It will help me shed my doubt about the decision I made to leave Alexandria. I feel more relaxed now than I have for the past several weeks. Working with Gamaliel will be an honor, and I am sure that you will enjoy your time with him as you fulfill your destiny in Jerusalem."

Oh, no! Father believes I intend to make Jerusalem my permanent home. I must not mention my plan to return to Alexandria in three years. The truth would be too hurtful now. It will come later.

"And, Father, Grandfather has contacted a friend in Jerusalem asking him to give us any help we might need. He is a Pharisee named Nicodemus. Grandfather has known him for many years as a faithful and reliable friend."

Silas paused again. He could see that his father's demeanor had been transformed completely. He was almost smiling! Silas was relieved that his father's attitude had appeared to improve so rapidly and so dramatically. Perhaps he had found peace with his decision at last.

Of course Silas loved his slim, tall father and would do almost anything for him. He knew Thomas followed the Law even though he had no desire to interpret it. He was a conscientious lay scribe, dedicated to his career. His kind eyes testified to the free legal service he provided those unable to pay his modest fees.

His hairline had begun to recede early in life, probably because of the stress and strain of his job. Silas wished his father would wear proper robes like his grandfather and not look like one of the most humble of Pharisees, but Silas respected his father and admired him in spite of his plain clothing.

The next day Silas said, "Father, Passover is only three weeks away. I hope that we will be in Jerusalem for the celebration and not somewhere along the way."

"Unless the two donkeys I bought this morning slow us down too much we will be there before the festival begins. Of course, being the owner of these animals is a new experience for me. Lawyers in Alexandria usually have no need for pack animals. I will observe them carefully for the rest of the day to get acquainted with them."

"What will you look for?" Silas asked.

"I have no idea, but I'll let you know what I find." Silas could see that his father was enjoying ownership of the two animals.

At the end of the day, Silas asked his father, "Are you and the donkeys good friends by now? And what did you find out about them?"

"Well they seem to know me, and because I've seen nothing alarming, I assume they are fit to go on the long journey with us.

We will start out early the day after the Sabbath." After making this important decision, Thomas suggested they join Deborah for dinner.

Two mornings later Silas and his father began to pack all their belongings and enough food for two weeks into four large wicker baskets. They included a tent to sleep under in case it should rain. In fair weather they would sleep under the stars, using their cloaks for cover if needed. They placed leather groundsheets over the backs of the donkeys, suspended ropes over the groundsheets, and attached one basket on each side of the two animals.

As soon as Thomas and Silas had finished loading the donkeys, the three travelers started off. They would stop on the way to bid Silas's grandparents good-bye. As they approached his home, Silas could see his grandfather standing in the courtyard reading a small scroll. After greeting the family, Matthew handed the scroll to his son and said, "I just received this message, and it's for you."

Silas was worried. For the first time ever he could see a sign of distress on his grandfather's face. Apparently, Thomas saw the worried expression as well because his hands shook as he took the scroll from his father, but as soon as he started to read, the nervousness disappeared.

"Why, it's a message from your friend Nicodemus. This is what he has to say: 'I was pleasantly surprised to hear that you and your family have decided to move to Jerusalem. I have known your father for many years and am looking forward to continuing our friendship through you.

"'I will do everything possible to help you get settled comfortably. Unfortunately, because of the great influx of pilgrims into Jerusalem for the Passover, it will be impossible for you to find suitable living quarters in the city until after the festival. If I had known earlier, I would have been most happy to accommodate you in my own home.

"'I have, however, been able to obtain temporary housing with a family in Bethany, a quiet town just two miles southeast of Jerusalem. I regret that the people are not Pharisees, but they are very religious and follow the strict dietary laws and most of the important Pharisaic rules and regulations.'"

Silas was not happy to hear this. He had never associated closely with common Jews and was not looking forward to living with them, even for just a few days. He was surprised to learn that his grandfather's friend was so liberal-minded, and he wondered if this was how Pharisees acted when they moved to Jerusalem.

Thomas continued to read. "'Because it is mandatory to have the Passover meal within the city walls, I am pleased to invite your small family to my home for the feast.'"

Silas was thankful to hear this. He only hoped that his grandfather's friend would observe Passover properly.

Silas realized that the letter had not caused the worried look on his grandfather's face. Only their move to Jerusalem had troubled him.

The travelers said good-bye to Matthew and Sarah, and started off on their journey. They had not gone far when Silas asked his father how long it would take to walk to Jerusalem.

"Even though we will not be traveling on the Sabbath, I reckon we will cover the two hundred miles in about twelve days and arrive in Jerusalem a full week before the Passover."

Silas was pleased to hear that. He was looking forward to celebrating the festival in the holy city. He was forced to admit to himself that he now recognized one more advantage of living in Jerusalem—being there for important celebrations.

Before long they left the Jewish quarter of Alexandria, and Silas reflected on a previous journey to the Promised Land that had begun thirteen hundred years earlier.[1] Led by Moses, the entire nation of Israel had left Egypt and wandered in the wilderness for forty years before reaching their final destination.

He was very thankful that he and his parents would not have to endure such a hardship. They would take a much shorter route, would not be pursued by the Egyptian army, and would not have to cross the Red Sea. Their journey would take a great deal less than forty days, let alone forty years. The conditions prevailing on their arrival would be much different also. They would not encounter armed resistance from the people living in their adopted country.

That would not guarantee that their arrival would be trouble free. Silas had been told at synagogue school that there was often some exhibition of hostility against Rome in Jerusalem, especially during Passover.

Later that morning, just after they had been ferried across the Nile River, they met a caravan of Jewish traders who had stopped to replenish their water supply. Thomas went to the leader to find out where the caravan was headed. When he discovered that it would pass near Jerusalem on the way to Syria, he asked permission to join the other travelers.

Although Silas did not relish the thought of traveling with so many disreputable-looking people, he was still relieved when the leader agreed. Traveling with a large group would offer more protection from thieves who might be waiting along the way. The only weapons of defense that he and his father had were the flimsy staffs they intended to use for support in walking, and Silas was sure their staffs would be useless to ward off an attack by armed robbers.

As soon as they attached themselves to the caravan, it started off into the midmorning sun to follow the narrow corridor along the shore of the Great Sea. Although they met other travelers from time to time, the road was lonely. They passed milepost after milepost seeing no one, but the road was a good one; the Romans were builders, and building roads was their passion.

When the caravan stopped at the end of the day, a few fellow travelers wandered over to talk to Silas. One of them said, "We don't have young boys traveling with us very often. Where are you from?"

"Alexandria."

Silas was not anxious to become friends with any of his rough-looking traveling companions. He had hoped his curt reply would send them away, but that was not to be.

"Alexandria," another man said, "I've heard that it's an amazing city. Aren't there some wonderful things there?"

"Yes, there are many wonderful things there. Alexander, a famous Greek king, hired the greatest architect in the world to create the greatest city in the world in a place where nothing had existed before. Deinokatris used the wealth of Egypt to build a library, museums, and theaters—all of them treasures. Alexandria is the most wonderful place in the world in which to live."

One of the crowd asked Silas, "Did you bring anything of value with you from this famous city?"

Anxious to get away from the obnoxious nobodies, Silas replied, "Yes indeed, I left Alexandria with a valuable treasure." He walked off to join his father without explaining that the treasure he referred to was his heritage and his education. Having had his fill of annoying travelers, Silas asked his father if they could set up camp away from the others.

"Silas, I think that's a good idea, and not just for tonight. We are the only Pharisees in the caravan, and I would not be comfortable camping so close to the others. I believe we should isolate ourselves when we stop each night."

Often, during the first two days of what had been an uneventful journey, Silas talked to his father about the Passover feast that would take place soon after their arrival in Jerusalem. The fervent desire of every male Jew over the age of twelve was to attend the Passover in Jerusalem at least once during his lifetime, and neither he nor his father had yet accomplished this goal.

Thomas reminded Silas that when they were settled in Jerusalem they would be able to attend every year. "In fact," he said, "we will *have* to do that because it is mandatory for all male Jews of age who live within fifteen miles of Jerusalem to observe each and every Passover celebration there."

Silas was still unhappy about leaving Alexandria, but he was beginning to understand that Jerusalem did offer some interesting opportunities. The festival was important, not only to Silas but to all Jews, because it commemorated their delivery from slavery in Egypt under Moses' leadership. At that time, God's tenth and final plague brought death to the firstborn of the Egyptians, but it passed over the homes of the Israelites because they were identified by blood of the lamb smeared on their doorposts.

This event was the origin of the Passover celebration. Silas had learned at a very early age that it was the most important of three compulsory annual feasts. The other two were the Feast of Pentecost, which was a harvest celebration, and the Day of Atonement, a very important day because it was a time to mourn for Israel's sins. When Silas had learned about the feasts, he had had no idea that the day would come when he would celebrate all of them in Jerusalem.

At the end of the third day, Thomas found an isolated spot as usual where they could enjoy their evening meal in peace far from the noisy group of travel-hardened companions. He tethered the donkeys to a tree some distance away from the camels of the caravan and the place where they would be eating and sleeping.

He and Silas untied the ropes and lowered the baskets from the donkeys' backs, placing them on the ground. They took their leather sheets, cloaks, and food for their dinner to the place where Deborah was waiting.

She portioned out some bread, cheese, and dried fish, making sure that enough was left for the rest of their journey.

Thomas poured the wine and wished Silas a happy birthday. Silas couldn't believe that he had completely forgotten about the day that should have been so important to him. After they finished eating, Thomas began to speak of Jerusalem, but his attempt soon came to an end.

Silas said, "Father, I'm very tired tonight. Do you mind if I retire now?"

"No. I understand. In fact I think it's time for all of us to get some sleep and rebuild our strength for tomorrow's walk. The weather's clear so there's no need to raise the tent."

"I'll spread my ground sheet under the tree over there," said Silas. "I'll keep my cloak nearby for cover in case the temperature should drop more than usual during the night."

Thomas and Deborah did the same and soon the family was settled down for some much needed rest. After a while, the usual soothing night noises of nature began to have their effect and Silas's eyes closed. He had not slept long when not knowing why, he woke with a start. At first he could only hear the same peaceful noises that had sent him to sleep. Then he heard a different sound. It was not loud, and it was not made by night insects or leaves fluttering in the breeze. A minute or two later it came again. He had heard the same noise somewhere before a short time earlier but perhaps because he was only half-awake now he could not remember where it had been. Deborah and Thomas still slept.

The next time he heard the noise, he jumped up fully awake. "Now I know where it is coming from," he said to himself. "It's coming from the direction of the tree where we tied the donkeys." The sliver of moon that he had seen in the sky when he retired was now covered by a dense cloud and the night was pitch-black. "I'm afraid some wild animal is attacking our donkeys. But that can't be because if the donkeys were being attacked by a wild animal, they would be braying fiercely." Instinctively, Silas reached for his flimsy staff, and shivering with fear, forced himself to stand and take his first step into the darkness.

Now the only sound came from the usual night noises, but they were no longer comforting. Silas wanted to think he had been dreaming, but was unable to convince himself that this was so. His next thought was somewhat reassuring. *If the sound I heard had been made by humans, it would have been made by bandits who had come to steal the donkeys, and they would have left with the animals by now. So there is no danger of humans still lurking in the area.*

There's that noise again and now I know what it is. It's the creaky noise our wicker baskets make whenever we handle them. I should have recognized it before. I've heard it every night when my father and I unload the donkeys. Now I'm really worried. The thieves are still here. They're loading the baskets on the donkeys preparing to steal not only our means of transportation but all of our worldly possessions as well.

He began to creep silently away in the direction from which the occasional basket-stretching sound came. He had not gone far when the moon peeked out from the cloud cover and he could see several feet in front of him.

Thank God. There is only one man there. But he is much bigger than I am! He's kneeling down and gathering the spilled contents of one of the baskets. Silas assumed the thief did not want to leave without stealing everything. That's why he was taking so long. If the intruder had not dropped one of the baskets he would have been gone long ago. *I must do something to salvage my family's possessions and I have to do it now*, he thought.

Summoning up his courage, Silas decided to rush the man. With a sudden lunge and the most blood-curdling yell he could manage, he attacked. The startled and weaponless thief turned, ducked under Silas's staff, kicked him in the groin, and ran. Silas fell to the ground, doubled up with pain. Silas's frantic screaming brought Thomas running. Deborah was not far behind. Silas's father knelt and held his son until the pain wore off, then he listened to Silas's story.

A few minutes later most of the camp came stumbling through the darkness to see what all the fuss was about and Thomas proudly explained what his son had done. When he finished his tale, he looked directly at the leader of the caravan, "You obviously misinformed us when you assured us earlier that there were no bandits near this area."

"That was no local bandit who attacked the boy," the leader replied. "I was afraid this would happen sooner or later. One individual traveling with us talked constantly about the riches he knew were in one of your baskets. I believe he was the assailant, and he was searching for the treasure your son said he had brought from Alexandria. When we return to our campsite we will most likely find that he is no longer with us, and that will be good news."

For the first time ever, in spite of his show of courage, Silas was humbled and embarrassed—and on his fifteenth birthday. He apologized to his father for the danger he had subjected them to by his bragging, and then listened sheepishly to a lecture on a few topics that he had never been taught at the synagogue school. At the end of the lecture, though, his father smiled broadly and said, "Already, this journey is making you a man!"

Silas woke up the next morning, a much more mature boy because of his nighttime learning experience. When the caravan began to assemble, Silas thought his father looked taller, stronger, and more secure than he had the night before. His robe looked clean and almost sparkling white. His beard was well brushed, but of course, without either oil or perfume. His receding hair line and the touch of grey in his beard made him look distinguished indeed.

Thomas showed his pride in his son, and it seemed to Silas that he and his father were both receiving more respect than usual from the other travelers as they greeted them with a friendly smile. When the caravan started out, the leader told Thomas that they were leaving with one man less than had been with them on the previous day.

Early on the eleventh day, the leader of the caravan informed Thomas that it would be their last one together. He estimated that they would part in late morning when they reached the east-west crossroad that led to Bethany. Just before the sixth hour, Silas and his family left the caravan as it continued on its way north toward Damascus. By the ninth hour of the following day they could see Bethany in the distance.

A short time later they walked into what to Silas looked like a sleepy little town. No people milled around as they would in Alexandria in the late afternoon. Then, just as he thought the place was deserted, he saw a lone man walking toward him and his family. When the man was close enough, Thomas greeted him and asked if he knew where the Jerusalem-Jericho Road was.

"You're walking on it," the man replied. "The east-west road takes on that name as it enters Bethany."

"Thank you," Thomas replied. "That makes our job easier. This is the road the house we're looking for is located on."

"Good luck," was all the man said as he continued on his lonely way.

Silas was beginning to realize that his father had known what he was talking about when he promised that Bethany would be a peaceful town because it was located on the quiet eastern slope of the Mount of Olives. It would be a comfortable retreat they could return to each evening to escape the hectic activity in Jerusalem, less than an hour's walk away.

As they moved along, Silas was happy with all he saw. The town where they expected to live for a few days would at least be safe and secure. Nothing disturbing would be likely to happen. Silas actually began to look forward to some peaceful time to adjust to his new life and get over the disappointment he felt because he had left Alexandria. He anticipated that Jerusalem would soon give him all the excitement he could endure.

Before long Thomas said, "Here it is. This looks like the house Nicodemus described."

"Father, I must admit that our temporary home seems to be well located and I'm sure that it will be quite comfortable for the short time we will have to stay there. Look, it shares a courtyard with the house next door, and both houses have been built with field stone. There must be lots of them on the Mount of Olives. I can see the top of a tree showing up over the rear of the house. We can tether the donkeys there."

An elderly man met them at the door, gave Thomas a warm welcome, and told him to bring his family in to meet his wife and to prepare for the evening meal. After dinner with John and Mary, Silas and his father unloaded the donkeys where they were tied to the tree behind the house. For the first time in almost two weeks, the weary travelers would not be spending the night outside under the stars. They would sleep comfortably in a bed inside one of the four rooms of their guest home. Visitors to the festival were not charged for accommodations no matter where they lived, but Silas knew that his parents would find countless ways to repay their host and hostess.

Silas woke up the next morning refreshed and ready to celebrate the Sabbath when it would begin at sunset. His mother spent the preparation day helping Mary with her chores. Silas and his father, on John's advice, sold the two donkeys in nearby Bethphage and received more than Thomas had paid for them in Alexandria.

After the sale, on their way home, Silas said, "Do you see that man about to tie an ass and a colt to the tree right at the edge of the road? That seems like a strange place to leave his animals; they could be stolen by anyone passing by."

"Perhaps that's a good sign, Silas. The people here may be more honest than some we have run across recently."

Silas and his father returned to Bethany just before sunset. When they entered the home, they removed their shoes and washed their feet in preparation for the observance of the Sabbath. John anointed their heads with scented olive oil, and they joined the others at the table which had been lighted by two candles and set with the wine cup and the Sabbath bread.

After John said a blessing, he sanctified the wine and offered a prayer of thanksgiving for the bread. Next the wine cup was passed along so that each person could drink from it. Then Mary brought in the lentil stew, and one after another those at the table dipped a piece of bread into the pot for a serving. The two families finished the meal with a fish and more bread.

The following morning the five of them went to the synagogue. Although it was somewhat different from the one Silas had attended for so many years, he still felt comfortable there. John, Thomas, and Silas joined the men in the main inner room, while Deborah and Mary went with the women to the loft above. Silas was relieved to see that the inferior position of women was recognized in Bethany just as it was in Alexandria. Apparently, the liberal thinkers had done nothing to disturb the rightful position of men in Bethany. He wondered what conditions would be in Jerusalem.

The service began with several blessings offered to God, followed by a recitation of the Shema. "Hear, O Israel: the Lord our God, the Lord is one. Love the Lord your God with all your heart, and with all your soul, and with all your strength."[2] Next the hazzan, the assistant to the synagogue's ruler, brought out scrolls of the Torah. Then several members of the congregation, one by one, read assigned portions of the Law. Then came a reading from the Prophets and a short sermon. The Aramaic blessing, given as a benediction, ended the service.

When they left the synagogue, Silas said, "Father, it's a comfort for me to know that wherever in the world we might be, the rituals of the Sabbath meal and the synagogue service will be the same."

"Yes. That's very true. And now, again, as we usually do, we will spend the remainder of the day in quiet meditation, but this time we will do it in the comforting silence of Bethany. After that we will look forward to another peaceful night's sleep."

"And what about tomorrow, Father?"

"It will be a very special day. You and I will leave the early-morning peace and quiet of Bethany and take a leisurely stroll into Jerusalem. Then we will visit the Temple for the first time and spend the day in meditation and prayer away from the noisy city outside."

Chapter 3

False Prophet

SILAS WAS AWAKENED by shouting and yelling in the distance. It seemed to come from up the road toward Bethphage. He dressed quickly, opened the door, and saw a crowd of nondescript people milling about outside. Bethany was no longer a deserted town. People were shoulder to shoulder along the road that was covered with a blanket of garments and tree branches. This puzzled Silas. He knew from the Scriptures that the pathway of a king or a warrior was often covered with articles of clothing or branches from trees,[1] but whom could this crowd be waiting for? They seemed to be looking for someone up the road where all the noise was coming from. Suddenly they began to cheer. He heard his name being called, and when he looked around he saw his father rushing toward him to see what the commotion was about.

When the cheering became still louder, Silas turned from his father to see that a procession, led by a lone man riding on a colt and leading a donkey, had just come into view.[2] It didn't seem possible that such a peaceful-looking man could cause such a disturbance. As the man got closer to where Silas and his father were standing, the crowd in front of them began to chant, "Hosanna to the Son of David! Blessed is he who comes in the name of the Lord! Hosanna in the highest."

Silas could not believe what he heard. He knew *Hosanna* was a plea to be saved, but he also knew that his people would be saved by a warrior mounted on a horse, the symbol of war, and not by a man sitting on a colt, the symbol of peace. *Son of David* was the name reserved for the Messiah who they must know would come as a conquering military hero to defeat the Romans and drive them out of the country. Surely this mild-mannered man could not claim to be the Messiah. "Father, what do you think about all this?" Silas turned to get his father's reaction to the farce they were witnessing only to find that he was no longer beside him. They had become separated by those milling about around them. He heard him, though, sounding very disturbed and asking someone in the crowd, "Who is he that you are screaming about?"

The reply came from a noisy person next to Silas. Pointing to the man riding on the ass who was now almost directly in front of them, he said, "He is the prophet Jesus from Nazareth of Galilee."

Silas rushed toward the area from which his father's voice had seemed to come. When he found his father, he was about to tell him that the two animals with the leader of the procession looked very much like the pair they had seen tied to the tree in Bethphage, suggesting that the man riding the ass had stolen them, but he kept still. Thomas had been so agitated by all that he had heard that he was trembling. Silas had never seen his father so upset. The expression on his face had changed from the usual one of kindness to one of terrifying rage.

Silas and Thomas continued to stare at the man riding on the ass and the ten or twelve others walking behind him who seemed to be attendants. The procession passed by and disappeared into the distance. The crowd began to disperse.

Thomas seemed to be in shock, but when he recovered he told Silas that he would leave as soon as possible for the city. "I must find Nicodemus," he said. "I'm sure that my father's longtime friend will know something about this man who has upset me so much. I want you to go with me."

Silas was elated to be treated like an adult and invited to go with his father. Although he was still beardless, he was almost as tall as his father. Silas wondered if his height was the reason he was being treated like a man and an equal for the first time, or if his father was acknowledging his maturity to help him further overcome his disappointment about leaving Alexandria. At any rate, Silas thought it was wonderful to be considered a mature Pharisee and he was anxious to join his father and help him find out what they could about this strange man called Jesus.

As they walked back to the house Silas said, "Father, I believe that the man we saw riding the ass is one of those false prophets we heard about in Alexandria."

"Nicodemus will know whether he is or not, and that is why we are going to visit him."

Silas was relieved to see that his father had calmed down and the expression on his face was not nearly as hostile.

"Perhaps your grandfather did not tell you, but Nicodemus is much more than just a very dear friend. He is one of the most prominent Pharisees living in Jerusalem at the present time and he is a member of the Sanhedrin. Although most of the members of the Jewish Supreme Court are Sadducees, even the few, like Nicodemus, who belong to our Pharisee party would be fully aware of any matter brought before it.

"I believe it's highly likely that the behavior of this Jesus person has already come to the attention of the court. If this is so, Nicodemus will be familiar with all that was said and will tell us what he knows about the man. Neither your mother nor our hosts came out to see what was causing the disturbance, so let's return to them and let them know what we have seen and heard and have decided to do."

Silas was surprised by the lack of reaction from John and Mary when they heard what his father had to say, and he wondered if it was possible that they were sympathetic to the group that had been cheering a false prophet. He was not surprised by his mother's reaction. She was worried that her husband and son were headed for trouble because they were going into Jerusalem so soon after the demonstration had taken place.

Nevertheless, Silas and his father bade Deborah, John, and Mary good-bye after morning prayer and set out to Nicodemus's home. Peace and quiet had returned to Bethany.

As they started toward the city, they followed the same road that the procession had taken just a short time before. They walked without either one saying a word until Silas told his father about his suspicion that their hosts were supporters of the heretic. When Silas received no response, he realized that his father was lost in thought about the very upsetting scene they had witnessed earlier.

For the remainder of their walk, neither one of them made an effort to talk. Silas climbed the gentle slope almost mechanically, placing one foot in front of the other. As they reached the rounded top of the Mount of Olives the silence was broken by a surprising shout of joy from Thomas. Silas looked up and there, spread out in front of him was the Kidron Valley and beyond it the city of Jerusalem. The view was magnificent, but the thrill he experienced was caused by the realization that he was seeing the holy city of his people for the first time. The panorama of beauty that he saw as he looked toward the walls of Jerusalem was dominated by Herod's Temple.

Silas then understood what Jeremiah was talking about when he asked, "Is this the city that was called the perfection of beauty, the joy of the whole earth?"[3] He was describing the very sight that now mesmerized Silas, and this thought brought him another step closer to accepting Jerusalem as a temporary home.

Silas would have been quite content to spend an hour or two on the crest of the Mount of Olives basking in the beauty below them if that were possible. In fact, on the previous day Silas's father had suggested that they do that before visiting the Temple, but the morning disturbance had caused him to change his plans.

As they walked down the slope, Thomas said, "Silas, I believe that our eagerness to find out more about Jesus is not the only reason that we should visit Nicodemus. I have been wondering as we walked along if that man riding on an ass is on his way to start an uprising in Jerusalem during the Passover celebration. I must warn Nicodemus that I think this is a possibility."

"Father, your suspicion reminds me that Grandfather told me overcrowding and excitement at annual festivals often results in riots, especially if a false prophet happens to be present to stir up the crowd. Perhaps Mother was right when she said we might be headed for trouble."

Silas and his father left the Mount of Olives and were soon entering Jerusalem through the Eastern Gate. Silas understood at once why they had not been able to get lodgings in the city. A teeming mass of humanity filled the streets. His grandfather had told him that the population of Jerusalem would be swollen to four or five times its normal size during the Passover festival with Jews from almost every country in the world participating. In spite of the huge crowd, however, the city appeared to be peaceful. Silas yearned to visit the Temple, but he realized they would have to pass by the entrance to that most holy place without stopping. Like his father he was anxious to meet Nicodemus and tell him about their early morning experience. Following the directions Thomas had been given, Silas and his father were able to weave a path past the Temple and through the crowded shops of the marketplace toward a residential section in the northern part of the city where Nicodemus lived.

As they walked along, Silas thought how fortunate he and his parents were that Nicodemus had invited them to his home for the Passover feast. He felt privileged not only to fulfill his desire to celebrate the festival in Jerusalem, but to do so at such an early age and with a great friend of his grandfather.

Silas remembered that during the last thirty days of his final year at the synagogue school much time had been devoted to discussions of the meaning of Passover. Although the festival was mainly a religious celebration, it also commemorated agriculture and the history of the Jewish race. The celebratory meal must be eaten on the first day of the weeklong Feast of Unleavened Bread. That day and the seventh day are kept as sacred holidays. The first day represents the day the Israelites left Egypt. The seventh day represents the day they reached the Red Sea. The symbolic foods of the many meaningful steps in the Passover meal represent historical events that take those participating from a memory of the past tragedy of slavery to the expectation of a better future.

Silas thought that because of the apparent liberal bent of Nicodemus he would perform the Passover service as prescribed in a book very recently prepared called the Haggadah. It contained many new prayers, blessings, songs, and readings from the Scriptures as well as comments by famous rabbis.

Silas suddenly realized that this was one departure from conservative tradition that he approved of. He wondered if being in Jerusalem was already influencing the way he thought. He knew about the many preparations that had to be completed by sundown—at which the day begins. He was sure that his parents (and perhaps he) would have much to do to help Nicodemus's household prepare for the festival.

When father and son arrived at Nicodemus's home they entered the stone-paved courtyard and walked up to the entrance of a two-story stone house. They introduced themselves to the kind-looking man who greeted them. In return they received a warm welcome from Nicodemus, the lifelong friend of Silas's grandfather. Silas was surprised that in spite of his lofty position in Jerusalem, Nicodemus seemed much less formal and even less holy than his grandfather. His dress was simpler and more like his father's. A stranger meeting Nicodemus on the street would have no idea that he was an important member of the Sanhedrin. He looked much like an ordinary Jew, but he was a close friend of Silas's grandfather, so Silas was sure that Nicodemus was a very special Pharisee even if he was a more liberal one.

As soon as they were settled, Nicodemus told his guests that he had spent many pleasant hours discussing the Law with Matthew, and now he was happy to have the opportunity to talk to his friend's son and grandson and give them whatever assistance they needed.

After an hour of enjoyable conversation, Thomas described the disturbance he and Silas had witnessed earlier in the day and asked Nicodemus what he thought about it.

Silas noticed that when Nicodemus heard his father's story the expression on his face changed from one of joy that their visit had brought to one of concern. He waited anxiously to hear what Nicodemus would tell them about the event that had upset his father so much just a short time before.

"As you have been told, his name is Jesus," Nicodemus said. "He is a poor carpenter's son from Nazareth, a backwater village in Galilee. The people there are inclined to be somewhat rebellious and often ignore our laws, especially the dietary ones. I first heard about this man some call the *Teacher*, although I'm sure that he has had no formal education of any kind, about three years ago when he spoke at the synagogue near his home. According to the report I received, he did have a small following at that time.

"But as strange as it may seem, I was told that his own family did not believe his bizarre message, whatever it is. Then, when he began criticizing the people of his village, he was forced to move away to Capernaum. Before long he became so offensive to so many that only a small group of twelve men, most of them simple fishermen, paid much attention to him. After a while his popularity began to increase again because of the miracles he claimed to have performed—but I'm sure that most of these have been exposed as fakes by now. I think that he is just a clever charlatan."

Nicodemus continued, "He doesn't seem to care about what kind of sinners he associates with, whether it is a dishonest tax collector[4] or even a despicable Samaritan[5]. His poor choice of companions certainly confirms his poor character. He even receives some support from women, if you can believe that. I've heard the names Joanna and Susanne but the one most often mentioned is Mary who came from the little fishing town of Magdala.

"I must admit that he has not been violent and does not seem to be organizing any attempt to seize power, but he has embarrassed us Pharisees by belittling our explanatory laws in public.[6] Strange as it might seem, he said he did not come to abolish the Law, but that's difficult to believe.

"Silas, your own grandfather helped to formulate some of the rules and regulations Jesus made fun of. As you well know, without them no one would understand the Law.

"We Pharisees who meticulously obey each and every one of these laws recognized some time ago that this man was a very annoying nuisance. Before long he became a real troublemaker for us, and we knew that soon we would have to do whatever was necessary to silence him. What you saw this morning worries me. I do not believe that the shouts of the people prove that he is guilty of blasphemy, but it seems that his support has begun to grow again. The time may have come for us to take action of some kind to keep him quiet and make him go away.

"I believe he should be arrested and tried before the Sanhedrin. That would silence him and put an end to his making fun of us. Of course, this cannot be done until after the Passover season. It would not only be illegal to take action during the celebration, but very dangerous. His followers could be incited to riot.

"I was amazed when I first heard that our opponents in the government agree with us that this man Jesus is a troublemaker. We seldom see eye-to-eye on anything with the party of the rich and famous—those Sadducees. Why, they only accept the first five books of the Torah and have no belief at all in the resurrection of the dead! It is most unfortunate that our priests come from their party.

"With all their faults it's no wonder that the Sadducees have lost influence and we Pharisees now control the mass of people because of our rule over the synagogues. Of course, these puppets of Rome outnumber us on the Supreme Court, but we still have our say. They hate Jesus because they fear he will further weaken the priesthood and lessen their control of the Temple. If this happened, the Sadducees' income could be drastically reduced. I fear that they may want to take more severe measures than I believe appropriate to silence Jesus.

"What you have reported seeing this morning disturbs me. It's difficult to determine exactly what Jesus believes and what kind of mischief he might have planned to make fun of our laws. I did not think he would have the audacity to celebrate the Passover in Jerusalem. I will tell you one more thing about Jesus that bothers me, but it should remain our secret. Several times notable wise members of our party have challenged Jesus about his weird beliefs, and each time they came away embarrassed as if he were the one in the right. I just don't understand it. I hope that some day I will get my turn to challenge him."

After further disturbing discussion about the problem Jesus was causing for the Pharisees, Thomas and Silas thanked Nicodemus for his hospitality and mentioned that they were going to finish their first day in Jerusalem with a visit to the Temple.

"I would not recommend it," Nicodemus said. "I would suggest that you delay your initial visit to the Temple until you have a full day available. Why don't you spend the few remaining hours on a tour of the Upper City? You should see where the wealthy families of Jerusalem live. That will help you forget about Jesus for a while."

Nicodemus described some of the sights that Thomas and Silas might marvel at. After father and son thanked him again for his help they set off, following the directions he had given them. While they walked slowly along the streets of the middle-class neighborhood where Nicodemus lived, neither Silas nor his father said a word.

Silas contemplated the strange orderly progression of the events he had encountered during the past two weeks. He realized that he now knew a great deal about Jesus. He was not only a false prophet, but a menace to the Pharisees and therefore a danger to him. If Jesus was allowed to continue his opposition to the Pharisees' interpretation of the Law, Silas's career would be in jeopardy. Silas knew Jesus must be forced to remain silent if he was to achieve his goal.

As Silas continued to think about his recent past, it became clear that all that had happened to him was meant to be; he had been led to Jerusalem for a purpose. He now knew that here, in the holy city, he would begin to fulfill the promise he made to his grandfather. He would do this by pledging his support to the Pharisees to help them expose this troublemaker called *Jesus* to be the fraud he was.

Silas and Thomas turned a corner and Silas was dazzled by the sight ahead of him. The broad avenue lined with white marble villas and the occasional palace began to wipe away his concern about Jesus. Without any doubt this was the Upper City Nicodemus had described. He had told them that Sadducees, chief priests, high-ranking Jews, and Roman officials lived in this area. One very ornate palace matched the description Nicodemus had given them of the high priest's domain.

Further along they entered a market where they passed in front of shops dealing in fine goods such as oils and perfumes, frankincense and myrrh, silk, ivory, and silver. Silas was overwhelmed by the quantity of luxury goods displayed for sale to the very wealthy living in this section of Jerusalem. The display of costly items forced the fading thought of Jesus still further away.

As they left the market, Silas realized that the huge structure facing them had to be the palace where Herod resided while he was visiting Jerusalem. He thought it was strange that no sign of life showed in the courtyard, but the absence of people near the unadorned building that looked more like a prison than a palace seemed appropriate for a king who was loathed by most Jews. Silas could see the two separate main buildings Nicodemus had described. He had said that there were large banquet halls in each of them where Herod entertained his supporters with elaborate dinners.

Then Silas saw the fortifications that had been added to protect the Upper City. Herod was not concerned about the safety of the rest of Jerusalem. After Silas's father pointed out the two arched passageways that gave the king access to the Temple, he and Silas agreed that they had seen enough of Herod's Jerusalem home, and they left the eerie tranquility of the place to head for Bethany.

"Silas," Thomas said, "I know that Herod's ancestors converted to Judaism many years ago, but he is still an Idumean and a foreigner as far as I'm concerned."

"Well, he certainly doesn't come from a respectable family. His father, Herod the Great, murdered his own wife and three sons, and I'm not sure that Herod Antipas is any less of a sinner than his father."

"And as most Jews know, Silas, he holds the position of king only because he is a collaborator with Rome."

"Yes, but he has been working on one project for some time that is very important to those same Jews."

"Of course rebuilding the Temple, like his many other projects, was done for the purpose of increasing his importance to Rome and not with the intent to restore Jerusalem to its former grandeur. Nevertheless, I know that you are anxious to see it, so we will start off early tomorrow morning and we will make one more attempt to spend the day at Herod's Temple."

Silas was looking forward to the worship and prayer at the Temple that would help him forget for a while the Alexandria he had left behind and give him the wisdom to expose the man Jesus as the false prophet he was.

The next day right after morning prayer, and just as Thomas had promised, he and Silas left Bethany, and before long they were once more on the crest of the Mount of Olives. This time they did not have to hurry on but could relax, basking in the beauty spread out below them. As Silas looked across the walls of the city, he focused on the centerpiece, the Temple. He was quite familiar with the history of the center of Jewish worship and sacrifice. He knew that the first Temple, built by Solomon about one thousand years before he was born, had been destroyed five hundred years later by Nebuchadnezzar during the Babylonian invasion. Then when the Israelites returned from captivity in Babylon, King Zerubbabel's first concern was to build a new Temple. That one had survived until Pompey took Jerusalem less than one hundred years before the present time. Now he was looking down at Herod's restoration that had been going on for forty-six years, and in spite of the efforts of hundreds of thousands of workers, the construction was still not finished.

Silas and his father left the Mount of Olives to get a closer look. Soon they were passing through the Eastern Gate once more. This time, instead of walking by the Temple, they stopped. Silas was overwhelmed by the sight of the cloister, known as Solomon's Porch, with its stately Corinthian columns and the even more splendid Royal Cloister with its four rows of white marble columns. He soon turned his thoughts to the interior. What was inside the Temple was most important to him.

Solomon's Temple had been built to house the Ark of the Covenant,[7] the sacred chest that secured the Ten Commandments Moses received from God. It grieved Silas that the precious vault and the core of his belief which it contained no longer existed. Like most Jews, he believed that the Holy Ark had been destroyed by Nebuchadnezzer six hundred years earlier when the Babylonians plundered and burned Jerusalem.

Animal sacrifices had always been the principal rite of the Temple. Of the five fundamental offerings (burnt, grain, peace, sin, and guilt), all except the grain offering required bloodletting of animals or birds that have been declared to be without blemish. The high priest had always been the dominant figure in the sacrificial system of the Temple, and Silas realized that he must be respected even though he was a Sadducee. He alone was allowed to enter the Holy of Holies, and then only on the Day of Atonement when he offered sacrifices for the sins of the entire nation. He was the Jews' only advocate with God, and he alone could intercede for them. The curtain that hung in front of the Holy of Holies was there to preserve its sanctity by preventing the exposure of the sacred shrine inside. In so doing, it separated the people from God. The people's relationship with God could only be through the high priest. Silas believed that this was exactly as it should be.

Silas felt uneasy as he and his father entered the Temple. It did not seem proper that their entrance was through the Court of the Gentiles. The area was teeming with people of all sorts. Anyone could come into this part of the holy place. But when Thomas pointed to the sign that warned of death to any Gentile who dared to venture into the interior, Silas relaxed. He was comforted to know that he would not be defiled by associating with Gentiles after leaving this area and going further into the Temple.

A lot of business was being transacted in this court and Silas knew why. Nicodemus had explained that every Jew over the age of nineteen had to go to the Temple before Passover to pay the annual tax. The half-shekel levy could be burdensome because it was equivalent to two days' wages for most common working men. Thomas would have to pay the tax before going any further into the Temple, but because he had nothing but Roman money he had to go to one of the moneychangers to get the necessary Jewish coins.

Nicodemus had suggested dealing with a particular banker who would not take advantage of Thomas and charge an exorbitant fee. Silas's father located the right man and got the necessary coins to pay the Temple tax and to purchase a dove to give as a thank offering for the safe journey they had made from Alexandria.

Then Thomas and Silas proceeded to the place where the merchants were located. They soon found the one recommended by Nicodemus. Like the moneychangers, some of the dove and lamb merchants took advantage of worshippers. Those who arrived without a sacrificial offering had to purchase one and pay several times the normal market price. Those who came with a sacrifice were no better off, because inspectors could easily imagine some little flaw that would make their offering unacceptable. Nicodemus had said that much of the profit from these outrageous practices went to the Sadducee Temple priests, which made them very wealthy. Silas's father purchased a dove and they went on.

Next, they both performed the ceremonial washing that must be carried out before they could participate in the approaching festival. With this done, they would only have to wash their feet when they went to Nicodemus's home for the Passover meal. Then they walked into the Court of the Women where they could see several women depositing coins into the contribution chest. Silas hoped that his mother would have free time to visit the Temple soon. Each court they walked through was more sacred than the previous one.

Next they entered the Court of the Israelites, where several men had already assembled for prayer and sacrifice and where Silas and his father would spend the remainder of their time. Silas watched while Thomas gave his offering to the priest there who took it into the Court of the Priests where only he was allowed, and where the burnt offerings were made. As he watched, Silas gave thanks to God that he and his father were morally good and not like either those in the Court of the Gentiles who cheated the poor, or that man they called Jesus.

When father and son returned to Bethany after an inspiring day, Silas thought once more that perhaps three years in Jerusalem would be tolerable, especially if the Jesus problem was solved. The divine peace and quiet of the Temple would continue to comfort him.

Chapter 4

True Prophet

AS SILAS AND his father walked into the Court of the Gentiles early the next morning, Silas heard a terrible crash and then another and another as if a violent storm was sweeping through the Temple destroying everything in its path. Wherever Silas looked he could see tables thrown upside down, coins rolling around on the floor, bleating sheep roaming about, and doves flying overhead. Silas had no idea what was happening. Then Thomas pointed to the cause of the commotion. When Silas turned to look, he could see a man who he thought must be insane, upsetting the tables and stalls of the moneychangers and merchants. He could not understand why no one had tried to stop the terrible destruction. Then he heard the crazy man shout in a loud voice, "It is written, my house will be called a house of prayer, but you are making it a den of robbers."[1]

Thomas asked the man next to him, "Who is that lunatic?"

When Silas heard the reply, "He is the one they call Teacher," he realized the horrible truth. The demented man was Jesus, the very person he had vowed to silence and had come to the Temple to forget. He and his father had risen with the sun, planning to spend the day at the holy place and to worship in peace and quiet. Now that seemed like a forlorn hope. It had become clear to Silas that Nicodemus had not known what he was talking about when he said this weird person was not violent.

As Silas surveyed the damage, he recalled that Nicodemus had said most, but not all, of the moneychangers and merchants in the Court of the Gentiles were dishonest. Now he wondered if Jesus had heard the same story. Perhaps he imagined himself some kind of a do-gooder and a protector of the poor pilgrims who had been cheated, and he had decided to take action. Silas was surprised to see that the tables of the men Nicodemus had recommended as honorable were still upright. This was either a strange coincidence, or Jesus had a very good source of information.

Something else bothered Silas about Jesus' action. Nicodemus had said that although a large percentage of the money raised in the Court of the Gentiles went illegally into the pockets of the dishonest Sadducee priests, some of the income was needed for necessary Temple operating expenses. Silas could not understand why Jesus, a Jew, would deprive the Temple of income unless he wanted to destroy it, but then he remembered that Jesus had called it a den of robbers. Perhaps he was just trying to rid the Temple of all the cheating businessmen and leave the honest ones for its support.

Silas's father shouted out, "If there is a problem here, this man should not try to solve it by a wild attack against these merchants and bankers. Who does he think he is? Why didn't he report his complaint to the Temple authorities and let them take care of it? That wild creature deserves to be punished. Someone should take care of him." Once more Thomas was shaking with anger.

His father's words made Silas wonder why the Sadducees had not already summoned police to arrest Jesus. They were in charge of the Temple and must have seen what had happened. The Pharisees would not allow such a thing to occur in the synagogue without taking suitable action. At first Silas wondered if the Sadducees might fear this man too much to accost him.

Then he heard a loud, strong voice ask, "By what authority are you doing these things?"[2] Silas realized that at last some responsible Sadducee was going to make an appropriate response. He could hear what sounded like an argument, but with all the noise in the court, neither he nor his father could tell what was being said.

Then, hoping that the situation would be taken care of by the Sadducees, Silas, with his father, left the Court of the Gentiles. Hurrying through the Court of the Women, they entered the Court of the Israelites where Silas could see a large group of men engaged in a heated discussion.

Silas heard one man say to the others, "If you don't know the man's name I'll tell you what it is. He's the one they call Teacher, and his name is Jesus. Some call him the Son of David. I saw him enter Jerusalem on the day after the Sabbath. He did not seem like a revolutionary then. He was riding on an ass, which was a sign he was a peaceful man, not on a horse, which would have been a sign that he was a warrior. It seems strange to me that he was so violent today. He must have had a very good reason for the mayhem he created in our holy Temple."

Many in the group told weird tales that they had heard about him. One man said he had heard that Jesus had claimed to have healed a leper.[3] Another man related the most preposterous tale of all when he said, "I'm from Galilee where he was born and raised, and I heard that he had fed thousands of his followers with just a little bread and a small fish or two."[4]

The man who had been speaking had barely finished relating this unbelievable tale when Silas heard his father's voice, "Now I know why so many are attracted to Jesus. They are not interested in his message; they are duped by the miracles he has claimed to perform."

"You're right, Father, and that's the explanation for what we saw at Bethany," Silas replied. "It's just as Nicodemus told us. He said Jesus was only a clever magician who had been successful in fooling many common people with fake healings. Then, however, he told us something puzzling. He said Jesus had defeated prestigious Pharisees in debate. I can't understand how that could happen. Nicodemus would like to talk to this strange man. I hope he is able to do that. If he does, I'm sure he will expose him in debate as the fake that he is. When he hears about the destruction in the

Temple today, he will realize that Jesus is a serious threat as well as a troublesome charlatan."

Silas and his father left the Temple; there was Jesus on Solomon's Porch surrounded by a large crowd of people, many of whom seemed to be afflicted with crippling illnesses. One man, who appeared to be sightless, approached Jesus as they watched.

They heard the blind man say, "Jesus, Son of David, have mercy on me!"

To this Jesus replied, "What do you want me to do for you?"

The blind man did not hesitate before responding, "Lord, I want to see."

With that Jesus told the man, "Receive your sight; your faith has healed you."

The man who had claimed to be blind walked away unescorted. Silas realized then just how clever Jesus was. He worked with a fellow conspirator who pretended to be blind in order to deceive the crowd by helping stage fake healings and attract a large following. Misleading his supporters was serious enough, and, regardless of Nicodemus's opinion, Silas thought that allowing them to think Jesus was the Son of David was blasphemous.

At that point, a small group Silas recognized by the dress of its members as Pharisees approached Jesus. "About time," Silas said to his father. "If the Sadducees are afraid to stop this lunatic, let our good people do it." Then one of the Pharisees said something to Jesus, but he spoke in such a low voice that Silas could not hear what it was.

When he moved away from his father and closer to Jesus, Silas was able to hear his reply to whatever it was that the Pharisee had said, "Woe to you, teachers of the Law and Pharisees, you hypocrites! You shut the kingdom of heaven in men's faces. You yourselves do not enter, nor will you let others enter who are trying to. Woe to you, teachers of the Law and Pharisees, you hypocrites! You travel over land and sea to win a single convert, and when he becomes one, you make him twice as much a son of hell as you are."[5]

Silas could not believe the Pharisees' lack of response to this horrible insult. Instead of disputing what Jesus said, they just slinked away, looking defeated and helpless.

Then it occurred to him that the Pharisees had not tried to challenge Jesus because they feared the reaction of the crowd. That made sense to Silas. The Pharisees did not fear Jesus. They feared those gathered around him who had been misled and seemed to worship him as a prophet. The crowd had grown larger. Many of the multitude that had come to Jerusalem for the Passover, and had probably never heard of Jesus before, had been attracted by the throng assembled around him and had heard all that had gone on.

Yes, the Pharisees had acted wisely by doing nothing that might start an uprising. That would have brought the power of Rome down upon the Jews during the important Feast of Unleavened Bread, which would be the worst possible time for a disturbance. Silas realized that he had a few things to learn before he joined the Pharisees to help them silence Jesus.

"Silas," said Thomas, "I'm disgusted with Jesus' sinful behavior, and I'm anxious to visit Nicodemus again and tell him all that we've seen. But first we must say the midday prayer."

"Before we do that let's get further from Solomon's Porch so we can't hear Jesus addressing the crowd. I've suffered enough exposure to that man for one day."

After they had said their prayer in a quiet corner away from the Temple, they left to consult with Nicodemus. They had not gone far when Silas was surprised to see Nicodemus walking toward them.

When he was close enough, Nicodemus began to speak. "I heard there's been a disturbance in the Temple and I'm headed there to find out what it's all about."

"There certainly has been," Thomas replied. "Silas and I witnessed everything that happened and I'll tell you what we saw." Thomas gave a detailed account of all that they had seen and heard.

When Thomas finished his tale of destruction, Nicodemus said quite calmly, "That's all I need to know. I won't bother to go to the Temple."

Silas was surprised by Nicodemus's mild reaction until he heard what he said next. "Now I have something important to tell you. The authorities will soon take care of Jesus. I have just been informed that the Sanhedrin has scheduled an emergency session to determine the best way to silence him. Whatever action they decide is appropriate will take place immediately after the Passover celebration."

"Thank you for the good news." Thomas said. "Now our walk back to Bethany will be more pleasant."

Silas said nothing. He would be happy to see the end of Jesus, but he hoped he would somehow be given the opportunity to play a role in silencing him.

Silas did not expect to see Nicodemus again until the Passover meal at his home, so on their way to the Temple the next morning, he was very surprised to hear that now familiar voice say, "I've been watching for you at the gate. I have important news. I've talked to him! Of course, I could not risk being seen with him or my life would not have been worth much, so I met with him secretly last night. I had some trouble finding him without exposing myself, but I finally managed to locate him in Bethany not far from where you are staying.

"I addressed him with the respect he did not deserve and words that I did not believe. 'Rabbi,' I said, 'we know you are a teacher who has come from God. For no one could perform the miraculous signs you are doing if God were not with him.' He did not acknowledge what I said, but instead replied, 'I tell you the truth, no one can see the Kingdom of God unless he is born again.' I asked what that meant.

"His answer did little to end my confusion! 'I tell you the truth, no one can enter the Kingdom of God unless he is born of water and the Spirit.'[6] When I told him I didn't know what he was talking about, he mocked me saying that, although I was supposed to be a learned Pharisee, I could not recognize the truth when I heard it.

"Certainly he both embarrassed and enraged me, but after we parted I began to understand at least a little of what he was talking about. I recalled that when we accept a pagan into our faith, we regard him as newborn. Maybe what Jesus was talking about was something like that. Perhaps if I'm able to meet with him again I will get a clearer concept of what he believes.

"As I told you before, the ease with which he outwitted our brothers in debate bothers me, and because of that what he said to me last night troubles me even more. The more I see of him and hear from him, the more I doubt that he is as deranged as we think him to be. Now I must leave, but please remember that all I have told you must remain our secret."

Silas and his father resumed their walk to the Temple. Silas could not understand Nicodemus. His attitude toward Jesus seemed to be changing to become more understanding and accepting. Surely his grandfather's friend was not beginning to believe that Jesus was a prophet!

After saying their prayers at the Temple, Silas and his father walked to the lower city before returning to Bethany. Thomas ordered a lamb they would pick up the next morning. Silas was glad when this was done and they could leave the repulsive area with its crowded streets, unattractive houses, and rundown shops. He certainly would not want to live in this part of Jerusalem.

Chapter 5

The Passover

SILAS WOKE UP on preparation day eager to help his family prepare for Passover. He was excited to be celebrating the rite as it was performed in modern-day Jerusalem. After the sacred event had come and gone, the Sanhedrin, hopefully with his help, would take care of Jesus. With this done, Silas's father would be free to look for permanent housing and he would visit Gamaliel. If his grandfather had made the necessary arrangements, he would begin to study under the famous rabbi.

Silas and his father left Bethany early in the morning. Deborah started out later to go to Nicodemus's home to help with the preparation of the celebratory meal. There was much to be done and the familial duties of the women of the household took precedence over Temple sacrifices and were considered equally sacred.

At the time of the first Passover the Israelites had been ordered to leave Egypt within a few hours. There had not been enough time for dough to rise, so the bread the fleeing slaves took with them was unleavened. In remembrance of that, the bread eaten at every Passover meal since then has been unleavened. To increase the significance of this, the day traditionally began with a ceremonial search throughout every nook and cranny of the house for any trace of leaven. This was the duty of the women. The task was called complete when all those in the search party agreed that every last bit of leaven had been found and destroyed. Once that was accomplished, the unleavened bread was prepared and baked for the Passover meal.

When the two men arrived at the Lower City, the unpleasant sight of the limestone houses crowded together on the narrow unpaved streets that had disturbed Silas the day before bothered him again. He well knew that the people living on the crooked alleys in the rundown area they were walking through would have the same passion for the Passover celebration as the rich and famous who lived on the wide, crisscrossing avenues of the Upper City.

Finally, they reached the section where the vendors of sacrificial animals were located. As soon as Thomas inspected the lamb to be certain that it was without blemish,[1] he paid for it, and he and Silas started out for the Temple.

After the lamb had passed inspection at the Temple entrance, Silas's father took it into the slaughtering area where he prepared to kill it himself as mandated by the ceremonial law. Sacrificial offerings which gave back to God the life of an animal that had been his creation had been made from the beginning of time and were an important part of the Jewish sacramental worship, especially during Passover.[2] Thomas was given a sharp knife free of nicks and scratches and was told to proceed.

With one quick movement he plunged the blade deep into the lamb's throat, bringing instantaneous and merciful death. The gushing blood which was considered sacred to God[3] was caught in a golden bowl by the first of many priests who were lined up in a row for the ceremony. He handed the bowl of blood to the priest standing next to him. Then the procedure was repeated with the bowl being passed from one priest to another down the line. Finally it reached the last one, who took the bowl and splashed the blood on the altar in the Court of the Priests. The sacrificial offering had been made in obedience to God's will. Done in faith, it would remove the last remaining taint from the forgiven sins of Silas's family. This accomplished, the lamb was opened up, the fat was thrown into the fire at the altar, and the skin was removed.

The carcass, fully drained of blood as required by ritual law, was given to Thomas to be eaten at the Passover meal that would start at sundown. Silas was relieved to leave the Temple. The slaying of lambs had been going on in the Court of the Israelites for some time and blood and nauseating odors were everywhere. His father carried the lamb to Nicodemus's home, where he placed it on a pomegranate spit over an open fire with legs and head attached, following a ritual that had been repeated over and over through the centuries since the first Passover.

When Silas returned from the Temple with his father, he was invited to contribute to the commemorating meal that his mother and Nicodemus's wife had been preparing. First he added sticks of cinnamon to the Charosheth paste of crushed fruit and nuts, just as the Israelites had added straw to moistened clay to strengthen the bricks they were forced to make for the pharaoh. Then when he stirred salt into a bowl of water, his thoughts went to the parting of the Red Sea. He placed the brine beside the mixture of herbs with horseradish, chicory, endive, and lettuce his mother had prepared as a symbol of the bitterness of captivity.

Just before the twelfth hour, Nicodemus's wife poured the four cups of wine to represent the four promises God made to the Israelites that are recorded in the Torah. All preparations for the meal had been completed. Finally it was sundown, the beginning of the fourteenth day of the month, and the time for all to proceed to the upper room carrying the food and wine. The guests assembled at a square table around which they reclined on couches.

Nicodemus read the first promise, "I am the Lord, and I will bring you out from under the yoke of the Egyptians."[4] Then he took the first cup of wine and said the sanctifying prayer over it before passing it around the table for each guest to drink from the cup.

Next Nicodemus washed his hands ceremoniously for the first of the three times prescribed. Once his hands had been freed of any obvious surface dirt, he picked up a stone jar and handed it to Thomas. This stone jar was used only to hold the ceremonial hand-washing water and had been kept free from contamination. Nicodemus held his hands with the fingers pointing up and

Thomas poured the specified quantity of water over them so that the water ran down over Nicodemus's wrists. Then Nicodemus rubbed his hands together for further cleaning. Because this action contaminated the water on Nicodemus's hands, he changed their position so that the fingers pointed down. Then the second specified quantity of water was poured over them from the wrists downward. Failure to follow this procedure exactly would be considered a most serious offense.

Next Nicodemus took a piece of parsley, dipped it in the salt water and ate it. The parsley represented the mint-like hyssop that was used to smear the doorposts of the Israelites' homes the night that the angel passed over them. Then Nicodemus blessed the unleavened bread saying, "Blessed be thou, O Lord, our God, King of the Universe who brings forth from the earth." As he broke the bread he continued, "This is the bread of affliction which our forefathers ate in the land of Egypt. Whosoever is hungry, let him come and eat. Whosoever is in need, let him come and keep the Passover with us."

After each guest had eaten a tiny piece of the bread, Nicodemus related the complete history of the Israelites down through the ages to the time of their deliverance from Egypt. This proud story had been told exactly the same way year after year since the first Passover, never to be forgotten in any detail. After this lengthy oration a psalm of praise was sung, "Praise the Lord. Blessed is the man who fears the Lord, who finds great delights in his commands."[5]

When the psalm was finished, the second cup of wine was passed around. Nicodemus read the second promise that God had made, "I will redeem you with an outstretched arm and with mighty acts of judgment."[6]

When this was done, everyone participated in the second hand washing in preparation for the main course which would begin after the grace: "Blessed art thou, O Lord our God, who brings forth fruit from the earth. Blessed art thou, O God, who has sanctified us with thy commandments and enjoined us to eat unleavened cakes." After that was said, pieces of bread were served and each guest made a bitter herb sandwich to eat with the lamb. Any lamb not eaten would be destroyed by burning it after the meal was finished, as directed by the Scriptures.

Nicodemus read the third promise, "I will take you as my own people."[7] The third hand washing followed, and then the last of the bread was eaten so that none would remain. The next prayer that was said in thanksgiving was also a plea for the coming of the warrior Messiah, who would defeat the Roman army and free Israel from domination.

Then a blessing was said over the third cup, "Blessed art thou, O God, King of the Universe, who has created the fruit of the vine."

Nicodemus read the fourth promise, "I will be your God."[8] Another psalm was sung, the fourth cup of wine was passed around, and the final prayers were said. The Passover Feast was finished.

Silas gave thanks that at last they had celebrated this very special occasion in Jerusalem as their tradition dictated, and he was pleased that the order of service chosen by Nicodemus was exactly as he believed it should be, including the readings from the Haggadah. The Passover celebration had brought a wonderful sensation of contentment to Silas. He felt it had reinforced him so well that he was strong enough to ward off any external frustration that he might encounter—even one caused by that false prophet, Jesus.

Chapter 6

The Trial

THE PASSOVER FEAST had been lengthy and had followed a very busy day. Silas fell into the peaceful sleep that always followed an event as sacred and meaningful as the Passover. For the first time in recent days he was not confused with thoughts about that strange man, Jesus.

The next day he and his father left Bethany to say the midday prayer at the Temple. The route they followed would take them past the city's praetorium—the residence of the military governor. Silas was anxious to see the building where the notorious Roman governor of Judea, Pontius Pilate, lived while he was in Jerusalem. Silas did not expect to get a view of Pilate, although Nicodemus had told him that it was the governor's custom to come to Jerusalem from his headquarters in Caesarea at Passover time, and he had added that Pilate always brought special troops with him because of the increased possibility of a disturbance during the festival.

Silas had only been in Jerusalem for a week, but that was long enough for his interest in the history of Judea to be revived, and his concern about Jesus did not affect his memory. He recalled that Pilate's appointment was relatively new. Before he was named governor, the province had been ruled by a pseudo Jew named Archelaus, a brother of Herod Antipas and son of Herod the Great.

When Rome recognized Archelaus's incompetence, the senate deposed him. Rather than take a chance on another Jew, the Roman government put Pilate in charge. Even though he had only been in office for three years, his reputation for being anti-Semitic had spread throughout the Diaspora. Silas had heard the rumor in Alexandria that Pilate's goal was the destruction of the Jewish race.

Silas had also received a warning from Nicodemus. He was familiar with Pilate's treachery and advised his friends to be very cautious while they were in the city. He said that Pilate often had some of his soldiers dressed as civilians and circulating in the crowd. He warned Silas and his father that any remark they made that sounded the least bit suspicious to the soldiers could bring the arrest of both of them. Now Silas's recollection of Pilate's reputation and the memory of Nicodemus's warning made him a little bit nervous as he and his father walked toward the praetorium.

Just before they reached the governor's residence, Nicodemus rushed excitedly toward them and motioned to a secluded spot away from the crowd. Silas could not imagine what would have upset their friend so early in the day, but he didn't hesitate to follow his father to the protected doorway Nicodemus had pointed to.

As soon as Nicodemus took his last step, he began to talk. "I'm so glad that you told me where you were going this morning. Otherwise I might never have found you, and it's very important that I did. I know that you are headed for the praetorium, and I have a great deal to tell you before you reach it. Jesus has been arrested by the Temple police and is appearing there before Pilate now!

"I know that you two must think that the high priest has taken a terrible risk to arrest Jesus during the Passover, and I agree. The streets are teeming with people, and no one knows how many are supporters of Jesus who might protest his arrest and create a disturbance. So far Caiaphas, the high priest, has been very lucky; there has been no sign of a riot. As you know, the slightest hint of an uprising could result in harsh reprisals by Rome. It is difficult to believe, but the high priest was given an opportunity to seize Jesus during the night with no risk to himself.

"Here is what happened. One of Jesus' disciples, *Judas*,[1] I believe he called himself, came to the authorities after the Passover meal. He offered to take the Temple police to an out-of-the-way place where they would find Jesus alone with just a few of his friends. He assured the high priest that his men could charge Jesus with some minor offense, take him off without interference, and have him in custody before daylight. The man must be crazy. He offered to do this for a paltry sum of money. The high priest said he could not believe his ears. At first he hesitated to even discuss the proposal with Judas, because regulations forbid the Temple police from making an arrest during Passover. But the temptation was too great, and before long he decided to accept the offer. Judas grabbed the betrayal fee and escorted the police to a garden on the Mount of Olives where they took Jesus without causing a disturbance of any kind. It is unbelievable, but his companions offered no resistance at all.[2]

"Now when Caiaphas dispatched the police to arrest Jesus, he gave them what seemed to me to be a strange instruction. Instead of ordering them to bring Jesus to him, he directed them to take him to the home of his father-in-law, Annas, to be interrogated. In case you don't know, Annas preceded Caiaphas as high priest and is still very influential in the Sanhedrin. I believe Caiaphas sent Jesus to Annas to flatter his father-in-law, hoping to gain the support he might need from him later in the Supreme Court. At any rate, after a brief session, Annas had heard enough from Jesus, so he ordered the police to take him to Caiaphas at his home for further questioning.

"In the meantime I had been summoned to the high priest's home along with a few others to be informed of those events which I have just described to you. I was there when they brought Jesus in along with some willing witnesses they had hurriedly rounded up. The high priest's questioning of Jesus was not productive and the witnesses' testimony was useless. At that point it seemed to me that it would be impossible to successfully lodge a charge against Jesus.

"Although I was disturbed by the illegality of the proceedings, I felt that it would be unfortunate if Jesus slipped away. We might not get another opportunity like this to chastise him for some time to come. As you know, I do not think that he is a serious criminal, but he has caused us trouble and deserves minor punishment of some sort for ridiculing us Pharisees. If he would only realize how beneficial our rules and regulations are, I believe he could be very helpful to our cause.

"Then, when it seemed that we had no case and Jesus' release was imminent, the high priest showed how clever and devious he is when somehow he managed to trap Jesus into making the ridiculous claim that he is the Son of God. When I heard Jesus' words, I knew that no matter how I felt before, I now had no choice but to join the others to shout blasphemy and demand his death. The ancient Law of Leviticus gave me no alternative.[3] I could not understand why Jesus had been so foolhardy. His preposterous claim had to be false, but there was nothing that I could do until he recanted his statement. I thought he would do this eventually and then we would be free to place a legitimate and much less serious charge against him. Until he retracted his words I knew that the accusation must stand.

"Nevertheless the high priest was now faced with a dilemma. The Sanhedrin cannot issue a death sentence and the Roman court will not try a case of blasphemy. It is not a civil offense in their opinion. The high priest knew the solution to his problem was to falsely accuse Jesus of committing a serious civil crime punishable by death, but first the charge of blasphemy had to be formalized and made legal in the Jewish court.

"Once it was daylight, the high priest ordered the police to take Jesus to the Hall of Hewn Stone in the Temple. He asked all of us who were with him to follow along because he would convene a meeting of the Sanhedrin there to officially charge Jesus. When we got to the Temple the roll call proved that we had more than the twenty-three members required for a quorum.

"Nevertheless the session was illegal, because it is forbidden for the Sanhedrin to meet during Passover. Ignoring the fact that the procedure was being conducted outside the law, the court confirmed that Jesus had committed a blasphemous sin and deserved the death penalty. Jesus refused to protest. I could not believe it. Why did Jesus remain silent when he could have been released with just a few words of confession? This man continues to baffle me.

"By that time I was quite upset by the way the high priest had duped Jesus into making that ludicrous claim. I don't know why he would ever say that he was the Son of God. I suppose he was so upset that in the heat of the moment he said the first preposterous thing that came into his head, and now he's too stubborn to back down. I protested our condemnation of him in the court, because I believe that he will disavow his statement if we give him a chance at a fair hearing after he calms down. Then, once the false charge is out of the way, we can bring a much less serious complaint against him to punish him for his attack on our ceremonial laws.

"My protest was overruled in the Hall of Hewn Stone, and I am probably now considered disloyal by members of the court. The Sadducees and the high priest are not interested in fair treatment. They believe that they have already achieved their goal with the confirmation of the blasphemy charge. Now they are determined to see the end of Jesus.

"Because the high priest knows that only the Roman governor can pass the death sentence in Jerusalem, he ordered Jesus to be taken before Pilate where he will present a charge that the governor will recognize as deserving the supreme penalty. That is where he is now. I feel very uncomfortable about everything that went on during the night, especially because I could not prevent such a miscarriage of justice. Nevertheless, I still hope that Jesus will recant before it is too late.[4]

"Before I leave, let me tell you about one other thing that bothers me. It is that Caiaphas ignored the law more than once in order to arrest and interrogate Jesus during Passover. He risked losing his position to do this, so he must have had a very strong reason for taking such unprecedented action. As I told you earlier he has been made exceedingly wealthy from illegal sales in the Court of the Gentiles at what is sarcastically called the *Bazaars of Annas* because his father-in-law Annas perfected the thievery.

"I believe he fears that if Jesus remains on the scene, his share of the profits from the vendors and moneychangers will disappear. As an honest Pharisee, I do not approve of Caiaphas's methods and I do not believe that Jesus deserves the death penalty for his threat to the Sadducees or for offending the Pharisees. I must leave now, but I wanted to tell you this before you reached the praetorium."

Nicodemus's tale left Silas more puzzled than ever about Jesus. He could not understand why he would claim to be the Son of God; an offense he must have known would bring an end to his life. Of course, Jesus could not be given the death penalty unless the high priest could satisfy Pilate that he had committed a crime against Rome that warranted a punishment of death. But from what Silas had heard about Caiaphas he was sure that the high priest would solve that problem somehow. He agreed with his father that if Jesus did not take back his words he would deserve the death penalty he was sure to get. That would certainly put an end to his mockery of the Pharisees, although not in the way either Nicodemus or they desired. As Silas approached the praetorium with his father, he could hear rumblings from what sounded like a very agitated crowd.

A large number of people had congregated in the courtyard in front of the palace. Whatever had been going on must have excited them, because they were busily jabbering away noisily to one another. The stage for the performance they had come to see was the balcony above them and they stared at the small group that had gathered there.

Silas recognized Jesus. He was standing there looking helpless, but somehow he did not look defeated. Silas assumed the stern-looking official next to Jesus was Pilate, and the woman beside him was his wife. A small contingent of soldiers completed the scene on the balcony. Silas knew that Jesus must have been taken to the balcony by force because he was a Jew, and no Jew would appear in a gentile dwelling without a struggle. He would have defiled himself by passing through an unclean gentile building.

As Silas and his father looked on, Pilate ordered those accusing Jesus of committing a crime against Rome to state their case. A spokesman for the Sanhedrin responded. He accused Jesus of trying to stop citizens from paying taxes to Rome. "Not only that," he added, "he declared that he was the king and true ruler of the Jews." This last remark seemed to upset Pilate. Silas wondered if this was because he realized that the Jewish authorities were attempting to trick him into settling an internal problem that they could not handle themselves.

Silas was not surprised then to hear Pilate try to put an end to the proceedings by announcing, "I find no basis for a charge against this man."

The Sadducee did not wait long before bringing out an additional charge. This time he accused Jesus of setting the people in turmoil, not just in Judea, but also in Galilee, his own country.

Silas recognized the craftiness of this allegation. He knew that Pilate would be deadly afraid of an uprising. A severe disturbance, regardless of the cause, would mean his recall to Rome and the end of his career. So Silas was shocked to see that when Pilate heard this accusation, he did not appear to be affected at all by the hint of trouble.

Pilate said in what sounded like a voice of joyful surprise, "So he is a Galilean!"

Now Silas knew why Pilate was not upset by the latest charge. Because a crime had been committed by a Galilean, Pilate would turn the case over to Herod, the king of Galilee, who just happened to be in Jerusalem for the Passover.

Pilate sent Jesus off under guard with his accusers to the king's nearby palace to have the case tried there. Silas had heard a rumor that Pilate despised Herod. This made him think that Pilate was not only relieved because he avoided making a decision, but also pleased with himself because he was putting the king in a very uncomfortable situation.

Silas left his father and followed the procession to Herod's palace. Jesus and a few of the Sadducees were escorted inside soon after their arrival. Then, after a long, tiring wait, the small group came walking out and Jesus was with them.

Everyone returned to the praetorium where the Sadducees' spokesman requested another audience with the governor. When this was granted, he once more addressed Pilate. This time he said they were returning their case to him because Herod wanted nothing to do with the accused man.

For a brief moment Pilate looked very perturbed, but then his expression changed. Pilate announced that because both he and the king of the country of the accused agreed that Jesus had committed no serious crime, he would set him free. To appease those gathered below him, he added that he would have him flogged first. Apparently flogging a man in whom he could find no crime did not bother Pilate's conscience.

By this time the crowd in the courtyard, which had grown larger while Jesus was appearing before Herod, had learned about Jesus' claim to be the Son of God, and they were not ready to agree to his release. They did not wait for the spokesman of the Sadducees to protest Pilate's decision. They answered it themselves with loud, angry shouts of disagreement.

Signaling for silence, Pilate addressed the Sadducees and the crowd surrounding them. "It is my custom to release one prisoner each year during the Passover celebration. I am ready to do that now while so many are assembled here in the courtyard. This time I will allow all of you who are here, not just your leaders, to choose for release one of two men—either Jesus, the man who now stands accused before you, or a man named Barabbas."

Silas recognized the name of a man Nicodemus had described as a notorious murderer. Then Pilate continued, "I want you to think carefully about which one I should release." Silas saw still another example of Pilate's ingenuity. He was letting the people make the decision he wanted nothing to do with, and at the same time he assumed that he was ensuring the release of the man he seemed to believe was innocent. Even though the mob was enraged against Jesus, Silas knew they would have no choice but to release him rather than a condemned murderer. Then Jesus would recant and Silas would do everything possible to help the Pharisees silence Jesus without physically hurting him.

As Silas watched the crowd, waiting for their response, he saw a great many of the leaders rushing from person to person saying something to them. When one of the Sadducees approached a group close to where Silas was standing, he could hear what it was, just one word, "Barabbas". As the Sadducees walked among the people encouraging them, chants of "Barabbas, Barabbas," began.

Silas was stunned. He was no supporter of Jesus, but how could Jesus be more of a threat to the people than a notorious convicted murderer? Then he realized that the Sadducees must have convinced the mob that Jesus was guilty of blasphemy, and if he was kept in custody long enough they could convict him of a fabricated crime bearing the death sentence. Where were all those who supported Jesus as he rode through Bethany? Were any of them here today accusing him of blasphemy?

Silas noticed a lone Pharisee going through the crowd saying the same one word, "Barabbas." What was the Pharisee thinking about? Jesus could still be given a legitimate trial later if he was released now and the notorious criminal kept where he belonged.

Silas had been taught to respect the party of his ancestors and follow their instructions, just as he followed their rules and regulations without question. Did this one man represent the party? Must he do as he was told even if it was obvious that it was wrong? Silas didn't know what to do. Yesterday's feeling of maturity had disappeared.

The shouts for Barabbas had become a deafening roar, and Silas knew the time had come to choose. A lone cry for Jesus would not bring his release, only an attack by the angry mob.

Without conscious thought Silas became part of the rabid crowd for one decisive moment and, as if hypnotized, he joined them crying for Barabbas's release. A moment later Silas tried to rationalize his action by assuming that although Jesus would be retained, he would still have a chance for the proper trial that both he and, he was sure, most of the Pharisees believed he deserved. Nevertheless, Silas had helped put a convicted murderer back on the streets of the city.

When at last Silas emerged from his daze, he realized that he had not seen his father for some time, and began to wonder where he was and how he had responded. Then he heard Pilate's voice once more.

"Herod has found nothing wrong with this man Jesus, nor have I," Pilate said. "He should be the one released." Silas began to relax. Pilate was about to overrule the crowd's decision. Jesus would be freed and censured in a proper court for his indiscretions. But when the crowd heard Pilate renege on his promise they shouted all the louder.

The Sadducees began to circulate through the mob again. They were still hoping to get the death sentence for Jesus. When Pilate made his third appeal for Jesus' release the mob exploded with a different demand that had been put into their minds by the Sadducees. "Crucify him! Crucify him!"

Silas was appalled. By this time the crowd had been convinced by the authorities that Jesus had committed blasphemy, and they were demanding the death penalty because one of their ancient laws specified that punishment for the great sin of blasphemy. That Roman law did not cover blasphemy was of no concern to them.

Silas had not joined in with the plea for crucifixion and he prayed that it would not happen, but Pilate thought that he had no alternative but to grant the crowd's wish, even though he would be acting illegally. A riot would doom him. It had become a choice between crucifying a man he knew was innocent and losing his comfortable position as governor of Judea. He surrendered to the threat of the demanding mob. With a consenting wave of his hand he announced, "I am innocent of this man's blood. It is your responsibility!"[5] Jesus was taken away to be scourged.

Silas left the crowd, and Thomas came to him. "Silas, remember how Nicodemus questioned Jesus' reason for refusing to recant the ridiculous false statement he had made? I have been struggling to determine Jesus' motive for his action ever since Nicodemus told us about it. Suddenly, one explanation for what seems to be his suicidal behavior occurred to me. What if his claim is not false? What if Jesus is the Son of God? That would justify his action. What if the Son of God is about to be crucified? Silas, I am distraught. I don't know what to do except to go to the Temple and pray for guidance. You stay here for now if you think you must, but join me there as soon as you can."

Silas was speechless as his father hurried away. He thought that the excitement of the day must have driven him mad. How could his father believe that Jesus was the Son of God? Every Pharisee and even most ordinary Jews knew what the Messiah would be like. He would be a conquering military leader capable of freeing his people from Rome's domination. He would not come riding on a little ass, but on a horse. Surely Thomas did not believe Jesus had restored the blind man's sight or healed a leper.

Silas realized that he had not only helped to condemn a man without a fair trial, but he had been unable to prevent that man's death by crucifixion. He knew that it was the most painful and degrading form of capital punishment that had ever been devised by man, made much worse by the mandatory scourging that preceded it. Even the crime of blasphemy should not bring death this way.

Crucifixion had become a common form of punishment in the Roman Empire to discourage crime. It was illegal to crucify Romans, but perfectly legal to crucify Jews. He recalled his father telling him about the mass crucifixion of eight hundred Pharisees some years before he was born.

Silas realized that Jesus had probably already been beaten with a deadly whip made of thongs with bits and pieces of metal attached at the ends. Just a few blows would expose his bones, perhaps splintering them, and cause massive bleeding. Very few human beings could withstand the excruciating pain. He could not imagine how a man as frail as Jesus appeared to be could live through such harsh and cruel treatment. He did not think that Jesus would survive to be crucified.

Then Silas was shattered by a new thought. His father was a very intelligent man. What if he wasn't going mad? What if his father was right and he, Silas, had helped sentence the Son of God? No, he knew that was impossible. Silas stopped to take a deep breath. He must get hold of himself. He was a proud, intelligent, well-informed, fifteen-year-old Pharisee. He knew the truth. He knew what he should believe. He knew what his grandfather would believe if he were here. Silas decided to reason with his father at the Temple.

Then, as he was about to take his first step away from the site of so much confusion and injustice, he saw Jesus staggering from the military quarters of the praetorium. Silas could hardly believe his eyes. In spite of the condition of his mangled body, with so much raw flesh exposed, he was somehow still alive and able to walk. He was even bearing the heavy crosspiece on which he would hang. Silas knew that Jesus would be paraded through the streets of the city as long as he managed to cling to life, to demonstrate the fate of criminals to the Jewish citizenry.

Once more he doubted that Jesus would survive until he arrived at the crucifixion site, but he shuddered to think about what would happen there if he did. The crosspiece would be laid down on the ground and Jesus would be placed on it with his arms stretched across its length. Then crucifixion nails would be driven through his wrists and into the crosspiece. If they drove the nails through his hands the smaller bones there would not be strong enough to support the weight of Jesus' body. Next a rope would be attached to the crosspiece so it could be raised to the top of the upright that had been planted in the ground waiting for him. Jesus' mutilated body would sway from side to side as he was hoisted up the pole until the crosspiece fit into the groove that would support it in its death-dealing position.

Silas had been told that loss of blood circulation and heart failure would bring an end to life on the cross, but that this might not happen until after several days of terrible pain.

As Jesus was led away Silas was relieved to see a man from the crowd take the crosspiece and carry it himself.[6]

Chapter 7

The Crucifixion

NOT KNOWING WHY, Silas changed his mind about joining his father. Instead, he followed the infamous procession through the many streets of Jerusalem as it made its way to the crucifixion site outside the city.

Three times Jesus fell, and three times he struggled until he rose and walked again. Silas could not believe that the fragile-looking, bleeding man was still alive. He had been interrogated from the time of his arrest in the middle of the night throughout most of the morning. He must have already been exhausted by the time he suffered those body-piercing blows of the scourging. Now this tortuous forced walk must seem endless to him. Silas felt relieved when Jesus finally reached Golgotha, but then he remembered the cruel torture that waited there for him. Out of compassion for the doomed man, Silas wished that he had succumbed on the way to the cross.

When Silas reached the top of the hill, he saw Jesus' crosspiece laid out on the ground lined up with two others. He wondered who the other two were who had been sentenced to a merciless death on this day. He remembered being told that Jesus did not hesitate to associate with sinners of the worst kind, but crucifying him with criminals seemed to be a cruel mockery of his life.

Jesus was the first to be nailed to his crosspiece and hoisted into position. Silas found at least some little relief when he saw that his feet would be bound and not nailed and were rested on a support to make it less likely for the nails to rip through his wrists. The other two men were treated in the same way, one placed on each side of Jesus.

Many of those who had demanded crucifixion, Sadducees and even a few Pharisees, had come to the site to confirm that the crucifixion had taken place. Some were there because they had nothing better to do. Others who were disillusioned followers of Jesus were there to make sure the false prophet they had believed in would be given the punishment they thought he deserved.

As Silas began to wonder if there were any here who still believed in him, he saw two women standing in the distance weeping. He did not know them, but remembering Nicodemus's words he thought one must be Mary Magdalene.

Many of those standing around at the foot of Jesus' cross ridiculed him because he did not save himself as everyone knew the Son of God would be able to do. When Silas heard their taunts, another possibility came into his mind. What if, for some very strange reason, Jesus believed that the cross was meant for him, that his true place was there on it?

He was startled to hear Jesus, beaten raw and bleeding, say, "Father, forgive them, for they do not know what they are doing." He could not understand it. What did it mean? He longed to talk to his father and Nicodemus, but he was alone.

Silas was terrified at midday when complete darkness closed in on the crucifixion site. It was only the sixth hour, and yet there was not a trace of light. It seemed as if the terrible spectacle before him was not meant to be seen by human eyes. For three hours fear paralyzed Silas's body. He remained there below the dying crucified figure in a trance. Then at the ninth hour, the darkness was swept away by a voice from the cross that shattered the silence with a cry that almost seemed to ring with victory, "Father, into your hands I commit my spirit."

These words freed Silas from his stupor. Now in panic, he struggled to escape from the scene. He longed for his father and the sanctuary he hoped the Temple would offer him. He had experienced much in one day that defied explanation. He had to pull himself together and realize that what he had been subjected to was only the death of a false prophet who had been found guilty of blasphemy.[1]

As anxious as Silas was to leave the site, he needed every bit of his strength to lift one foot ahead of the other as he trudged back toward the city. He had lost all track of time. Darkness had come and gone, but he knew that it could not be the beginning of a new day.

As he walked on and on toward the Temple he remembered Jesus' plea for forgiveness for the crowd while he was suffering on the cross. He wondered what the words could possibly mean. Then, when those last words of Jesus, "Father, into your hands I commit my spirit," came back to him, they brought a surprise. He could not understand why he had not recognized them sooner. They were the words that he, like every other Pharisee boy, said every night at bedtime to pray for a restful sleep. He wondered if it would be possible for Jesus to have a restful sleep after the terrible torture he had endured. Perhaps. The day had been one of extreme suffering for Jesus, and yet he had refused drug-laden wine to numb his pain.

Thomas was coming from the Temple. "Silas," he said, "you should have come with me. You would have witnessed the most extraordinary sight imaginable. As you know, I returned to the Temple for solace and guidance. I remained in prayer in the Court of the Israelites facing the Court of the Priests for what seemed like many hours. Instead of feeling relief, I became more confused and tormented by doubt.

"Then, at the ninth hour, the curtain covering the Holy of Holies was suddenly torn, split down the middle. This was strange enough, but it was not ripped from the bottom to the top as would have happened in a wind storm, but from the top down.[2] Silas, I hope you understand what this means. You know that the Holy of

Holies is a place so sacred that only the high priest can enter, and then only after ceremoniously cleansing his whole body. Even he can only enter on the Day of Atonement, that one day in the year when the high priest offers an animal sacrifice for all of Israel's sins. Our only way to reach God has always been through the priest who enters this sacred place to intercede for us. Now that most holy part of the Temple is exposed to all of us. It is just as if the way to God has been suddenly opened to everyone."

Silas listened spellbound to all that his father had to say, and then it was his turn. "What you have told me is only part of the story. When I tell you my experience, you will realize just how amazing the sight you saw was." Silas described his incredible day at the foot of the cross, right up to that unbelievable ninth hour when he and his father unknowingly shared a remarkable experience. The darkness enshrouding Jesus on the cross and the barrier separating the people from God disappeared at the same time.

Silas and his father left the Temple in stunned silence. They passed a Roman centurion talking to a Jew who had apparently just come from the Temple. Silas heard the Jew tell the centurion about the curtain, and then he heard the centurion's response, "Surely he was the Son of God."[3]

Just as they were about to leave the area of the Temple, Nicodemus saw them. "I have been waiting for you two. I knew that you would come here. I'm sure that both of you, like me, saw enough today to cause you much concern. The three of us have a lot to think about.

"But first, I have something that I must do and I want you two to know about it. There is no one else whom I can talk to about such an important matter. Regardless of who Jesus really was, I don't think that his body should be left for the animals to dispose of, as so often happens. If any action is to be taken it must be completed before the twelfth hour when the Sabbath will start. That means the body must be removed within the next two hours.

"It is my good fortune that a friend of mine from Arimathaea who supported my feeble action at the infamous meeting of the Sanhedrin will help me. Although Joseph did not tell me, I believe he is secretly a disciple of Jesus! He is as uncomfortable as I am with the Supreme Court's action, and we both regret we were not able to prevent a great injustice. Now we feel that the least we can do is to treat Jesus' body with respect. Joseph has already gone to Pilate to get permission to remove the body. If he is successful, I will help him take it to his own tomb, which is located in a peaceful garden. We will wrap it in a clean linen shroud and I will provide sufficient myrrh and aloes for burial. Then when all is done, we will roll the huge stone over the opening and Jesus' body will be safe.[4]

"If all goes well, we will have much for which to thank Joseph. He is a most wonderful man. Fortunately for us, he is very wealthy or we would not have had access to such a beautiful burial site, but his wealth is the least of his assets. I hope that somehow you will be able to meet him before he leaves for his home away from the city. You will soon discover that under his full head of grey hair lies a very keen mind—one that is able to distinguish right from wrong and good from bad, and under his gold-trimmed cloak you will find a heart richer than all his wealth. If I am correct that he was one of Jesus' followers, his name will go down in history as not only the first Pharisee, but the first member of the Sanhedrin to become a believer in whatever Jesus' message was.

"Now we must part, but I am anxious for us to share our experiences of the day, so please meet with me right after the Sabbath."

Chapter 8

The Empty Tomb

AS SILAS WATCHED their friend walk away, he turned to speak to his father. "I may not know who Jesus really was, but the thought of his abandoned body hanging on the cross exposed to wild animals tears me apart. He does not deserve this cruel treatment. I hope Nicodemus and Joseph will be able to rescue him from this terrible humiliation and give him the burial he should have."

"I don't know if that will be possible, Silas. From what I've heard, Pilate's decisions are based solely on what he expects to get in return. Whether they succeed or not will depend on Joseph's ability to supply whatever it is that Pilate will demand."

"Father, that's not all that's bothering me. Who was this Jesus?"

"Neither one of us will have peace until we know the truth about Jesus, and right now, I have no idea how or when we will find that truth."

Silas was weary beyond belief when they reached their temporary home just in time for the Sabbath meal, and neither it nor the service of worship and prayer in the synagogue the following morning brought the sense of peace Silas usually felt. The day after the Sabbath, Silas and his father left Bethany and started on their way to meet with Nicodemus.

They had not gone far when Silas said, "Father, so much has happened in Jerusalem that it seems like an eternity has passed since we arrived."

"That's how I feel too," Thomas replied. "We must search for the truth regarding this man who humiliated the Pharisees and threatened the Sadducees; and what we find may change our lives."

Two days ago Silas had thought he was mature and at peace with the world. He had no doubt in his mind about what he should do or how he should think. His religion supplied him with a rule for every circumstance. Now, he wasn't sure about anything; his self confidence had left him. He wished that his grandfather could be with them to help him and his father with the question that demanded an answer.

When they arrived at Nicodemus's home, they were given the usual warm welcome, and Nicodemus said, "I have a special surprise waiting inside for you. Please come in.

"This is my very good friend Joseph. He has been waiting here with me to meet you before returning to Arimathea. We are both anxious to hear your account of all that you saw the day before yesterday, because there must be some things that we missed." An exciting hour followed as Silas and Thomas told their stories.

Then it was Joseph's turn, and he began this way, "Nicodemus and I were at the trial of Jesus and at Golgotha when he was nailed to the cross, but we left before his final hour and did not witness the miraculous events you two have described.

"Nevertheless, what you have seen does not surprise me. Our story begins where your stories end. As you already know, Nicodemus and I planned to give Jesus the burial we believe he deserved. Well, we were lucky. Pilate was most cooperative and gave me permission to take Jesus' body from the cross. I think he was anxious to help because he regretted his part in the tragedy. I thanked him and left hurriedly to meet Nicodemus; we had very little time for what we needed to do, but God was with us. We were able to give Jesus a decent burial in my tomb, and roll the heavy stone against the opening just before the Sabbath began."

Joseph paused and then said, "This morning I passed the burial place on my way here. The stone was rolled away and the tomb was empty!"[1]

Silas gasped in disbelief. Thomas looked dazed. Silas realized by Nicodemus's lack of reaction that he had heard the story earlier.

When Silas's father was able to talk, he asked, "What on earth happened?"

"Well, I was told that when the chief priests heard that two of Jesus' supporters had given him a decent burial in a garden tomb, they feared that the same two supporters would return to the tomb later, remove his body, and claim that he had risen from the dead. To prevent this from happening they persuaded Pilate to post Roman soldiers at the site. When the tomb was reported empty, Pilate allowed the chief priests to question the soldiers. They claimed some ruffians had overpowered them and removed the body. The chief priests agreed that only Jesus' deceitful supporters would have a motive for making such a bold and disgraceful theft."

"Why would Jesus' supporters do that?" Thomas asked. "They could see that he had been given a proper burial."

"I'm sure the guards did not tell the truth," Joseph replied. "I'll tell you what really happened. First of all, let me explain that with great risk I attended several of Jesus' teaching sessions, and I learned a great deal from him and about him. I witnessed him perform acts of healing that without any doubt were miracles, but his real attraction for me was his message. Although he belittled many of what he called our meaningless rules, his basic belief is somewhat similar to our Pharisaic belief, and I must admit that the regulations he made fun of are a little far-fetched.

"He said that he came not to abolish the Law of Moses but to reject improper interpretation of it, and I believe that. His message is one of repentance, asking for forgiveness, obedience to God, faith in God, and love for God and man. He even teaches that we should love our enemies. Can you imagine loving the Sadducees?

"As I told you, I heard Jesus several times. I could not help but notice that the same group of twelve men had attended every session. Curious, I asked one of them, a man called Peter, to tell me about him and his friends. He explained that they were students of Jesus who had followed him from Galilee and were busy trying to learn all they could while he was still with them.

"Peter told me many things, some of which I did not accept at the time, but now they all seem quite believable. Just listen to this one. A short time ago he told me that Jesus had said that he must go to Jerusalem and suffer many things at the hands of the Jewish authorities and be killed, and on the third day be raised![3] What the four of us witnessed the day before yesterday was the crucifixion of the Son of God!"

Then, as if in a trance, Joseph began to walk away from the shocked father and son. As he got to the door, he stopped and turned to speak. "I must leave you now, but please go to this man, Peter, and listen to him. I have told Nicodemus where I think he will be." Joseph left without another word.

Silas felt as if he had been struck by lightning. Had the grave been robbed, or was Jesus resurrected as he prophesied? Could Jesus really be the Messiah? The Roman centurion thought so. Joseph of Arimathea said so.

Just minutes after Joseph left, the three men were on their way to the Lower City where the working people of Jerusalem lived in a crowded, noisy area. They wanted to find Peter before the leaderless disciples decided to return to their homes in Galilee.

The city was bulging with celebrating pilgrims on this the third day of the Feast of Unleavened Bread. Many had left their temporary quarters to spend a few shekels on the streets of Jerusalem. Nicodemus had said that the festival, besides being a paramount religious event, gave the business health of the city a welcome boost because all those fortunate enough to have money could not wait to get rid of it; and, of course, the demand for sacrificial animals was a big contributor to the economy.

The Temple was a good customer of local merchants, and the demand for such things as priestly robes, incense, and altar ornaments increased during any festival. The taverns were kept busy serving visitors salted fish, soup, fruit, and even well-cooked locusts and wild honey with local wine. Nonessential businesses were shut down, and many who normally left the city to tend crops or olive groves chose instead to walk the city streets and participate in the celebration. Everywhere, dishonest men with quick hands were looking for careless shoppers, but nowhere was there any visible interest in what had happened at the crucifixion at Golgotha.

With much difficulty Nicodemus, Thomas, and Silas forced their way through the crowd and into the Lower City. For some reason, Silas was not repelled by the sights of this depressed area of Jerusalem as he had been previously. Following the directions they had been given, they located a place that matched Joseph's description.

Silas had never visited a home such as this before. Nicodemus knocked at the side of the curtain-covered open door, but no one came to answer. Finally, the curtain parted just a crack and after a slight pause a muffled voice asked, "What do you want?"

"We are looking for Peter," Nicodemus answered.

"There is no one here by that name," came the reply. And then, "I can tell by your dress that you do not belong in this part of the city. Who is this man that you are looking for?"

"He is Peter, a friend of Joseph of Arimathaea, and we are friends of Joseph."

With that the curtain parted slowly and the three were motioned inside.

"Why do you seek my son-in-law?" the woman asked.

"We are anxious to talk to him about all that we have seen and heard in recent days. Perhaps we can even help him now that his leader is no longer with him."

"Then you have not heard everything."

"What more could there be?"

"Their leader is still with them. Jesus is alive! This very morning Jesus' friend, Mary Magdalene, visited the tomb with another woman and found it empty. But before they left the area an angel told them, 'Don't be alarmed. He has risen! But go; tell his disciples and Peter he is going ahead of you into Galilee. There you will see him, just as he told you.'"[4]

Silas looked at his father wondering how it could possibly be true, but Nicodemus said, "It's all beginning to fit together. Now, more than ever, we must talk to Peter. When will he be back?"

"He will not be back. He is on his way to Galilee. Fortunately for you he is still not very far from here. Because you have come from Joseph of Arimathaea, one of Jesus' most trusted disciples, I feel safe in telling you where you can find him. He and the others are in Bethany. They are with friends of Jesus, Mary and Martha.[5] I will tell you how to get there, but do not go today because the eleven have much to discuss and plans to make. Be sure that you do not wait any longer than tomorrow, because soon they will leave for Galilee to be reunited with the Master."[6]

Silas and the two men were speechless for the first few minutes after they left Peter's mother-in-law. When they began to talk, they agreed that it was difficult to believe what she had told them, but it was just as difficult to dismiss what she had said as being untrue. They must leave to search for Peter early the next morning.

The following day, the three men met on the Jerusalem-Jericho Road and started off to find the home of Mary and Martha. They had only gone a short distance when Nicodemus said, "This is it. The place where I met Jesus is not far from here."

"I can't believe it," Silas replied. "For almost two weeks we have been within a stone's throw of Mary and Martha's home. Do you think that it is possible that Jesus visited there while we lived nearby?"

"I have no doubt about it," Nicodemus said. "Peter's mother-in-law said they were friends and it was in this area that I talked to him."

When they went up to the door, Mary met them. As soon as she was satisfied that they were friends of Joseph of Arimathaea, she greeted them warmly and invited them in. Once inside, they met Martha, Peter, and ten other disciples of Jesus.

Silas felt out of place in the presence of those who obviously believed in Jesus without question. When he looked at his father and Nicodemus, he sensed that they were uncomfortable also.

Peter described how each of them, of humble background in Galilee, had been chosen by Jesus to be his students. When Jesus started on his teaching mission they followed along, witnessing many miracles, and listening to all that he told them. Peter said that some things had been difficult to understand at first, but eventually the picture began to clear, and then the final answer came with the resurrection.

"For much of our time with him we did not know his true identity, although he had often tried to tell us. Then the truth came through to me alone. It happened one day when Jesus asked, 'Who do you say I am?' At that precise moment, the answer to that question was revealed to me and I answered him, 'You are the Christ, the Son of the living God.' And Jesus replied, 'Blessed are you, Simon, son of Jonah, for this was not revealed to you by man, but by my Father in heaven.'[7]

"Although I knew then that he was the Messiah we had been waiting for, I did not understand until a few days ago what his true mission was. Like most other Jews, I believed that the Messiah would come to us as a military leader whose sole purpose was to defeat the oppressive Romans with force. We did not perceive the Messiah as a gentle person who taught love and forgiveness.

"Some time later he took me along with James and John to the top of a high mountain and there before our very eyes he was transfigured and a voice from the cloud confirmed that he was indeed the Son of God. When it was over, Jesus ordered us not to tell this story until after he had risen from the dead.[8]

"So now you are able to hear it and believe it. Since that time we have learned even more. Now we know that he came to replace the sacrificial lamb that in the past has been offered in the Temple to redeem us from our sins. He was our true sacrificial lamb, and he offered his life on the cross for the sins of everyone. We must repent, ask to be forgiven, and if we have faith, then it will be so.

"Since yesterday, when the tomb was found empty, many have seen him. Just last evening he appeared in the midst of us, not coming to the door as you three did, but as a spirit. His first words were, 'Peace be with you.'[9] Then he ordered us to carry on the work he had started, explaining that he would always be with us because the Holy Spirit would be there to guide us. He told us that we should 'go and make disciples of all nations, baptizing them in the name of the Father, and of the Son, and of the Holy Spirit.'[10] When we see him next it will be in Galilee where we will be going soon.

"In the meantime, you three should stay in Jerusalem and go about your usual business, but keep in mind all I have told you. I have faith that you will soon believe as we do. When we return, we will need your help to teach the truth, and it will not be easy. We will have to meet secretly as we increase our number. The Roman government will be suspicious of us and see us as troublemakers. The religious leaders will be anxious to rid themselves of us. You must leave now, for we have much to do. Good-bye and the peace of the Lord be with you."

As the three men began their walk back to the Jerusalem-Jericho Road where they would part, Thomas was the first to speak. "I'm convinced that we will find it difficult to reconcile much of Jesus' belief with our Pharisaic faith, which we will have to do if he truly is the Messiah. It will take time to sort everything out. Unfortunately, once the festival week is over, most of our time will be taken by the daily problems of ordinary life, but three days are left before that happens. I don't know about you, Nicodemus, but Silas and I will spend much of that period in the Temple contemplating all that we have been exposed to and trying to find the truth in it."

"I can think of nothing better for you to do. I only wish I could do the same. Unfortunately, I have a duty to perform because of my position on the Sanhedrin. Nevertheless I will come to the Temple whenever I can."

"It's shameful," Thomas said, "that our worldly tasks prevent us from spending the time we need to discover the truth about Jesus."

"Thomas, remember that Peter told us that he and the other disciples would come back to Jerusalem. Let us hope that the message they return with will be the one we need."

"That's a wonderful thought to part with. Nicodemus, we have gone through much together in a very short time, and I believe that the friendship you extended to us has grown stronger because of that."

"I'm sure that it has. Peace be with you and Silas."

Chapter 9

Forty Days

THE FEAST OF Unleavened Bread was over, but Silas remained uncomfortable with the present state of his life. He wanted to believe what they thought was the truth, but feared that acceptance would destroy much of the Pharisaic faith to which they had been devoted.

Thomas took almost two weeks to find a permanent residence in the city. With John's help he was able to find the owner of an ox-drawn cart and negotiate successfully with him for a reasonable fee to transport the family's possessions to their new home. After thanking John and Mary for their hospitality and saying good-bye, the small family left the quiet town of Bethany for the noisy city of Jerusalem.

Once they were settled, Silas began to relax, expecting his life to become more like the one he was accustomed to, but he knew that was not to be when his father said to him, "I have decided not to contact Gamaliel about your education until we can become comfortable with Jesus and his belief. Once we have accomplished that, we must find out what the rabbi's position is. In the meantime, you can help me set up my business."

Silas was nonplussed. He longed for a simple and uncomplicated existence like the one he had enjoyed in Alexandria. He had believed then that what he had been taught from the Torah was everything he needed to know to lead a good life, and of course he had the oral law which the Pharisees had developed to guide him. Like his father and grandfather, he had been happy in the knowledge that he lived as morally perfect a life as was possible. He longed for the security he had enjoyed in the years when his father had told him so often that he was special.

Six weeks after witnessing that horrible crucifixion, Silas and his father went to the Temple as they often did. After prayers and meditation, they left to return home. They had not gone far when Silas saw Nicodemus coming toward them. When Nicodemus came closer Silas could see that Nicodemus was very excited. As soon as Nicodemus was sure that no one was close enough to overhear what he was going to say, he told his friends he had great news for them. "The disciples are back. They have just returned from Galilee and are in Bethany now. They are preparing to meet tomorrow with as many friends as can be found, and we have been invited. Let's go there together in the morning." Silas and his father agreed. Now they were just as excited as Nicodemus was.

The next day the three friends had much to talk about as they walked along the road toward Bethany. These three-way conversations reminded Silas of how fortunate he was that two learned Pharisees treated him, a fifteen-year old, like an adult. Once more he felt the maturity that made him the equal of his companions.

Thomas said that he was concerned about the security of the disciples. He reminded the others that it was only their claim to be friends of Joseph, which could have been false, that gained them entry to the disciples' earlier meeting. "We should warn the disciples to be more careful about letting strangers in. Of course, now that we have met them, we must be very cautious also."

"Thomas, you will realize how appropriate your comments on security were when I tell you about a recent experience that I had. Although I did not tell you before, I resigned from the Sanhedrin shortly after the crucifixion. Because of what I had seen and heard, I could no longer continue to serve on that body.

"Of course, I knew that because I had protested the lack of a fair trial for Jesus the Sadducees considered me one of his supporters. They were anxious to bring a legitimate charge against me, but had no grounds for interviewing me until I resigned my position on the Supreme Court. Resignations from that body are most unusual, so I was not surprised to be summoned to appear at a hearing to explain my action.

"I could tell from the members' questions that they feared I would support the followers of Jesus if they challenged the legality of his trial. After a lengthy session, the Sadducees realized that they could not prove that I had left the Supreme Court because of a relationship with Jesus or his disciples. I was astonished that they did not ask me what I knew about the disappearance of Jesus' body. They were unaware of the part I had played in giving him a decent burial.

"Now I will tell you why I did not mention my resignation before. I was about to be dismissed when one member interrupted the proceedings to ask a question that surprised me. He asked me to explain my close relationship with you, Thomas. The Sanhedrin paid someone well for that information. I answered by telling him about my friendship with your father and the promise I made to care for you and Silas as if you were my own.

"I'm telling you this now because I believe that you and Silas should know it, but I do not think it is any cause for concern. The fact that there were no follow-up questions convinced me that the Sanhedrin accepted the answer I gave them."

When Silas heard this he hoped it was true, but he knew that he and his father would be in trouble if the authorities found out where they were headed now.

Silas knew also that the Sanhedrin was not the only source of worry for him and his father. They lived in a Roman world held together by Roman legions and the Greek language and culture, but they were not Romans. They were Jews. Jews were despised by the Romans no matter where they lived in the widespread empire, and the suspicious government kept a careful watch on their behavior. So, for as long as the Jews didn't cause any trouble, they were ignored, but Rome would not tolerate any hint of disloyalty. Silas and his father would have to make sure they neither said nor did anything that the Roman authorities could interpret as being disloyal to the emperor. Silas feared that any relationship with the disciples of Jesus could be interpreted as being disloyal.

"Nicodemus," Thomas said, "thank you for telling us about your experience with the Sanhedrin. Now I want to tell you the conclusion I just reached after many days of careful consideration and prayer concerning all that we heard about Jesus and his message. I am finally proud and happy to say that as of today I truly believe in Jesus Christ."

"Thomas, I am pleased to hear that because I have been sure for some time that without any doubt Jesus is the Messiah. Now we can both call ourselves *believers*."

Silas knew that both men were waiting for him to say something, but he was still not quite ready to make a commitment.

Before long the three arrived at the outskirts of Bethany. Following the directions Nicodemus had received, they found themselves on a narrow winding street in what looked like a very poor neighborhood in a section of Bethany they had not been in before. Nicodemus remarked that they should be safe there; it would be unlikely that either Roman officials or Jewish leaders would frequent the area.

Nicodemus soon recognized the meeting place from the description he had been given. When he said, "This is it," Silas was surprised to see a large building in such a run-down section of Bethany, but after they climbed the outside staircase to the upper room,[1] he saw that a large meeting place was a necessity. At least one hundred people were already there, a few sitting, most standing. Silas recognized Peter standing behind a table at the front of the room. Standing nearby were the ten other disciples: John, James, Andrew, Philip, Thomas, Bartholomew, Matthew, James the son of Alphaeus, Simon the Zealot, and Judas the son of James.

Peter[2] spoke to the crowd. "A great deal occurred in the forty days our Lord was with us. During all that time he continued to teach and counsel us. We now know that all that happened to him was in fulfillment of the Scriptures.[3] We were instructed in great detail as to how we should continue the work that he began. One of our main concerns was that none of us thought we had the ability to carry on the mission he started, but he told us not to be worried about that, because the Holy Spirit would give us the power we needed to do God's work.[4] That gave us the confidence that we needed to go forward.

"Then before he left to return to the Father, he instructed us to go to Jerusalem because in that city we would be empowered by the Holy Spirit. Jesus told us that once we got that strength from heaven, we should go out as apostles to teach and spread the Word, first in Jerusalem, but then throughout the entire world.

"After Jesus entrusted us with this great commission, he suddenly disappeared from our sight, and we heard this message, 'Men of Galilee, why do you stand here looking into the sky? This same Jesus, who has been taken from you into heaven, will come back in the same way you have seen him go into heaven.'"[5]

Silas listened to all that Peter said, and when he had finished, Silas knew that at last he was ready to make a commitment.

"As you know," Peter said, "Jesus selected twelve disciples to represent the twelve tribes of Israel, but now because of the betrayal and death of one of us, we are only eleven and must select a replacement for Judas Iscariot. This man must be one who has been with us from the beginning of Jesus' ministry and was a witness to his resurrection. We have already identified two such men and now must choose one of them to restore our number to twelve.

"The men we have selected are: Joseph, called Barsabbas, and Matthias. After prayer we will choose one of these men by the same method used in the Temple to appoint all officials. The two names have been written on stones of equal size. The stones have been placed in a jar. The jar will be shaken until the first stone falls out and the man named on the stone will replace Judas Iscariot." After praying for guidance, Peter took the jar and shook it. Soon one stone fell out. Peter picked it up and said one word, "Matthias." This ended the meeting abruptly.[6]

When Silas left with the others, he felt that at last he had a chance to find the peace he sought. As he walked away he said to his father and Nicodemus, "I know now that without a doubt our Messiah has come. I believe in him and am anxious to learn more about what he taught while he was with his people. I also know now that the education I want and need will not come from Gamaliel."

Chapter 10

Pentecost

WHEN SILAS LEFT the large upper room at Bethany he was excited about his future, but he realized he had much to learn about the new belief. He feared that the rigid discipline of his Pharisaic background would be a handicap. He had led a life controlled by rules and regulations that had to be followed without fail. He would have difficulty in comprehending a belief based solely on love of God and love of neighbor, but he was confident that the new faith would soon bring him the relief he craved. He was already beginning to feel more comfortable about living in Jerusalem, because there he had found what he was sure would be the true way of life.

A few days after Silas and the others returned to Jerusalem from their meeting with Peter, the next great Jewish religious observance was to begin. The celebration was called Pentecost[1] because it occurred fifty days after the Passover feast. This festival honored two quite different events: the giving of the Law to Moses on Mount Sinai and the success of the annual harvest.

Peter had told them the disciples would meet for the Pentecost celebration in the same upper room where they had eaten the Passover meal with Jesus. Peter said that at that supper Jesus had taken the bread, blessed it, broken it into pieces, and given one piece to each disciple, saying, "Take and eat; this is my body." Next he took the cup of wine and after giving thanks to God, he said, "Drink from it, all of you. This is my blood of the covenant, which is poured out for many for the forgiveness of sins."[2] Peter had said that the covenant was a promise of a new relationship between God and man and that Jesus' death on the cross, which followed the last supper, opened the way to repentance and the forgiveness of sins.[3]

Because it was compulsory for all adult males living within fifteen miles of Jerusalem to attend the Pentecost celebration there, the city was once more teeming with worshipers from all the nearby towns. Visitors came from throughout the world again because it was the goal of every male Jew to attend at least one Pentecost festival in Jerusalem during his lifetime.

Silas was happy to be walking with his father on the streets of the city on such a special day. They passed by many strange-looking visitors who were speaking in languages Silas did not recognize.

As they walked along Silas saw a gathering of people who appeared to be very agitated. Coming toward them out of that crowd was Simon the Zealot who had met Silas and his father in the upper room at Bethany.

Simon was very excited. "I'm so glad I spotted you," he said. "I have exciting news to tell. As you know, we met again in the upper room. We had only been there for a few minutes when all of a sudden, as we were about to pray, we heard a roar like a most violent storm, and each one of us felt as if something sharp, but invisible, had stung us. Then Peter, who understood, shouted, 'The Holy Spirit has come to us just as Jesus promised.[4] Let's celebrate and go out onto the streets to proclaim our belief and share it with all.' As we left the room I recalled Jesus' words, 'Go into all the world and preach the Good News to all creation.'[5]

"When we were outside Peter said, 'What a great opportunity we have been given to bring our message to everyone from everywhere![6] Now we can give them something very vital to take home with them, the Good News of salvation through belief in Jesus Christ.'

"When we reached the crowd we separated, each of us preaching the Word with enthusiasm to as many persons as could hear us. Soon a few people started to shout that we must be drunk because they could not understand anything we said.[7] Others tried to silence them as if they knew exactly what we were talking about, and soon the crowd was stirred up. When I recognized you two standing here, I knew I must tell you about everything that happened this morning. I'm puzzled about all the confusion that has just developed. But wait, Peter is about to speak. Let's hear what he has to say. Perhaps he will have the answer for us."

"I understand what is happening," Peter said. "We are speaking to you in Aramaic, our native tongue, but those of you who want to believe in Jesus are hearing what we say in your own language.[8] This is because the Holy Spirit is speaking to you through us. Those of you who do not understand and accuse us of being drunk are so filled with unbelief that our words mean nothing to you. No, we are not drunk. Anyone drunk at this early hour of the day would still be asleep in the gutter.

"Furthermore, regardless of what language any of you use, I am able to understand what you say. We have been empowered by the Holy Spirit and have become apostles. Those of you who are familiar with the Scriptures will recall that the prophet Joel foretold what is happening at this very moment. He said, 'And afterward, I will pour out my Spirit on all people.'"[9]

Silas could see that Peter had the undivided attention of the huge crowd, even including some of those who had accused the apostles of being drunk at the third hour of the day.

After a slight pause Peter continued, "Jews of the world, let me tell you what horrible act you have committed and what the result of your sinful action has been. Just a few short weeks ago you condemned a Jew to the most horrible death ever devised by man, death by scourging and crucifixion. This Jew, who was so much more than mere man, was Jesus of Nazareth in Galilee."

Silas knew that Peter was talking to him, a new believer, as well as the others in the crowd.

"Now I will tell you, he was our Messiah, the true Son of God. You crucified him. Then on the third day he was raised from the dead and lived among us, his disciples, for forty days before returning to his Father in heaven. All this did not happen accidentally. It was foreordained by God.

"To you who may believe that because he was crucified, Jesus could not be your Messiah, remember that his resurrection confirmed who he was and still is. Let me remind you that God, speaking through David, your ancestral king, who was also a prophet, foretold the resurrection of Jesus, the Christ, just as I have reported it to you.[10] All that happened has been part of God's eternal plan."

Silas could see that many who listened had understood because they began to wail and cry for help. Peter took advantage of the situation and began to console the crowd. "Don't despair. You are not lost if you believe what I have told you, but you must take action. Repent and be baptized, every one of you, in the name of Jesus Christ for the forgiveness of your sins, and you will receive the gift of the Holy Spirit."[11]

After Peter finished speaking, Silas was baptized, along with a host of new believers that Thomas estimated later to be as many as three thousand.[12] Silas knew something very special had happened on this day.

Now that Silas had been baptized, he understood what Jesus had meant when he told Nicodemus, "Unless you are born again you cannot enter the Kingdom of Heaven." With his baptism Silas felt the forgiveness of his sins and the beginning of a new life.

What a life it promised to be! He already knew God from his years of study of the Torah, and he had met his Son on the Cross and talked to those who had been with him after his resurrection. Now on this day the Holy Spirit had come to the apostles and, through baptism, to him.

Silas turned to his father. "Father, I'm sure that Grandfather would have become a believer today if he had been present to witness the work of the Holy Spirit at the celebration of Pentecost."

"I believe that also," Thomas said, "but it troubles me that during the almost eight weeks that we have been searching for the truth, your grandfather in faraway Alexandria has been unaware of all that we have seen and heard."

"Thomas," Nicodemus said, as he approached his friends, "I have a suggestion. I see no reason why you cannot share what we have learned with your father, my faithful friend, by explaining to him in a letter the development of our faith just as it happened, taking him through our conversion step by step. I know your father well, and although it may take time to convince him that his Messiah has come, I know that some day he will no longer deny the truth."

"Nicodemus, I believe that your suggestion is a possible solution to our problem. A letter to my father could be very effective, especially if Silas is a part of it."

"Oh, Father. I would be thrilled to help. Let's get started right away. I now believe that the way to fulfill my obligation to Grandfather and enrich the lives of others will be through spreading the story of Jesus Christ."

"That's wonderful," Thomas said, "but I'm quite concerned about this daunting task. I am well aware that bitter feelings often developed in the past between those who took up a new belief and those who clung to their old way of life. In many families a change in faith pitted son against father and father against son. Our letter could cause an insurmountable barrier between my father and you and me. Before we start our task, let us pray together to ask that what we write will not tear our family apart."

When this was done and they were ready to begin Silas said, "The Holy Spirit will be with us, so if we do our best we will succeed. We must tell the truth, that belief in Jesus Christ, and not adherence to a host of meaningless rules and regulations, is the only way to salvation."

"Silas, let's discuss a small part of our learning experience each day. When we are satisfied with what we come up with, I will dictate my understanding of our discussion and you will commit it to writing. We must be careful because we are new to the faith and could easily make a mistake. Eventually the whole story will be told."

So they wrote the letter, with Thomas contributing parts and Silas, too, telling of what he had seen. Silas ended the epistle: "Grandfather, this is Silas speaking again. I promised to continue the family tradition of interpreting the Law for the enrichment of all who believe. I know now that I will be able to fulfill my promise, but in a way that neither of us anticipated. The proper interpretation can only come through the teachings of Jesus Christ with the guidance of the Holy Spirit, and not from anything that can be found in the library at Alexandria. I will continue to search for, find, and disseminate the truth now that I know where it can be found. My prayer is that you will join us and become a believer, as those who follow Jesus are called.

The grace of our Lord Jesus Christ be with you."

Chapter 11

Genesis

FOR THE NEXT few days after Pentecost the apostles continued to meet in public and preach to the crowd that always gathered to hear more about the message Jesus had left for them. Most often the speaker was Peter, but one of the other apostles would take a turn from time to time to give him a rest. Silas attended the sessions every day, but Thomas could not as he was struggling with his business.

Often, after the meetings, Silas would ask Peter to explain something about the new belief he didn't understand. One day Silas said, "Peter, at our very first meeting in Bethany you told us that as we grew we would have to meet secretly. Both the Roman government and our own leaders would be suspicious of a group they perceived to be different, if it continued to increase in size. We have many more followers now, yet we are still meeting in public without encountering any interference. This seems very strange to me."

Peter, as always, replied seriously. "For many years now various groups considered to be inoffensive by the authorities have met in the first few days after each Pentecost festival. We are not perceived to be different from any of the others, and so we are left alone.

Unfortunately, most of the celebrants will be leaving Jerusalem soon, and then we will be conspicuous."

Soon after this conversation with Silas, Peter decided that they should no longer chance open-air meetings. He met with the apostles and presented an alternative to the public sessions. "First of all," he said, "it is most important that we follow the Law and continue to worship together on the Sabbath. The authorities should not object to that. Then we should meet again on the following day in small groups in private homes. We will need to find believers willing to offer their homes for this purpose and then instruct them how to conduct a service. As time goes by and our number continues to grow, I'm sure that more homes will be offered, so that we will be able to take care of everyone."

Before many days had passed, all known believers had been contacted and enough homes to accommodate them had been offered. Thomas was happy to offer his home and suggested that a group of twenty or thirty people would be comfortable meeting with him.

The plan worked well. On the Sabbath the members of the group either went to the Temple to worship or to the synagogue if they lived too far from the Temple. Then as soon as possible after sundown on the Sabbath, just as the first day of the week began, the faithful gathered at the homes of their friends to give thanks and to praise and to learn.[1] The homeowner or someone else would volunteer to be the leader.

At Thomas's home as well as in the homes of others a pattern of worship soon emerged that took advantage of the believers' rich Judaist heritage. The main meal of the day was part of the service. Each worshipper brought his own food. If an apostle was present he would bless some of the bread and wine and reenact the last supper he had shared with Jesus in the upper room.[2] After they ate, they said prayers, read from the Torah, and sang hymns or psalms. Often the leader would give a message. Following the practice of the synagogue, one or more of those present might also address the gathering before the service was concluded. Many of the believers contributed to the informal meetings.

Toward the end of a meeting at his home, Silas watched the speaker, who was carried away by his enthusiasm, inflame the congregation. They began to argue with one another about what the speaker had said. Silas worried because the meeting was about to end in confusion. Something must be done. He went to the front of the room, stood on a bench, and raised his hand to show that he wanted to speak. One by one the members of the congregation saw Silas and became quiet. Then one man said, "Let's hear what the boy has to say."

"Friends, do not let the essence of the message you heard this evening be lost in the turmoil you created. When you go to your homes, think about the speaker's words and pray for understanding. Then, when we next meet, enter into quiet discussion and grow in knowledge and love of God." One by one, the silenced believers left the meeting; the confusion was replaced with reverence. When Peter heard about what had happened, he asked Silas to become more active in leading the home service.

One day when Peter was teaching at one of the home meetings, he spoke about the two great commandments, mentioning that the second one, 'Love your neighbor as yourself'[3] is often ignored. At the end of the service, just as Peter had hoped, one of the men suggested that they should begin to show their love for one another by helping those in need.

At first those with more than necessary to cover their own expenses began to help those who were less fortunate, and as time went on more and more families sold everything that they did not absolutely require and contributed the proceeds to a general fund.[4] Someone was appointed in each group to accept the responsibility of distributing from this fund as was necessary.

Pleas for healing were increasing as well. When the apostles were not teaching, they were kept busy curing all who had faith, whether the sickness was of the body or the mind. Important also to the new movement that some called *The Way*, was the growth of fellowship that developed through close association of the members with one another, especially during the breaking of bread together.[5]

As Thomas's business began to grow, Silas spent more time helping his father with some of the details. One day as he walked along the east side of the Temple, on his way to deliver a document, he saw a cripple sitting at the Beautiful Gate begging for alms. Then he noticed that Peter and the other apostles were about to pass through the gate and enter the Court of the Gentiles. Silas heard the cripple's request for money and then, Peter's answer, "Look at us! Silver or gold I do not have, but what I have I give you. In the name of Jesus Christ of Nazareth, walk." With these words Peter grabbed the cripple's hands and pulled him to his feet.

The man stood, completely healed, laughing and shouting and jumping on legs that a minute before had been useless. When Peter and the others resumed their walk toward the Temple the healed man went with them giving thanks and praise to God as he went.[6] The crowd that had witnessed the miraculous healing followed, singing praises and amazed at what they had seen. Silas recalled that he had witnessed a similar miracle a short time ago that he did not believe. He was ashamed now that he had thought the blind man was an accomplice of Jesus.

When Silas saw the reaction of the crowd to the miracle that had been performed, he wondered if Peter would take advantage of the situation and conduct an open-air meeting. Then he saw the apostles stop walking and heard Peter say, "Men of Israel, why does this surprise you? Why do you stare at us as if by our own power or godliness we made this man walk? The God of Abraham, Isaac, and Jacob, the God of our fathers has glorified his servant Jesus. You handed him over to be killed, and you disowned him before Pilate, though he had decided to let him go. You disowned the Holy and Righteous One and asked that a murderer be released to you. You killed the author of life, but God raised him from the dead. It is Jesus' name and the faith that comes through him that has given complete healing to this man."[7]

Silas was not surprised when he heard Peter continue to address the crowd in a similar manner to that which he had used at Pentecost. "Now brothers, I know that you acted in ignorance, as did your leaders. But this is how God fulfilled what he had foretold through all the prophets, saying that his Christ would suffer. Repent then, and turn to God, so that your sins may be wiped out, that times of refreshing may come from the Lord, and that he may send the Christ, who has been appointed for you—even Jesus. He must remain in heaven until the time comes for God to restore everything, as he promised long ago through his holy prophets."[8]

Silas had been listening to Peter's words with such attention that he did not realize some Sadducees, along with a few of their chief priests, had approached the gathering, until he heard their leader ask, "By what power or what name did you do this?"[9] They had heard Peter refer to the resurrection of Jesus, and unlike the Pharisees, the Sadducees did not believe in resurrection.

On the Temple grounds the high priest's question was all the authorization the police needed. They arrested the apostles and led them away. Silas could do nothing. Because the arrest happened at the mid-afternoon hour, no hearing would be held until the next day and the apostles would be in prison overnight.[10] Those who had witnessed the miracle and heard Peter's words began to leave, dismayed, but many told Silas they were sure the apostles would be released soon, and they declared that when this happened they would return to repent and be baptized.

Silas looked forward to the baptism of these new believers, but he also recognized the increased burden they would bring. Additional leaders had been trained and were doing well, but they would have difficulty carrying on with a larger following if Peter and the other apostles were imprisoned for any length of time. Many thousand Jews now realized that their Messiah had come and were eager to hear the message he had left for them. Silas feared that the believers might begin to drift away unless Peter and the apostles were released very soon.

Silas learned the next day that the apostles had been freed and were assembling at their upper room to report what had happened to them.[11] When he and his father entered the meeting place, Peter was just beginning to speak:

"The authorities seemed astonished when we confessed that we had no formal training for what we were doing, and that we showed no fear of them when we answered their questions. They knew we were followers of Jesus, but they didn't seem anxious to repeat the interrogation made of him at the home of the high priest that had been so useless and embarrassing for them. Their chief concern seemed to be that a large crowd had witnessed the curing of the cripple who was now standing in front of them, healed. We believe they feared that there would now be an increased demand for healings, and because they did not want the people to witness any more miracles, they forbade us to teach or heal in the name of Jesus.

"In their arrogance, they assumed we would agree. But with John's support I told them that we must listen to God and not to them, and must pass on to all the Word we had received from Jesus and the Holy Spirit.

"At that point they seemed very frustrated and embarrassed and could think of nothing else to say except to threaten us more. I believe they feared what the crowd that witnessed the healing would do if we were punished, and so we were allowed to go free."[12]

When Peter finished speaking, those assembled offered a prayer of thanksgiving for the apostles' release from those who opposed Jesus. Then they prayed for help in spreading the message and for protection from their enemies. The warning of the leaders of the Jews was clear. Those who believed in Jesus would be suspects, and every movement they made would be closely followed. The authorities, both Sadducees and Pharisees, now feared the apostles just as they had feared Jesus.

Peter said that in spite of the Sanhedrin's threat, they must take their message to the streets more often to reach those who did not yet believe and urge them to attend the home meetings.

Several days later the apostles decided to follow Peter's directive and boldly take their message out to all the people of Jerusalem. They chose Solomon's Porch for their regular meeting place. It was one of two great porticos or colonnades that went around the outer court of the Temple, an easy place for all who wanted to hear the message to find, but within sight and sound of the Sadducees and chief priests, who wanted to get rid of them.

Silas was kept busy helping Thomas. There was a greater need for lawyers in Jerusalem than in Alexandria, and the influx of visitors attending festivals resulted in a temporary increase in the demand for Thomas's services. Many business people requiring legal assistance came to Thomas for the first time, recommended by Nicodemus.

One day, however, when Thomas did not need him, Silas left to attend a session on Solomon's Porch. More and more people were coming now for healing and to hear the apostles' message. Pilgrims were arriving from other cities and towns of Judea.[13]

Silas was surprised that the apostles had not been bothered at the Temple by the Jewish authorities. Thomas said that their great success had protected them.

The Sadducees were afraid to interfere openly lest the large crowd that supported the apostles would rise up against them. They were beholden to Rome for their favored position and they knew that Emperor Tiberius would not tolerate any reaction that might develop into a riot.[14]

Silas was still far from Solomon's Porch when a friend rushed up to him and said that the apostles had been apprehended by the Temple police and taken off to prison.[15] Silas was horrified to hear this, but there was nothing for him to do but return home and give his father the news. Silas and Thomas endured a restless night.

The next morning Silas was flabbergasted when the same believer who had given him the disturbing news the previous day came to the door to announce that Peter and the others were back at work on Solomon's Porch.[16] Once more Silas left for the Temple, but this time his father went with him. They had not gone far when they saw Nicodemus coming toward them.

"Nicodemus, what a wonderful surprise," Thomas said. "It's a real treat to see you. My business keeps both of us off the streets. The reason we are outside today is that we heard the apostles had been imprisoned but were released and were back on Solomon's Porch teaching, and we're off to see if that's true."

"Yes, it is true, and I'll tell you what I heard about the arrest of the apostles from a friend of mine, a Pharisee and member of the Sanhedrin. Fortunately he still trusts me in spite of my recent resignation.

"They were all seized yesterday when they were isolated from the crowd and taken off to the Jewish High Court's prison. Then, when the Sanhedrin met this morning to discuss what crimes their prisoners could be charged with, they were informed that a group very much resembling the apostles was preaching on Solomon's Porch. In disbelief the high priest sent messengers to the prison to confirm that the Galileans were still there.

"When the messengers returned, they told the court that everything appeared normal and secure when they arrived at the prison, but when they went to the apostles' cell they discovered that there was no one inside. At this point word came that the group on Solomon's Porch was indeed the same one that had been imprisoned the previous day.

"In fear of retaliation by the crowd, the high priest did not order the apostles taken by force, but just sent a summons demanding their appearance before the Sanhedrin. When the apostles received it, they obliged and went to the court at once without protesting.[17]

"The high priest acknowledged the apostles' presence, but ignored their mysterious escape from prison as he began to speak. 'We gave you strict orders not to teach in the name of Jesus. Yet you have filled Jerusalem with your teaching and are determined to make us guilty of this man's blood.'

"Peter and the other apostles replied: 'We must obey God rather than men! The God of our fathers raised Jesus from the dead—whom you had killed by hanging him on a tree. God exalted him to his own right hand as Prince and Savior that he might give repentance and forgiveness of sins to Israel. We are witnesses of these things, and so is the Holy Spirit, whom God has given to those who obey him.'

"Of course this enraged the Sanhedrin, but before the high priest could respond, Gamaliel, a Pharisee you are familiar with, requested that the court adjourn for a private session. Away from the accused, he proposed a solution. He suggested that if the apostles were fakes as he believed, and allowed to go free, they would lose favor with the people and soon disappear from sight. If the accused were who they claimed to be, which he believed was impossible, no one could do anything to stop them, and all who opposed them would be sinning against God.

"The members of the Sanhedrin were relieved to hear these words, and when the apostles were brought back the high priest merely repeated his order to them to cease their preaching and healing and dismissed them.[18]

"This is all that I found out from my friend. He said he had no idea how the apostles escaped from their cell."

Silas, Nicodemus, and Thomas went on to the Temple, and there on Solomon's Porch as they expected, they saw Peter speaking. When the meeting was over they went along with the apostles to their upper room.

Peter told them what had happened. "We escaped from prison during the night when the doors mysteriously opened. We found a messenger standing outside the cell who instructed us to leave and return to the Temple early in the morning to continue our ministry to the people. As you have discovered, that is what we did."[19]

Nicodemus told the apostles about Gamaliel's part in their trial.

"Gamaliel is an honest Pharisee," Thomas said, "and well-known to my father. Before Silas became a believer, he had intended to study under him. Silas and I are also Pharisees and we can assure you that we, unlike Sadducees, have no political ambition and no desire to become puppets of Rome. None of our fellow Pharisees have yet believed the message of Jesus. They are content to live by adhering to every little one of their thousands of rules and regulations, but I am sure that as time goes by members of our party will recognize the truth, and I cannot help but think that Gamaliel is already beginning to see the light."

Outside the upper room Silas spoke: "You told us, Nicodemus, that the leaders of our Supreme Court feared that Jesus would expose their dishonest operation of the Temple and eliminate their ill-gotten gains. Now it seems to me that they fear the apostles for the same reason, but no matter what persecution the apostles suffer in the future, I know they will continue with their teaching and healing at the Temple, on the streets, and in the homes of the believers, and I predict that in spite of the threat of persecution, the number of believers will continue to grow."

"I hope that the persecution you refer to will never become a reality. I believe that the lack of success the Sadducee leaders have had abusing the apostles will convince them to stop their attacks, not only against our leaders but against all members of The Way as well. The Pharisees are not likely to be violent with us even if we continue to deny their life of rules and regulations. As long as we do nothing to upset the Roman authorities, we should be able to look forward to a peaceful coexistence with those who do not believe as we do."

"Nicodemus," Thomas said, "you are an optimistic pacifist."

"You must remember, Thomas, that I met Jesus shortly before the crucifixion. Although I may not have understood his words, I saw only love and peace in his eyes. Keep that thought with you until we meet again."

Chapter 12

Stephen

AS SILAS PREDICTED, the number of believers continued to increase, but as Nicodemus also predicted, the apostles were no longer threatened. Peaceful coexistence seemed to be a possibility.

Silas received great satisfaction whenever a truth-seeking Pharisee appeared among the new arrivals, but he was overwhelmed one day when a Sadducee priest became a believer. He had not expected that ever to happen.

As the number of believers in The Way continued to increase, the apostles thought they should have a better name to distinguish their belief from other Jewish sects. They decided to use the word *church*[1] from the Greek meaning assembly or gathering.

One day, Silas's friend Stephen asked him, "Have you heard that I've been given a new assignment?"

"No I haven't. Tell me about it."

"Peter came to me yesterday to discuss a problem that is a result of our rapid growth. It involves a group of Greek-speaking Jews among the new believers from distant lands who had decided to stay in Jerusalem after their Pentecost experience. They live comfortably in an area where the synagogue service is conducted in

Greek, and because they have not yet been able to find employment in Jerusalem, the church is supporting them financially.

"The Hellenists, as Peter called them, were satisfied with the assistance they were given until they discovered that the church leaders were not treating them as well as they treated those native Jews who also needed help. They came to Peter accusing the leaders of discrimination.[2] When he heard their story, he knew something had to be done, so he came to me with a plan.

"He said he realized that the church had grown to the extent that a provision for managing the details of daily living must be provided. What he would not do, he told me, was to involve the apostles with administrative details, because their days should be limited to spreading the message of Jesus Christ.[3]

"He said he had asked the apostles to select seven capable men from among the members of the church to take care of grievances such as the one he had just described. Then he asked me to be the leader of this group.[4] He said that if I accepted, my first task must be to resolve the complaint of the Hellenists.

"Of course I accepted the challenge, and am anxious to go to work."

Stephen did go to work, and cries of discrimination faded away.

Silas was not surprised with his friend's success, but he was surprised, one morning, to see him on the streets preaching and performing miracles along with the apostles.[5]

"What are you doing out here?" Silas asked him.

"I have no intention of limiting my time to the care and feeding of the flock. I want to go to where the need is greater. I know the church is growing rapidly, but the majority of the Jews in Jerusalem have either not heard or do not believe the Good News. Like the apostles and other leaders of the church, I want to reach as many of these non-believers as possible."

"Stephen, that's wonderful. I will be glad when I have learned enough to help The Way as you do," Silas said.

"I have an idea," Stephen said. "I'm leaving here now to speak to a group of devout Jews in their local synagogue. Why don't you come along as an observer?"

Silas began to worry as he looked around the synagogue at the diverse group Stephen had chosen to speak to. He recognized many of them. The congregation was made up of Libertines, also called *Freedmen,* because they were freed slaves, Cyrenians from North Africa, a group from Alexandria, and Jews from Cilicia and other of parts of Asia.

Why, Silas wondered, did Stephen come here? He has made a terrible mistake. He should not be speaking to these people. Most of those in attendance come from a culture very different from his. And why is he speaking to these people in Aramaic, a language unfamiliar to them?

He should be able to see from the puzzled expression on their faces that they do not understand much of what he is saying. Why does he continue to talk, and why are the people listening quietly? They must be intimidated because they perceive Stephen as speaking with authority.

Silas was relieved when Stephen finally stopped talking, but he soon became concerned again. Many of those who had been listening quietly began to shout out criticism. They had recognized a few Aramaic words, especially *Law*, but had misunderstood what Stephen had said about them. They had not understood Stephen's message at all and were very unhappy about what they thought he had said.

He had tried to explain that because of the sacrifice Jesus, their Messiah, had made on the cross, the sacrifices in the Temple had become meaningless. They interpreted this to mean that Stephen had recommended the destruction of the Temple. They also believed that he had suggested replacing the Law of Moses, which they considered untouchable, with some new law they thought this person Jesus had made up.

Silas heard first one and then another from the hostile audience demand Stephen be brought before the legal and religious court of the Jews and charged with heresy. Three ruffians responded to the demands of the crowd, and no authorities were present to stop them. They jumped up, grabbed Stephen, and led him away.[6]

Silas followed along behind the mob, confident that Stephen would convince the Sanhedrin that he had been misunderstood.

Although the court was in session when they arrived, the size of the group convinced the Sanhedrin to grant an audience. Several witnesses claimed that Stephen had said that this Jesus he worshiped would destroy the Temple and change the Law of Moses.

When the high priest heard the accusations, he asked Stephen if the charges against him were true. Silas could not believe Stephen's response. Instead of denying the false testimony, he chose to make a very lengthy speech, this time in Greek, in which he recounted the history of Israel from the time of Abram to the crucifixion and resurrection of Jesus. He emphasized the continued disobedience of the Jews in spite of the opportunities they had been given to obey God. He said that although they should have known better, they had continued their sinful ways throughout history, down to the present time. He accused those he was speaking to of worshipping the Temple as a building instead of worshiping the God it represented. He finished by blaming them for murdering the very Son of God, their Messiah.

Silas was shocked by what happened next. The enraged mob ignored the Sanhedrin, and, unchecked by the Temple police, seized Stephen and dragged him off. Members of the court were not concerned. No Roman soldiers were present to halt the violent reaction, because they were worried about the possibility of a riot. As the mob left the area Silas heard Stephen shout, "I see heaven open and the Son of Man standing at the right hand of God."

Silas followed the Jews as they pulled Stephen along beyond the city walls. He had no idea what they intended to do to his friend until he heard them begin to chant, "Stone him, stone him, stone the one who accused us of being murderers."

Silas was terrified, but he did not know what to do. Then he saw a man, too far away to be identified, rush out to the front of the procession and try to stop the angry mob from going further. At first they just ignored his cries of peace and love and orders to stop what they were doing, but when he persisted, they began to beat and push him, and he fell. The frenzied crowd rushed forward over him and crushed him. Finally someone dragged his dead body off the road. Silas realized now that protest was foolhardy. He could do nothing but pray.

Silas was jostled by the crowd that had continued to grow. The noise of the shouting and hollering had attracted many who had not heard Stephen speak and didn't understand what he had done to anger the crowd. But they joined in anyway, hoping to enjoy free entertainment, and watch the brutal murder they assumed would take place. Even young boys followed, and as soon as they found out where the procession was going, they ran on ahead gathering stones of all sizes to make a stockpile of ammunition for the angry approaching horde. One bloodthirsty bully gathered enough stones to fill a large pouch at his waist.

When the angry mob arrived at a suitable spot, they tied Stephen upright to a tree so he would make an easier target to hit, and Silas remembered the sight of Jesus being raised to the cross.

Those who chose to do the stoning shed their outer garments to make their throwing easier and more accurate. They placed their robes at the feet of a Pharisee they called Saul. Silas recalled that he had seen him earlier at the hearing watching all that was going on.

The signal was given to start. The first few stones missed the target, and the crowd mocked the throwers, but when one found its mark on Stephen's forehead Silas saw Saul lead the crowd in cheers to encourage the stoners. Another stone hit Stephen, and he cried out in a loud voice, "Lord, do not hold this sin against them." Other stones hit in quick succession. The throwers had found the proper range at last. Small stones seemed to be more accurately thrown than the larger ones. Then, gathering all his strength so as to be heard above the cheers of the crowd, Stephen cried out once more! "Lord Jesus, receive my Spirit."

Just as he said this a large stone struck him on the head and the last sign of life ebbed away.[7] He was finally at peace.

When Saul returned the robes to the stoners, Silas noticed that his face was lit by a bright smile. Silas knew the Sanhedrin would be smiling also. No riots had been caused for Pilate to hear about. The event had been orderly, and the spectators departed satisfied.

As Silas walked away he could see that Stephen's body was still tied to the tree, but that the body of the man trampled to death by the mob was being removed for burial by two men. One of them, answering a question from a bystander, said, "He was a Pharisee named Nicodemus."

Chapter 13

A New Era

A SOLEMN GROUP of mourners walked back to the city after removing Stephen's body from the stoning tree. Silas spoke to Thomas, "Stephen was murdered by his own people who had become an enraged mob when they were confronted with the truth they could not accept. They killed Nicodemus, too, when he tried to stop them."

"Silas, I don't believe that we will ever have the peaceful coexistence that Nicodemus died trying to achieve."

"I agree with you, Father. I'm worried that Stephen's disastrous mission may have taken our infant church into a new era—the beginning of persecution of the believers, not just by the Sanhedrin and the Roman government but by non-believing common Jews who have been encouraged by their success with killing Stephen.[1]

"Unfortunately, ordinary Jews can quickly become a hateful mob when they attempt to justify persecution by their ancient law, 'Stone him to death, because he tried to turn you away from the Lord your God.'"[2]

A former friend of Saul told Silas much about the man who had smiled at the stoning of Stephen. Saul had learned the trade of tent making at Tarsus, the capital of the Roman province of Cilicia, but before that, he had been well trained in his home in the Scriptures and in the traditions of his belief. Then he entered the synagogue school and became fluent in Hebrew, Aramaic, and Greek. After attending both the university and the school of philosophy he moved to Jerusalem to study under Gamaliel, a member of the Sanhedrin.

He kept to himself and was unaware of the emergence of what he perceived to be a new sect until it came to his attention during the Pentecost celebration. He was told that its members wanted to do away with the Law that was the foundation of his faith. He immediately branded the believers, as he heard they were called, as heretics, and he prayed for the day to come when God would give him the power to rid Jerusalem of sinners such as those. He would have no qualms about inhumanely destroying anyone like them. His feelings were as calloused as his hands had become from sewing the leather of his trade.

One day, he went to the Hall of Hewn Stone, as he often did, to observe whatever cases might be presented to the court. When he arrived, he discovered that a member of that new sect with the contradictory name of believers was on trial and was presenting his defense.

He heard the defendant, a man called Stephen, charge his accusers with the impossible crime of murdering the Son of God. When Stephen was dragged out of the court by his accusers Saul followed along behind the procession. As he watched the stoning he calmly stroked his beard. He had a plan in mind and he was resolved not to let his small size or poor health prevent him from accomplishing his mission. He wanted the Temple police to arrest and the Sanhedrin to try those he knew to be sinners, and before long he won the approval of his plan by the Supreme Court.

Once the Sanhedrin gave Saul their blessing, the persecution began. Silas knew the rest of the story. He was devastated by what was happening to the church. Members were seized and taken to prison in droves, and their homes were confiscated.

Saul went from house to house with the Temple police to drag off to prison anyone he suspected of believing in Jesus. As day of terror followed day of terror, makeshift prisons soon bulged with prisoners held in chains. As long as sufficient space was left to hold those arrested, Saul would not stop.

Persecution spread like a fire out of control throughout the church in Jerusalem. Believers could no longer appear in public. Members of the church fled the city for their own protection. If suspects were not at home when the police came, their homes were taken and given to those known to be loyal to the Sanhedrin. The rightful owners had no alternative but to join those fleeing the country.

The growing vibrant church that had boasted to have thousands of members was soon reduced to a few faithful who were living in fear. Silas and Thomas and a few others remained behind with the apostles, trying to live a normal life but ready to face whatever dangers might befall them.

For some time prior to Stephen's murder, Silas had been thinking more about the promise he had made to his grandfather. He knew without a doubt that it would be fulfilled through his belief in Jesus Christ as the Messiah, but he had not been sure until recently what role he should play in making it happen.

The persecution of the believers led Silas to make the decision. Once he was sure it was the right one, he went to his father to discuss it. "Father, even if I hadn't already decided not to study under Gamaliel, it would be impossible to do that now, because the famous rabbi probably approves of the persecution of the believers. Also, I now consider that my formal education was completed in Alexandria and that further knowledge can only come through study with the church leaders, which study I will pursue until I am qualified to function as an adult and as a scribe."

"Silas, I understand what you are saying, and it's exactly what I want to hear. Ever since we arrived in Jerusalem, I have been hoping the day would come when you expressed a desire to work with me as a scribe, and now my dream is to be fulfilled."

Silas knew that his reply would hurt his father, but he had to make it. "Father, I love you dearly, but I have no intention of entering your business. My fervent desire is to work for the church as a scribe somewhere away from Jerusalem. I intend to join the last of the believers who are now preparing to leave the city. I will do this not to escape the threat of violence, but to do my part to keep persecution from destroying the church."

Thomas was silent for a moment. Then he said, "Silas, of course I'm disappointed, but I have to admit that you have made the right decision, and I am very proud of you. We will both be able to make our contribution to the church, although each of us will make it in a different way. I will remain in Jerusalem and work to support the decimated church with the funds it will need to continue its existence, and you will bring Jesus' message to the countryside."

A few days later, after Silas said good-bye to his father, he joined those who were getting ready to leave. During the early days of persecution, leaders had emerged from among the believers. Philip, a member of the group of seven that was disbanding, was one of them and he was in charge of this last group. Silas had admired Philip for some time and believed that he would be a good person to follow. When he learned that Philip's group was about to depart on an eighty mile walk to Samaria, of all places, he was even more pleased with the choice he had made.[3] Philip would be ministering to those whom most Jews would have nothing to do with. Silas's choice would test his faith. He knew very well why the two races hated each other.

Seven hundred years previously the Assyrian army had conquered the Northern Kingdom of Israel. Although most of the Jews of Samaria, the capital city, were taken away as prisoners, many were left behind. Later, gentile exiles from other nations that had also been defeated by Assyria were taken to Samaria to live. After some time the Jews who were left behind began to intermarry with the Gentiles who had been brought in, producing a hybrid race considered impure and not at all Jewish by the Jews of the Southern Kingdom of Judea.

Judean Jews despised the Samaritans so much that when they traveled to the countries north of Samaria, they would not follow the shorter route through the city. They chose instead to take the much longer and more difficult road through barren land to avoid contact with the people they could not tolerate.

When Silas recalled the history of the Samaritans, he realized how remarkable it was that now he, a Pharisee, was going to participate in a mission to their country. Traditionally a Pharisee, much more than any other Jew, would refuse to even come close to one of those who he believed were despicable inferior beings. Just one year earlier Silas would rather have faced death than live with a Samaritan, but his life was no longer governed by hateful traditions. Now his decisions were based on what he had learned about Jesus' teachings. The Samaritans must be given the message, but should they be accepted as equals? Silas did not know the answer to that question.

Silas was sure that he had made a wise choice to follow Philip, but the venture might be dangerous. He worried that the Samaritans would drive Philip's group away, and that if the Samaritans did receive them, the apostles might not forgive them for associating with people they considered inferior.

As Philip and his followers approached Samaria, a gathering of Samaritans rushed out, surrounded the interlopers, and demanded angrily, "Who are you and what do want?"

"We are Jews from Jerusalem," Philip replied, "and we bring you a message of salvation through belief in Jesus Christ."

Silas was surprised to see that Philip's response brought a complete change in the attitude of the Samaritans. Their hostility disappeared in an instant, to be replaced by welcoming smiles. Silas was baffled by the sudden change, but Philip took advantage of the improved situation, entered the city, and immediately launched his first teaching session. When Silas saw how readily the Samaritans received Philip's message, his fear of rejection disappeared.

Just as Philip was finishing his talk, a Samaritan approached Silas and in a low voice said, "We've been expecting you."

"Why is that? What are you talking about?"

"Your leader, the man your speaker just referred to by the name of Jesus, came into our country two years ago. He stopped to get a drink at Jacob's well. This was a very strange occurrence; Jews do not often come into Samaria. In fact you Judeans are the first Jews to come here since your leader left. It so happened that one of the women of Sychar, a nearby village, was at the well also.

"Then the next strange event occurred. Your leader did what no other Jew would dare do. He talked to the woman in public. The fact that she was a Samaritan made this breach of conduct even worse. If one of your rabbis had seen him having a conversation with this woman, his reputation would have been destroyed. To make the meeting even more exceptional, he somehow knew the woman was immoral, but that knowledge did not stop him from talking to her. Because of her reputation not many of our own people would have anything to do with her, so she was overwhelmed that this strange Jew would discuss serious matters with her.

"He treated her with kindness as he talked about how she should conduct her life. He referred to water that was much different from the water in the well. He called it *living water* that would quench the thirst of her soul. He told her many other amazing things, and she believed everything that she heard.[4]

"When she left Jesus to return to the village she was so anxious to let others know about him that she forgot to take her water jar. She repeated everything she had learned to her neighbors, and for once they listened to her. Because they were intrigued by what they heard, they went to the well to meet Jesus themselves and hear him speak.

"They were so interested in all that he said that they invited him to come to their village and teach. This he did, staying with them for two days. He talked to them about many things and even claimed to be the Messiah. After he left, the men of Sychar came to the capital city to explain his message to all of us. They convinced us that he was the savior of all Samaritans. They said that he had predicted the time would soon come when his disciples would go out to teach the world. We were sure that this meant he would send them to us, and I believe that they are here today."[5]

Silas now understood why he and his friends had received such a warm reception, and he also knew the reason Philip had chosen to come to Samaria.

After the group had been in Samaria for almost two years, Philip sent a messenger to Jerusalem with a report on their progress and an invitation for the apostles to come and see for themselves what had been accomplished. A short time later Peter and John arrived.

The apostles prayed that the Samaritans would receive the Holy Spirit.[6] Peter praised Philip and his group and told them that Jesus had once said, "And you will be my witness in Jerusalem, and in all Judea and Samaria,"[7] and then later, "Love your enemies, do good to those who hate you."[8] Silas's fear that the apostles might not approve of their mission was unfounded.

Before the apostles left, Peter spoke to those who had come to Samaria with Philip. "The mother church in Jerusalem has not grown substantially in numbers since that terrible reign of terror forced you to flee, but it is still in existence. When you left, we did not know who the driving force was behind the persecution that imprisoned or killed so many of our number and brought you here. We know now that his name is Saul."

This announcement brought shrieks of disgust from the group. Silas alone was not surprised. Peter's announcement confirmed what Saul's embittered friend had told him. When the crowd became quiet, Peter said, "Although we have been less secure since Stephen was attacked, some good resulted from his stoning. It caused a dispersion of believers from Jerusalem, which has made possible a great spread of our faith. Your success in Samaria is proof of that. The church is growing elsewhere also. The number of believers is increasing daily in spite of the actions of our enemies."

Before leaving Samaria, Peter asked for the church's prayers to keep the apostles and the few others who were still free in Jerusalem safe from Saul.

After Peter and John left to report the success of Philip's group to the other apostles at Jerusalem, the Samaritan church continued to prosper. Silas had learned much as he continued to watch Philip teach and heal in the months following, and he was anxious to play a more important role.

One day at a meeting, Philip rose to address the group. "We have had great success at Samaria and have every right to be proud of our accomplishment. Not only have we brought many Samaritans into the fold, but we have developed some fine new leaders, so that we now have more than we need here. I believe that the time has come for some of us to go on to new areas that need our help."

Before Philip could say anything else, Barnabas, his chief assistant, rose and said, "I have been thinking about this very thing for some time now, and I agree. I propose to start out on my own tomorrow on the hundred-mile walk north to Damascus, the capital of Syria, and minister to the people there. I'm looking forward to it, but I will need some help. I hope to hear Silas say that he will go with me."

Silas jumped to his feet and shouted, "Why should we wait for tomorrow? I'm ready to leave today."

Silas's enthusiasm brought laughter from the assembly, but with a big smile on his fierce face, Barnabas assured him that the following morning would do just fine.

Barnabas, a native of Cyprus, was a Levite. Because of his priestly background and his teaching ability Silas believed that he could learn much from him. Silas had recently had his eighteenth birthday. He could already feel the stubble that would soon become a beard. Although he did not object to the more menial tasks he had been assigned, he longed for the day when he would be declared old enough to take his turn spreading the Word.

He had great respect for Barnabas, not only because of his background and leadership ability, but because he had sold all his property and given the proceeds for distribution to those less fortunate.[9] He looked forward to a new and different opportunity with Barnabas at Damascus. The city was a very important and busy business center because two major trade routes passed through it. Of course, although it was a gentile city, many Jews lived there as well. In fact, the first Jews to settle at Damascus came there more than one hundred years before the arrival of Silas.

Silas felt very safe on the road to his next home because of the burly man with whom he was traveling. Barnabas was much larger than most Jewish men. His deep and commanding voice suggested a muscular body under the cloak covering his large frame. His size and the fierce expression on his face would be more than enough to frighten any lone bandit away.

On their arrival at Damascus, Barnabas and his small group of volunteers soon found the Jewish quarter and rented suitable living accommodations. On their first Sabbath they attended a synagogue that was close to their temporary home. The men filled the large room on the ground floor under the loft for the women of the district.

To Silas, the synagogue had become the place to respect the age-old faith that had given birth to the new belief. The service was traditional, with the reading of the confession of faith in the one true God followed by prayers and readings from the Scriptures. In deference to the new arrivals, the ruler invited any of them who wished to speak to come forward. Barnabas asked Silas to be their speaker.

Without hesitation Silas stood and spoke: "Our belief is based on the teachings of Jesus Christ in whom we have complete faith. He died on the cross for our sins and your sins. He proved that he was truly the Messiah for whom we have been waiting for such a long time when he rose from the dead on the third day.

"After his resurrection, he lived on earth with his apostles for forty days. During this time he continued to teach them so they would be able to carry on his work after he left them. Before returning to his heavenly Father he commissioned his apostles to bring his message of repentance and the forgiveness of sins to the whole world. They brought the Good News of salvation to us, and now we are passing it on to you."

When Silas finished speaking, a man rose to respond. "We have heard something of this man, Jesus, of whom you speak, and of how two years ago one of his followers was stoned to death after he had maddened a crowd of Jews like us with his words. This tells me that not everyone who hears believes."

Before anyone else could say a word, the man pronounced the benediction. The service was over and the crowd was dismissed.

Silas was discouraged by what he interpreted as a failure at his first chance to teach, but Barnabas consoled him, and he was soon ready to try again. Fortunately, future meetings were successful, not only for Silas but for the other members of the group as well, and soon the church was well established in Damascus. Most of the converts became very active in the movement, and Silas soon had many new friends. After the group had been in Damascus for a little over a year, Ananias, a new and close friend of Silas, came to him at the synagogue with a strange story.

"I had a most unusual dream last night," he began. "God spoke to me! First of all he told me to go to the home of a man I had never heard of. He said that his name was Judas and that he lived on Straight Street right here in Damascus. Next came the most amazing part of all. Once there, I was to ask for a man I did not know but had heard a great deal about. Saul of Tarsus! God told me that Saul would be there and that he was now blind. Then, of all things, God ordered me to restore his sight!"[10]

"Oh no," Silas said. "If you go to that home, and if Saul is really there, you will be walking into a trap and going to prison, or worse. Saul is the most despicable Pharisee ever created. His goal is to exterminate the followers of Jesus. If he is here in Damascus now it will be for that reason. He is not blind. Do not go!"

"But I must go! God needs Saul, and he needs me. Let me finish my story. I truly believe that Saul is here and is blind and that somehow I will be given the power to restore his sight. God said that he had selected Saul to take the message of Jesus not only to Jews but to Gentiles as well, but his task will not be easy. I am to warn Saul that he will suffer in fulfilling his mission."[11]

"There must be some mistake. Saul is a very evil man. I first heard the name at the stoning of Stephen. I learned much about him later. Then at Samaria, Peter confirmed that he was the one responsible for the persecution of the believers in Jerusalem. Since then we heard he had received permission from the Sadducee priests to come to Damascus and repeat here what he did in Jerusalem. If what you say is true, he is here only to persecute us."[12]

"I'm familiar with all that," Ananias said, "but listen to me. I know it sounds unbelievable to you and I can understand that, but I'm sure that it was the voice of God I heard last night. I must go now and do what God has ordered me to do. I will talk to you later."

Silas could not believe the fantastic story he had just been told, but he could do nothing. Ananias was determined to go to the home of Judas where a trap might be waiting for him. As Silas thought about the dream his friend had just described, he realized that one part of it might be true. Saul could be here in Damascus now!

If this were so, Silas could think of a possible explanation for Ananias's dream. Perhaps one of Saul's supporters was a magician; there were many of them in Damascus. A clever magician working on orders from Saul could have hypnotized Ananias, forcing him to believe that he had dreamed the story he was told. The illusion could have been Ananias's death sentence.

Silas decided to consult a new believer by the name of Simon to find out if he thought hypnotism could be this powerful. Simon had been a magician who cast spells before he listened to Philip, became a believer, and was baptized.[13]

Silas found Simon after a lengthy search. His magician friend agreed that it was indeed possible that Ananias had been hypnotized to believe what he was told was a message from God. Silas thanked Simon and left. He was sure now that Ananias was headed for trouble, probably for death.

He had not gone far when he met Barnabas. Silas had just finished telling him Ananias's fantastic story when he saw Ananias rushing toward them looking very excited.

"I was right," Ananias exclaimed as he reached Silas and Barnabas. "The vision I received was truly a message from God. I found the home on Straight Street without any trouble and the man who came to the door identified himself as Judas. I introduced myself and asked for Saul. I admit that I did so with suspicion and fear.

"Judas gave me the sign of a believer and said that he was expecting me. I was amazed. Without hesitation or pausing to ask questions, he asked me to follow him into an inner room, and there I saw a blind man just sitting and staring into space as if he was waiting for someone.

"When Judas told him that I had come to the door and asked for him by name, his demeanor changed as if his wait was over and he said, 'You must be Ananias, because a voice told me that a man by that name would come to restore my sight. There is no longer any doubt in my mind—Jesus was the one who talked to me and he is just as those I have been persecuting have claimed. I have been a sinful, murdering monster and I must repent.'

"I was overwhelmed by what he said and to hear that he too had received a heavenly message. I was trembling because of the unbelievable things that were happening and barely able to tell him that, yes, God had sent me to him that he might have his sight restored and be filled with the Holy Spirit. When I laid my shaking hands on him, the miracle happened. His sight was restored at once and he begged to be baptized.

"After his baptism, Saul ate, telling me that it was the first food that he had eaten since losing his sight three days before as he walked from Jerusalem to Damascus.[14] When he spoke again, it was to ask us to no longer call him Saul. He said that was the name he bore when he persecuted the followers of Jesus and he did not want to hear it again. He now desired to be known only as *Paul*, the name that would acknowledge his rebirth as a believer in Jesus Christ.

"Then he told me what had happened to him. He confirmed that he had been given authority by the high priest to come to Damascus and arrest any who believed in Jesus and have them brought to Jerusalem for a mock trial by the Sanhedrin. But before he reached our city, he was hit by a bolt of lightning and knocked to the ground and blinded.

"Then a voice identified as that of the same Jesus he was persecuting spoke to him. He was told to rise and ask his companions to lead him into the city to the house of Judas who lived on Straight Street. The voice promised that he would get further instructions there. He said he did not know whether to believe the voice or not, but he did know that his sight was gone and that there was no alternative but to do what he was ordered.

"Paul said his fellow travelers escorted him as he requested to the home of Judas, whom he did not know. Once there they abandoned him in fear. They had heard the voice, but had seen no one. Paul soon learned that Judas was not surprised by his appearance. He, too, had received a message from God explaining that a blind man would come and three days later be followed by a believer named Ananias who would restore his sight.[15]

"After Paul finished telling me all this, he said that because he believed it was really God's plan and not the Sanhedrin's that had directed him to Damascus, he thought he should stay here and not return to Jerusalem. He has had a life-changing experience. He wants to join us, learn from us, and work with us.

"Jesus blinded him and then restored his sight for a very special reason. He chose him to take the Word to Jews and Gentiles alike. Paul is an apostle ordained by God. You must believe my story and accept him. He is anxious to get on with his new life and redeem himself for all the harm he has done. Now please come with me to meet him."

Silas and Barnabas accompanied Ananias to the home of Judas to meet Paul and to welcome him into the church.

Paul went through an amazing period of transition during the first few weeks of his new life with Silas and the others. At first it was difficult for him to comprehend the miracle that had transformed him. One day his goal had been the persecution of the believers, and three days later he was ready to give his life for the very ones he had vowed to destroy.

Nevertheless, Paul was hungry for the knowledge that he knew he must have to fulfill the mission he had been given. Both Barnabas and Silas spent a great deal of time helping him, and the three became close friends.

One day Paul came to Silas and Barnabas with a strange tale. "I have worked day and night since the restoration of my sight trying to learn all that I could about the belief I once thought was heresy. Before I am ready to join the two of you to teach and preach, I need to reflect on all that I have heard and evaluate what I have been exposed to. To do this I must be by myself for a time. I have decided to go outside Damascus to the district of Arabia to meditate and pray. I promise that I will return here, and when I do I will begin to work seriously with you, my two good friends."

Paul had only been with them a short time, but he had already become an important part of Silas's life and ministry. True to his word, he did return, and he was filled with enthusiasm and anxious to get to work. And he looked more robust and healthier than when he had left.

Before long, Paul was taking his turn with Silas, Barnabas, and the others preaching in the synagogue. In spite of the inspiring account of his conversion, many were still suspicious of him. They wondered how he could be sincere in urging everyone who would listen to embrace the same belief he had just recently sworn to abolish from the face of the earth. Bit by bit the sincerity that his firm speech conveyed began to win listeners over.

Although his voice was not thunderous like that of Barnabas, it was clear and penetrating. It possessed the strength that seemed to have bypassed his body. After some time most of those who heard him preach realized that because God had faith in him, they should also.[16]

One day Silas and Paul agreed to try something different. They preached one after the other in the same session. Silas began by talking about his experience at the cross and during the first weeks after the resurrection. Paul spoke next with the story of his conversion. With this evidence presented, that Jesus truly was the Messiah, he told the listeners the time had come to repent and ask to be forgiven and that if their faith was strong enough, forgiveness would come.

Then Silas spoke again to let the new believers know that they would receive salvation as a gift because of the grace of God. Paul finished by telling them that they should live by obeying what Jesus had said were the two greatest commandments—to love God and to love others.

All went well for Paul and Silas for some time, until a group from Jerusalem reached Damascus. News was leaked to Silas that these were enemies of Paul, and he learned what had happened in Jerusalem since Paul's departure.

As Saul, he had left Jerusalem on an important mission. The Sanhedrin had told him to go to Damascus and identify as many of the insurgent followers of Jesus as possible. The high priest told him he would send a detachment of Temple police a week after his departure to arrest all those he had exposed by then as a threat to Judaism.

The Temple police set out on schedule, but when they arrived at Damascus they found no trace of Saul, and after searching for several weeks they returned empty-handed to report his mysterious disappearance to their leaders.

Two years later news came back to Jerusalem that infuriated the Sanhedrin. Saul was alive and well and living in Damascus. Then the Jewish leaders learned that Saul had defected, joined the dissidents, and changed his Hebrew name of Saul to his Roman name of Paul.

The authorities were furious. When they asked for volunteers to go to Damascus and take care of the man who had deserted their cause, many came forward. Most of them had worked with Saul when he waged his campaign of death against the followers of Jesus. They felt betrayed and left Jerusalem anxious for revenge.

When they arrived at Damascus they initiated a well-organized attempt to find and destroy the man they had once worshiped. Their first task was to identify loyal Jews who were known to have nothing to do with the followers of Jesus. Because this included many of the Jews in Damascus, it was not difficult to find them. Soon they had located a sufficient number that the search for Paul was ready to begin, but not every recruit that had been chosen was loyal to the cause. So the news was leaked to Silas just before the search began. When Paul heard of the plot he realized that if he were to carry on with the work of the church he must survive, and to survive he must leave Damascus.

Just as he was preparing to go, word came that his enemies had anticipated he would attempt to flee, so had posted guards at every gate of the walled city to prevent him from getting out alive.

Paul had to leave Damascus, but he didn't know how to do it until Silas, the youngest man of the three, suggested that Paul could escape by going over the city wall. He explained that all they would need would be a basket large enough to hold a man, a heavy rope, and two strong men.

Paul and Barnabas thought this was a brilliant plan and they congratulated Silas for suggesting it. Their praise made the twenty-one-year-old Silas feel like a most valuable member of their three-man team.[17]

When Barnabas suggested that they start searching for a large basket, Paul surprised him and Silas by saying, "Not yet. I have one more problem, but I think that this time I have the solution. At first I didn't know where I should go if I did manage to get out of the city safely, but now I do. I'm sure that my destination must be Jerusalem.

"It is quite possible that the Sanhedrin and the non-believers I abandoned are not the only ones wanting my death. The head church may also believe that I should be punished for what I have done. If the apostles have either not heard or not believed the story about my conversion, they would still view me as their enemy, and of course the followers of Jesus still living in Jerusalem may despise me for my persecution of so many of their number.

"I must go to Jerusalem and appear before the apostles to clear my name. This will not be easy. First of all I will have to avoid the Sanhedrin and the Temple police. Then I must convince Peter and the others that I have truly become one of them. For that reason, I am asking you two, my good and faithful friends, to go with me and testify on my behalf."

Silas and Barnabas did not hesitate to agree to join Paul on his mission to clear his name, but now three people had to leave Damascus in a basket.

Chapter 14

Return to Jerusalem

BARNABAS, WATCHED CLOSELY by Silas, Paul, and two strong men in their prime, peeked out through the crack in the door. He pushed it open wide enough to have a clear view up and down the silent street. He peered into the distance and turned to reassure his friends.

"Now I know why they call this hour the *dead of night*," he said as quietly as his strong voice would allow. "It's just like a burial ground out there. The only men besides the five of us who are up and around now are those guarding the gates waiting for Paul to put in an appearance, but we won't apologize for disappointing them."

Barnabas led the way out onto the deserted street. Following him, Silas, Paul, and the two strong men wound their way through crooked narrow alleys, avoiding any area Barnabas thought might hide wide-awake souls, even friendly ones. Soon they reached the city wall at an isolated spot.

With more than a little difficulty, the men scaled the wall one by one until all five were on top along with a huge basket and a strong rope. According to the prearranged plan, Barnabas would go over first, so he moved to the edge, taking care not to kick any loose stones. He somehow managed to collapse his large frame sufficiently so that most of it fit into the basket. With care and without a sound the two strong men lowered him to the ground below.

When a tug on the rope told those on top of the wall that Barnabas had extricated himself from his cramped quarters and all was clear, they hoisted the empty basket up and prepared to send Paul down.

As soon as Paul was on solid ground, Silas had the first basket ride of his young life. When the basket was lowered for the fourth time, it was loaded with the food and the few belongings the three men would need for their hundred-mile walk to Jerusalem.

They remained silent after they started out until they were sure that their voices could not be heard at the city wall. Then they stopped to thank God for helping them to accomplish Silas's bold plan without a hitch. When they continued their journey, they trudged along at a good pace. The silence was broken by Barnabas's loud laugh.

Startled, and with one voice, Silas and Paul asked, "What's so funny?"

"I was just thinking about the reaction of the Sanhedrin when their servile assistants return empty-handed, and how embarrassed they would be if they knew that Paul had arrived in Jerusalem while their accomplices were still searching the back streets of Damascus for him."

"It is good to hear you laugh, Barnabas," Paul said. "Laughter has been out of our life for too long. Let's hope that you have brought it back."

When the three men started off again, their footsteps were lighter than they had been before. At dawn they rested at a place where they were hidden from the view of any travelers that might be headed for Damascus. After the initial tension caused by their daring escape had subsided, Silas realized how happy he was to be returning to the city he thought he would never grow to like. He was anxious to visit with his parents.

At the end of the fifth day of walking, the three men were very close to their destination. "We will have to be especially careful from now on," Barnabas said. "Let's stop and rest until the third watch and then enter the city in the early-morning darkness."

When they agreed that the time was right, the three men entered the city through the Eastern Gate, walking in the shadow of the buildings as quietly as their horsehide sandals scraping on the stone roadway would allow. Before they left Damascus, Silas had suggested that they stay with his parents while they were in Jerusalem, but Barnabas and Paul said they did not think this was a good idea. They had heard the reason Thomas's business was thriving was that his clients did not suspect he was a believer. The major portion of the church's income came from Thomas, and if the three men stayed with him, his cover might disappear and his business suffer.

One of the faithful in Damascus had directed them to go to the home of a believer who lived alone and seemed to be above suspicion, and that is where they were headed. They had never met this man, and of course he had no way of knowing they were coming. They had been given his address, but even with that, finding his home in the black hours of morning would be the first problem. The second and major one would be convincing him that Paul was no longer to be feared. They had agreed not to hide Paul's identity. Much darkness was left when the three men reached a small building in a back alley that without any doubt matched the description they had been given.

"Silas, you lead the way," Barnabas said. "Go up to that door and knock loudly enough for the man who lives in the house to hear you, but not so loudly that you might waken any suspicious neighbors."

"I appreciate your attempt at humor, but I will knock at the door the only way I know how." Silas's knock brought Jacob to the door. Silas gave the secret signal of The Way and the three men were ushered in at once. Their host seemed accustomed to receiving visiting believers in the dark of night.

Silas introduced himself, Barnabas, and then Paul who he said had been known as Saul of Tarsus before his conversion. When Jacob heard that hateful name, he started to tremble. "It's him. He hasn't changed. He's just been away for a while. Now he's come back and you are here to help him," he said, gasping. "All right. I'm ready. Take me away."

Silas hurriedly replied, "No. You are safe with us, believe me. I am the son of Thomas, whom I'm sure you know well and respect, and Paul is truly one of us."

Then Paul took over. "Perhaps you have not heard about my conversion, or have, and like many others, do not believe it. Let me tell you my true story." Paul related in full detail everything that had happened on the road to Damascus and during his life there since that experience. He was so sincere; the four men were soon friends.

After they had been fed and rested for a while, Silas left the others to visit his parents. Thomas opened the door and looked astonished to see his twenty-one-year-old son now a full two inches taller than he had been when he left home. Deborah seemed pleased that Silas was wearing only what he needed for warmth and modesty. Silas had long since abandoned his desire to dress ostentatiously like a hypocritical Pharisee. He had purchased a new plain robe and tunic for the visit to Jerusalem, and they were still reasonably clean. His only adornment, if it could be called that, was the leather writing kit Thomas had given him when he left home. No worthy scribe would go anywhere without his reeds and ink pot.

Silas worried that his father would be hurt when he found out that his son was going to stay with friends in Jerusalem and not with him, but when Thomas understood the reason for his decision, he did not object.

"Silas," said Thomas, "why don't you tell your story first. I'm sure that your life in Samaria and Damascus has been more exciting than my years in Jerusalem. I want to know all that has happened to you since you left home to spread the Word."

"I will be most happy to do that, but first I must know if you have heard from Grandfather."

"No, I have not," Thomas replied. "I sent letters to him on two occasions with reliable messengers, but did not receive word back either time. I wish that I could go to Alexandria to visit him and hope to reason with him, but I cannot. My presence in Jerusalem is vital to the success of my business, and the success of my business is vital to the life of the local church."

"I was afraid that would be your answer," Silas said. "I'm worried more than ever about him, but the responsibility should now be mine. I hope that some day soon I will be able to go to Alexandria to see him. If that happens, I pray it will be a happy occasion with his acceptance of the truth. Now I will tell you my story."

Of course Silas was very pleased to talk about the growth of his faith and the expansion of his work in the church. Without mentioning Paul's presence in Jerusalem, Silas told the story of his conversion as he had heard it and believed it. Silas's father said that they too had heard about Paul.

When Silas was finished, Thomas had his turn. He related the details of daily life in Jerusalem, assuring Silas that he had not been tormented by the non-believers for some time. He added that he regretted the reason for this. His life was peaceful only because he had kept his relationship with the believers hidden. Unfortunately, this was necessary for the church to survive, and he was thankful that Silas understood this and had decided to stay elsewhere while he was in Jerusalem. He explained that because the public did not suspect he was a believer, his business had become prosperous, and he was able to make substantial contributions to the church.

Thomas announced that he had one bit of information to disclose that was very important and indicative of the way the church was headed. "It involves an experience that Peter, the head of the Jerusalem council, had and told us about," he said. "Silas, after Peter left you at Samaria, he stopped at Lydda[1] on the way back to Jerusalem. He stayed there for some time teaching and healing. Then he went on to Joppa where he lived for a while with Simon the tanner. While there he performed a miracle. He restored to life a woman named Dorcas. This miracle and Peter's mission at both Lydda and Joppa brought many converts into the church.[2]

"And, Silas, while Peter was at Joppa, the most extraordinary thing happened. You told us about the dream that Ananias had at Damascus. Well, Peter had a very strange dream at Joppa, at a very strange time. It came at the ninth hour—in the middle of the day, so it was more of a vision than a dream. In the vision God told Peter that it was permissible to eat the meat that our religion taught us was unclean and must not be eaten. Three times Peter heard God say, 'Do not call anything impure that God has made clean.' Of course, Peter was puzzled by this dream and had no idea at the time what it meant.

"Two days later Peter had another unnatural experience. He heard a voice instruct him to go to the door and leave with the three men he would find there. It sounds unbelievable, but when Peter opened the door three men were indeed waiting for him there, just as he had been told. They explained that they had come from Caesarea, the Roman capital of Judea, forty miles to the north. They said that Cornelius, the centurion in charge there, had told them to go to Joppa and find a man called Peter.

"Peter could not understand how a Roman officer in Caesarea could know his name and where he was staying. Then the men surprised Peter once more when they told him that Cornelius was recognized by the Jews at Caesarea as a God-loving, charitable, and prayerful soldier.

"Silas, Cornelius was one of those we meet occasionally who tire of the horde of useless gods of the Roman Empire, yearn for the one true God that we have, and find him in our synagogues. As you know, we call them *God fearers*.

"Then the men astounded Peter by their next revelation. In it was the answer to his question, and it astonished him. They told him that at the ninth hour, two days before, Cornelius had had a vision in which God had instructed him to send three men to a certain home in Joppa, where a man named Peter was staying and to bring him to Caesarea to speak to him.[3]

"Peter knew something unusual was happening to him, and he had no alternative but to go to Cornelius. The next day, he and a few others left with the three men to start their journey to Caesarea. After a two-day walk they arrived at the capital city. Once there, Peter and his friends were taken to the centurion. Cornelius welcomed Peter and repeated the story the three men had told him about his vision.

"Then Peter began to talk. As I heard it, this is about what he said: 'You are well aware that it is against our law for a Jew to associate with a Gentile or visit him. But four days ago at the ninth hour I had a dream in which God showed me that I should not call any man impure or unclean. You, Cornelius, had a dream at exactly the same time. You were told to send for me. Without a doubt our dreams came from God, and they have taught me that in God's eyes all who believe in him are the same, and all who believe in him will receive forgiveness through his name.'[4]

"Cornelius thanked Peter for coming to visit him and for his understanding. Peter stayed on to teach at Caesarea for several days after this, during which time he offered baptism in the name of Jesus for all who believed."

Silas was shocked by what he had just heard, and amazed that his father did not seem upset by the acceptance of Gentiles into the church. Then his father added that the leaders in Jerusalem had criticized Peter at first, but when they heard the whole story, they agreed with him.[5]

Then Thomas said, "And we must agree with him also. God has given life-saving repentance to the Gentiles too."

Silas did not reply, but he had something new and very different to think about. It grieved him to admit to himself that he had not yet shed the prejudice he was born with as a Pharisee. In spite of his new belief, he was still a bigot. In his younger years gentile proselytes had been received into his own synagogue, but he had not accepted them.

Although he had admired Philip for his decision to serve in Samaria, and was happy with his decision to go with him, he had not been comfortable with the Samaritans even after spending two years in their country. Silas could not deny that God had sent Paul to minister to the Gentiles, but he was not able to treat those who were different as equals.

Silas left his father deeply troubled by what he had heard and the way he felt about it.

The next day Silas left the home where he was staying with Barnabas and Paul to visit his father again. He wanted to tell him that after a sleepless night thinking about Peter's experience, he knew he would eventually have to be reconciled to the acceptance of Gentiles into the church.

He also had another important matter to discuss with him. He knew he must tell his father that Paul had come to Jerusalem with him and Barnabas and confess that the real reason for the group's visit to the city was to convince the church leaders that Paul was sincere about his conversion. Then, hoping that his father would believe that Paul was truly one of them, he would ask for advice about helping him present his case to the church council.

When he arrived at his parents' home, his mother met him at the door. After a few words of greeting, Silas explained that he had come to talk to his father about bringing an important matter before the Jerusalem church. He was disappointed when his mother said that his father had just left on urgent business.

His mother said, "Silas, if it has to do with the conversion of Paul and your defense of him before the Jerusalem council, why don't you tell me what you plan to say to them? Think of it as a rehearsal of what you will tell your father later. Then you can make any changes that you see fit, so you will be more comfortable with the testimony you present to him and the leaders of the church."

Silas was amazed by his mother's insight and boldness. She was talking to him as only a Jewish man would do. She had always kept silent on important matters as their tradition demanded, but six years in Jerusalem had changed his mother remarkably. Somewhat reluctantly Silas agreed to do as she had suggested.

He related Paul's story once more, telling his mother all about his experience on the road to Damascus in detail, Paul's initial difficulty in convincing people that he had truly been converted, his eventual success at Damascus, and then his recent escape from the non-believers. Silas finished his story by explaining that Paul's future status would depend on whether or not he was accepted by the apostles and then the believers in Jerusalem and elsewhere.

Silas's mother listened to her son carefully, and when he was finished, she complimented him on his presentation, telling him that his father would be pleased at the way he had explained the situation.

Then Deborah surprised Silas once more when she said, "I assume that Paul came to Jerusalem with you. If this is so, what will you advise him to do if he does not get the full acceptance and support of the people?"

After Silas acknowledged that he had not thought about that, she said, "I think your father and I would suggest that if Paul is rejected by the people here, he will be rejected elsewhere where his sins of the past are known. You should get him out of the city and into a friendly community at once.

"One possibility would be Tarsus, the city where you said he was born. He should be comfortable there, and I think he would also be safe there. If there are believers among the Jews at Tarsus, they would not likely be aware of his vile deeds in Jerusalem. From what you've told me, I believe that Paul will become a great leader of the church, but he has to be alive to be effective."

Silas was impressed by what his mother had said. After he thanked her for her help and advice, she took the opportunity of his presence and began to talk again.

"Silas," she said, "other things have been happening in the church here besides the acceptance of Gentiles, but your father did not mention them last night. As you know we Jewish women have always lived in a patriarchal society, and our role has been restricted to home and family. Male and female have not been treated equally, and I understand that this inequality has been ordered by an ancient law. Even at birth a female baby is considered inferior to a male child.

"But when Jesus began his ministry almost ten years ago, things began to change slowly. He gave women a new identity and importance. And you told us he even talked to a Samaritan woman in her country. More importantly, Jesus involved women in his ministry, especially one called Mary Magdalene.[6] A few of these women traveled from town to town to help him.[7] They even supported him financially.

"And if you remember, it was women who were selected to announce Jesus' resurrection.[8] Now the church is beginning, at least, to welcome women as partners in spreading the Word. I hope that you will eventually accept this change as well as the entry of Gentiles into the church."

Later that same day Silas was able to meet with his father. Neither mentioned the time he had spent with his mother, nor did they discuss the position of women in the church. When Silas was invited to say what was on his mind, he confessed to Paul's presence in Jerusalem and then told the complete story of Paul's conversion and the difficulty he now faced to prove that he was a true believer.

Thomas listened to Silas deliver the supporting argument that he and Barnabas had prepared to present to the apostles. He congratulated Silas on their preparation. Then he surprised Silas when he said, "Even if the apostles accept Paul, it will still not be likely that the people on the street will believe him, and therefore you should adopt the plan that your mother suggested earlier."

Silas was flabbergasted to hear that his parents had discussed his problem and that his father agreed that his mother's suggestion should be followed, but he was also pleased. This was a welcome change from past practice.

As Silas walked away from his parents' home, he began to think about the problems confronting him and Barnabas. Paul had insisted on coming to Jerusalem to clear his name, they had agreed to support him, and that they would do. Although they had arrived at Jerusalem safely, they still had the most difficult part of their mission ahead of them—to get their friend accredited by the church leaders and accepted by the believers.

Even if the decision of the church council was favorable, Paul would not be able to roam the streets without fearing for his safety. He would still be the most hated man within the walls. Except for leaving his temporary home to appear before the apostles, Paul would have to stay hidden as long as he remained in the city.

The non-believers had wanted nothing to do with Paul ever since he deserted them at Damascus, and they would never feel differently about him. The Romans would be suspicious of an apparent turncoat, and the Jewish authorities who had given him permission to persecute the believers would consider him even more of a defector if the council believed his story. Yes, Silas was convinced that Paul would have to remain undercover for his own protection. He was glad that when he had left him with Barnabas at Jacob's home, he had emphasized the importance of his remaining out of sight.

As he returned to the home where the three men were staying, Silas thought of all that his parents had said to him since his arrival in Jerusalem, but when he entered the house, his thoughts were quickly displaced by what he heard Paul say.

"Barnabas, let me explain. I know that you and Silas thought I should stay cooped up here in Jacob's house like a prisoner, but I just could not do it any longer. The urge to make contact with a few of the faithful of the city, and convince them that I was no longer their enemy, was too strong to deny. I knew that I had many to fear in Jerusalem, but I was sure that I would be safe outside if I didn't wander too far away. In fact, Jacob assured me that most of those living in his neighborhood were believers, and they didn't go around looking for trouble. I decided that if I stayed close by, I would be all right. So while Silas was away and you were asleep I left the house and went for a short walk. I met several men[9] who I thought must be church members and attempted to talk to them. Each one refused to listen, and a few actually threatened me, so I returned disappointed. But I will try again tomorrow."

Silas stood in the doorway listening to all that Paul said to Barnabas, and then he spoke. "Paul, you made a mistake. The believers you tried to speak to recognized you. The memory of the persecution that many of their friends had suffered at your hands when you were known as Saul was still fresh in their minds. You are lucky you were not attacked. Now we have a new worry. The whole city will soon know that you are back and your enemies will be plotting against you."

"That will not matter. I am convinced that when our leaders hear my story they will believe it, and when this happens, the entire church will accept me. I am ready to meet with the apostles and ask you two to arrange for a hearing as soon as possible, and then be there with me to give the support you pledged before we left Damascus."

Silas and Barnabas knew they must act at once, and because it was late in the day they left immediately, hoping that Paul would remain inside with Jacob. Following the directions they had been given, they found the secret meeting place of the church council and were given an audience with them. They explained why they had come to Jerusalem and requested an early hearing for Paul.

Silas was surprised when the apostles suggested meeting on the following morning. They said that they were anxious to hear Paul's story and make a decision about his fate, because he was a very controversial person and the potential cause of unrest in the church.

Soon after the three men arrived at the hideaway the next day, Paul was asked to state his case.[10] He began by admitting to his attempts to destroy the church before he became a believer. Then he described in detail his miraculous conversion experience. Next he emphasized his true faith by telling about all the good work he had done during the two years he had served in Damascus.

He told the council that he had had daily opportunities to imperil the church, but never once during all that time had he done anything but the work of the Lord. He pointed out that the Sanhedrin had recognized him as a believer in Jesus and had sent agents to pursue him for that reason. Finally he told them that because of his value to their cause, his story must be accepted for the truth that it really was. After Paul finished, Silas was invited to speak. Then Barnabas had his turn.

After Barnabas finished giving his testimony, the apostles asked to be excused for a few minutes. In no time at all the three men were invited back into the meeting room to hear the announcement that Paul had been received into the church as a member in good standing. The three men gripped one another and left. Paul was elated. The leaders had endorsed him, and he was certain that the believers in the Jerusalem church would now accept him without question.

By the next morning, Paul was sure that the apostles' decision had become well-known to the few hundred church members who were still living in the city and that they would be ready to receive him and listen to what he had to say. Silas and Barnabas went with him to the hall where they knew many of the believers would be meeting to discuss the decision of the church fathers.

When Paul was given permission from the leader to address the gathering, he began by telling them the story of his conversion and the destiny that Jesus, the Son of God, had chosen for him,[11] but as he talked, Silas could tell by the reaction of the crowd that they had not forgotten the ugly part of his past. Apparently, they could not believe that a man so evil could become a man so good in such a short time.

The decision of the church leaders had meant nothing to them. Many of those he was talking to had had friends or family members persecuted by him, and they could not forgive him for what he had done. The longer he talked, the more agitated they became.

Silas was afraid that the crowd would soon become violent. When Paul stopped to get a drink of water, Silas took advantage of the break and rushed him out of the building to safety. Before those inside realized what had happened, the three men were well on their way to Jacob's.

Back in the safety of their temporary home, the three men discussed the disastrous meeting at the hall. Paul had been deeply hurt by the rejection of his fellow believers and did not know what to do next. "I realize now that I should get out of Jerusalem, but I have no idea where I could find a safe haven. I was threatened in Damascus, and my reputation as a persecutor is known throughout Judea."

"Paul," Silas said, "my mother suggested, and my father agreed, that if you decided you needed a safe haven the best place for you to go to would be Tarsus."

Paul thought for a moment before he spoke. "That is a great idea. I believe I could find safety in the city of my birth, but it grieves me that I will not be returning to Damascus, the city of my rebirth. I understand, however, that if I am to live to carry on the work of the church, I must protect myself. I will leave for Tarsus immediately, knowing that the time will come when I can safely rejoin you to deliver the message of salvation through belief in Jesus."

At nightfall, after just four days in Jerusalem, Paul left with an escort to return to the home of his youth.

Silas was sorry to be separated from Paul, but he knew his friend would be happy spreading the Word in the city that was his first home. He, himself, looked forward to the day when he would have gained sufficient knowledge and experience to lead a mission to Alexandria, the city of his birth. In the meantime, he yearned for the challenge to do something new and different for The Way.

Thinking about the distant city Paul was headed for, Silas began to ponder the fate of the believers in all those many places they had fled to after the stoning of Stephen. He wondered if the church had grown in some of those areas and withered away in others.

He remembered hearing that in at least one of the locations where the Jewish believers had settled, the Syrian city of Antioch, the church was doing well, but had followed an unusual path. As Silas heard the story, it began when Jews from two widely separated places left Jerusalem after the great Pentecost celebration and established churches in the countries they had come from—one on the island of Cyprus and the other in Cyrene. Some years later, believers from these two communities went to Antioch, each group with the intent to minister not to their own, but to the Gentiles of that city. As a result of the success of these newcomers, there were now many Gentiles in the church at Antioch.[12]

When Silas had first heard this report, he was reminded that his father had told him that, like Peter, all believers should accept members of other races. Although he was beginning to agree, he still felt uncomfortable about allowing foreigners into the church. Although he wanted to do something new and different for his faith, accepting Gentiles as complete equals did not appeal to him. In the meantime, he and Barnabas decided to remain in Jerusalem for a while. They were welcomed by the church and soon were well known to the leaders and members alike, and of course Silas enjoyed being close to his family.

One day after the two men had been in Jerusalem for two years, they were surprised to be summoned to a meeting with the apostles. When they arrived, Peter informed them that the council had been discussing a troublesome situation, which they would describe, and were prepared to take action.

"We are very concerned about a potential problem at Antioch," Peter said. "As you know, a very large number of Gentiles have become believers and been accepted by the church there." Peter's words did not surprise Silas. The council was finally going to take action to stem the flow of outsiders into the faith. "Of course, we are very pleased that this has occurred." Silas could not believe what he was hearing.

"But all is not well. We are worried about the safety of the Gentiles and the possibility of a serious problem. A few narrow-minded Jewish followers of Jesus in Antioch are beginning to resent the inclusion of Gentiles in the church and are threatening to create trouble. We on the council are fearful of what will happen unless action is taken immediately. We have decided that you, Barnabas and Silas, have the training and skill necessary to prevent this situation from getting out of control. We are hoping to hear you say that you are willing to travel north to Antioch and do whatever is necessary to prevent serious trouble from developing there."

As much as Silas wanted to help the church and work with Barnabas, he knew the assignment would be too difficult for him to accept because of the way he felt about Gentiles coming into the church. Barnabas would have to take the three-hundred-mile walk without him. While he was gathering courage to tell the council how he felt, Barnabas spoke.

"Silas and I are overwhelmed that the council feels we are worthy of this task and are happy to accept the challenge you have offered us."

Silas was dumbfounded, but he could only remain silent and pray for help.

Chapter 15

Antioch

THREE DAYS AFTER meeting with the officials of the mother church, Silas said good-bye to his parents and left with Barnabas for Antioch, the third largest city in the world. Only Rome and Alexandria were bigger. Teaching in such a large city would be a new experience for both men. For the first few days on the road neither Silas nor Barnabas mentioned the problem they had been sent to Antioch to deal with. That could come later on their month-long walk. In the meantime, other topics could occupy their time.

Then one day Silas started the conversation. "Barnabas, I have been thinking about our assignment to work in a church where the majority of members are Gentiles. I've now convinced myself that because I was able to work with people who are different at Samaria, I should be able to work with Gentiles at Antioch. As each day's walk brings us closer, I get more anxious to find out what's waiting for us there."

"I'm sure that you will get along very well with the Gentiles, but we will have other concerns to deal with. I learned quite a bit about Antioch just before we left Jerusalem. Although it is an inland city, it is still a busy port of the Great Sea because of its location on the Orontes River, and this makes it an important business center. It also brings in a great diversity of people, but its importance as a commercial city is not its only claim to fame. It is well known throughout the world that Antioch is the place in Syria to go to for what is known as a *good time*. Loose living and day and night immorality have made Antioch famous as a fun-filled city for some, and a sinful city for others. The height of its debauchery is located at the Temple of Daphne. I was told that the priestesses leave their daytime jobs at the temple to become sacred prostitutes in the laurel groves at night."

Silas agreed with Barnabas that accepting, integrating, and protecting the Gentiles would not be the only problem they would have to face at Antioch. He also agreed that they had a very exciting future waiting for them.

As soon as Silas and Barnabas arrived at Antioch, they found living quarters in the Jewish section of the city and went to work teaching a mixed group. Both men were readily accepted by Jews and Gentiles alike, and before long any evidence of trouble between the races had disappeared. The lack of competent leaders had been the cause of troubles in the past. Other problems they had anticipated did not develop. In spite of the evil diversions surrounding the church, it continued to grow.

Silas was still not completely comfortable associating with Gentiles. Because The Way was a sect of Judaism, he could not help but wonder if Gentiles should become Jews in order to come into the church.

He was surprised to discover that women of both races had become active in the church, and he felt quite at ease serving with the women. As the months passed he realized he enjoyed being with one of them more than any of the others. Her name was Rebekah. First he noticed her great beauty. Then he discovered how much more he enjoyed doing little jobs around the church when she was there to help him. Before long he was inventing reasons to help her. They talked about their interests and the beliefs and doubts of their faith.

When Rebekah learned how Silas felt about Gentiles coming into the church, she quoted Peter's words as she remembered them, "I now realize how true it is that God does not show favoritism, but accepts men from every nation who fear him and do what is right." After some time, she was able to convince Silas that what Peter had said was indeed true. With Rebekah's help Silas was able to get along more easily with those he still considered to be different, and he was sure that if the Gentiles would only become Jews, he could accept them completely.

Silas became happier at Antioch than he had ever expected to be, and he hoped that he would live there forever. He was able to make a living as a scribe, and he was satisfied with his leadership role in the church, but he knew something was still missing in his life. Bit by bit Silas began to understand what he needed to be completely happy was to marry Rebekah and raise a family. If this would happen, he was sure his life in Antioch would be more rewarding than it ever could have been had he stayed in Alexandria. When he told Rebekah of his love for her, she said she would like nothing more than to share her life with him and work with him to spread the Word.

After Rebekah's father gave his blessing, the couple followed tradition by announcing their intention to marry very soon by the will of God without disclosing the exact day and time. Of course they invited all the members of their church to attend the ceremony. The guests understood that, according to custom, the wedding would take place without prior notice at some time during a future day or night. This would challenge them to outwit the bride and groom and be present as the ceremony was about to start. To accomplish this, it would be necessary for them to be ready at all times to leave their homes and meet the bridegroom as he went to claim his bride. While Rebekah watched for Silas to come, several of her friends sang and danced in front of her home each day.

Then early one afternoon, not long after the announcement had been made, the best man gave the signal that the wedding was about to begin. Marching down street after street in front of the groom he proclaimed, "Here's the bridegroom! Come out to meet him!"[1] As the guests heard the summons, they left whatever they were doing and hurried to reach the bride's home before the groom got there.

Although Silas and Rebekah were both committed to the new belief, they still retained much of the rich heritage of Judaism. The ceremony took place in the open under the covering of a canopy of the type that had been used for centuries to represent the marriage chamber. Rebekah insisted on the *mikval*, the ritual bath, for herself because she believed that it was analogous to baptism and the *ufrif*, a reading from their ancient Scriptures, for Silas.

He made sure that he was the one to place the linen veil over Rebekah's face. This symbolized, that, unlike Jacob, he knew that he was getting the right bride.[2] At the end of the lengthy service, Silas presented the traditional small coin to Rebekah to express his commitment. Then a special prayer merged ancient practice into a new ritual of The Way.

After the blessing, the guests left to follow the bride and groom and gather outside the married couple's modest small home. Silas and Rebekah held a weeklong party with all their friends from the church coming and going. Everyone enjoyed a grand and glorious time inside and outside the new home with food and wine and dancing to the music of flutes and tambourines. At the end of the week, Silas went back to the work he loved.

Silas's busy life as a scribe and church leader was made much easier by Rebekah's very capable assistance. A year after the wedding the couple's life was made even more rewarding by the birth of their first child, a girl they named Martha. Silas recalled what his mother had said about some people thinking a female baby was less acceptable than a male child, but, looking at his precious daughter, he could not understand how anyone could feel that way. The following year the couple had their son, Joseph.

Rebekah was dedicated to Silas and the children, but she also took the church very seriously. One day she made a remarkable contribution when she said to her husband, "Because we worship the Christ, the Anointed One of our Scriptures, shouldn't we call ourselves Christians?"[3]

Silas continued to lead a busy but fulfilling life as he watched both his family and the church grow steadily. Rebekah was at his side helping whenever it became necessary. As the church continued to flourish, however, the proportion of Gentiles among the believers continued to increase. Although Rebekah had helped Silas feel more comfortable working with Gentiles, he still wished that they would somehow become Jews and be full-fledged members of the church. He had heard that some Jews in Jerusalem, especially Pharisees who had become believers, felt very strongly that Gentiles who entered the church should first keep the Law of Moses by being circumcised. Silas began to wonder if this could be the solution to one problem that concerned him.

He spoke to Barnabas about another problem.

"We have seen a great deal of growth without serious problems during our time here, but I believe much more could be accomplished if we had more qualified leaders."

"I couldn't agree more. There are many willing to help, but our need is for capable leaders and neither of us has the time required to give others the necessary training."

"What we need, Barnabas, is someone who is a qualified teacher, who has been brought up in the Jewish faith but has spent much of his life in a gentile community."

Silas had barely spoken these words when both he and Barnabas shouted, "Paul!"

"He would be the ideal person, and I'm sure that there would no longer be any ill feeling toward him at Antioch. Silas, you stay here with your family and do double duty, and I'll leave for Tarsus tomorrow."

Barnabas soon persuaded Paul to come to Antioch and work with the church. Both Jews and Gentiles welcomed Paul, and he immediately began to work with young men that either Silas or Barnabas had recommended. In no time at all, several of them were trained to assume leadership roles.[4]

About one year after Paul's arrival, word was received that the people of Judea were suffering from a severe famine. The church at Antioch responded in good Christian fashion. Each believer gave a gift, the size depending on his resources. The church members considered their contribution so vital that they asked Silas, Barnabas, and Paul to take it to Jerusalem for distribution.

The three men agreed to do this; confident that the newly-trained leaders were quite capable of taking charge while they were away and realizing that they needed the experience.[6] The fine acceptance of Paul at Antioch encouraged the men to believe that opposition to him in Jerusalem would have disappeared also.

Because of the urgency of the situation in Judea, the three men left the following day and arrived at Jerusalem in less than three weeks. Once more they stayed with their friend Jacob, but this time they were able to find his home much more easily because they did not think it necessary to wait for the dark of night to start looking for it. The relief they brought to Jerusalem was received with thanks to God. The gift from Antioch established the Christian custom of helping others in need and forged a sense of unity among churches.

The acceptance of Paul by the Christians of Jerusalem was one of the greatest rewards of the trip, but another one was Silas's reunion with his parents after eight years of separation. Thomas and Deborah were thrilled to hear all about their two grandchildren. Martha was now five and Joseph was one year younger.

Some time after Silas, Paul, and Barnabas returned to Antioch, John Mark, a cousin of Barnabas, also came from Jerusalem,[6] but he came as the bearer of disturbing news. John Mark had said nothing about coming to Antioch when Barnabas visited him in Jerusalem several weeks before, so his sudden appearance in the synagogue took Silas by surprise. Barnabas was conducting the service and, following protocol, he asked his cousin if he wished to address the assembly. John Mark took the floor.

"I bring you the most frightening news from Jerusalem," he began. "As you know, persecution of Christians has come and gone repeatedly ever since the resurrection. Recently it returned with a terrible consequence. After Herod Antipas, the ruler of Galilee, refused to do anything to save Jesus from being crucified, he went to Rome to ask Emperor Caligula to confer the title of king on him. Although he was considered to be king, he had never been officially given that title. But the emperor had no affection for Antipas and answered his request by deposing him and appointing one of his favorites, Herod Agrippa, to be king of Galilee instead.

"Agrippa was educated in Rome but, as I'm sure you have been told, he has been able to keep on the good side of the non-Christian Jews by observing the Law and all Jewish practices. Until recently he had ignored the Christians. Then, possibly because the Christians of Jerusalem had received the help you sent to them recently, the non-Christian Jews became more antagonistic toward the Christians.

"When Agrippa became aware of this, he saw an opportunity to improve his position with the non-believers still more by extending his authority into Judea and launching an attack on the Jewish believers there. The persecution reached a new height when Agrippa's ruffians killed the apostle James, the brother of John. It grieves me to bring you this devastating news, but you must be told.

"Then Agrippa took further action, but this time the result was not nearly so disastrous. When he saw how much James's death pleased the non-Christian Jews, he tried to gain even more favor with them by having Peter, head of the Jerusalem church, arrested and put in prison. By the time Agrippa did this, however, the Passover had begun, and he was clever enough not to have Peter murdered during the feast. He was content to leave him in prison until the celebration was over.[7] Of course, we knew that as soon as the time was right Agrippa would have Peter brought to trial and sentenced to death on false charges, and we would be faced with the tragic loss of a great leader.

"Then one night I was at the home of Mary, my mother and Barnabas's aunt, with a group of Christians praying for Peter's safety, when we heard a loud knock at the door. Rhoda, a maidservant, went to see who was there. Fearing that it was someone from Agrippa's command, she asked who it was without opening the door. She was startled when she recognized Peter's voice as he identified himself. Although she was positive that it was Peter at the door, she was so excited that instead of letting him in she ran back to where we were gathered to tell us that Peter had come. Because that seemed impossible we sent another of the believers to find out who was really there. He, too, recognized the voice, and on opening the door he saw Peter standing there in front of him.

"After greeting everyone, Peter told us an extraordinary story. He began by explaining that he had gone to sleep earlier that same evening chained and under heavy guard. Then he said, 'I was soon awakened by an angel who told me to get up, dress, and leave the prison. At that point the chains fell away from me.

"'The angel escorted me past the sleeping guards and out the door to freedom, and then vanished. I walked the streets of Jerusalem until I was sure that I was not being followed, and then I came here, but now for my safety and yours I must leave and go to Caesarea. I believe that I will be safer there with Cornelius than here in Jerusalem.'

"We found out later that when Agrippa heard that Peter had escaped, he ordered the execution of all the guards who had been on duty that night. Of course we praised God for Peter's escape, but the good news about his freedom did not erase the pain of James's cruel murder.[8]

"Just before I left Jerusalem to come here, Agrippa died and was succeeded by his son Agrippa II. We can only hope that our future will be less terrifying under him."

John Mark decided to remain in Antioch, and before long he was kept busy working with Silas, Barnabas, and Paul.

Chapter 16

Into all the World

ON SABBATH, THE three leaders and John Mark lingered at the synagogue after everyone else had left.

"It is wonderful to see so many of the congregation taking part enthusiastically," John Mark said. "It is just one more indication of the success of the church at Antioch."

"I'm very happy and feel well rewarded because of the substantial growth we have enjoyed," Barnabas replied.

"From what I hear, many other churches have not done nearly as well," Silas said, "and most cities of the world have no church at all. We know that many countries beyond Judea and Syria are waiting for someone to either introduce or strengthen Christianity. Every time we discuss the need for leaders beyond our city, a new location comes into the conversation. The Roman Empire is constantly increasing its territory. I heard recently that its army had pushed its way up into the far north to a country called Britain."

"Silas, there's much to be done by Christians in the expanding world," Paul said, "and there is a desperate shortage of leaders. We are lucky here, but when leaders do become available it will be difficult to decide which area needs help most."

Silas said, "We must remember that it was to us as well as to others that Jesus issued the great commission 'to go and make disciples of all nations, baptizing them in the name of the Father and of the Son and of the Holy Spirit.'[1] Don't you think that the men who took over for us when we went to Jerusalem are capable of taking charge permanently? Why don't we give them the opportunity they deserve and consider responding to the call?"

"I believe the Holy Spirit is prodding us through you, Silas," Paul replied. "There certainly are a few here ready to assume leadership, and I am ready to go. Your words have reminded me of my experience on the road to Damascus. They made me realize that when Jesus directed me to go out and minister, not only to Jews but also to Gentiles, he did not intend that I should spend the rest of my days in Antioch. I believe you have been inspired to tell me that the time has now come for me to be on my way. I will go, and I want the two of you to come with me."

"I'm ready," Barnabas shouted, "but where should we go?"

"To Alexandria," was Silas's excited reply. He had been waiting for years for this opportunity to take the message to the city of his birth. He was anxious to continue riding on the wave of success he was enjoying.

"I'm afraid not," Paul replied with a sudden show of authority. "I believe we are being directed to Asia Minor."

Now Barnabas became excited. "The best entry to Asia Minor is through Cyprus, the island in the Great Sea where I was born. I would be happy to lead the mission there."

Paul hesitated briefly and then said that Barnabas's proposal was fine with him. After Paul's earlier criticism of his suggestion of Alexandria, Silas was in no position to object. John Mark asked to be included, and now Barnabas showed his authority by his reply, "Welcome to the group, cousin."

Although Silas was the one who suggested the mission, he was beginning to have second thoughts about it now that it had suddenly become a reality. He did not know how he could leave Antioch even for a short time even for such an important reason. He dreaded saying goodbye to Rebekah and the children.

That evening he told Rebekah about the group's plans, and she reassured him the children and she would be well taken care of by the Christian community of the city.

"Silas, because of what you have committed yourself to, our love will grow stronger during our separation."

Comforted by Rebekah's support, Silas began to look forward to a new and exciting adventure. He had never been on a boat of any kind before, except small river boats, and now his first experience on the water would be a voyage across the Great Sea that he used to admire only from a safe distance.

All that he knew about ships and sailing came from stories that had been read to him as a child. He had heard that most vessels were manned by competent seamen. He prayed that the ship they would be sailing on to Cyprus would be such a one. His grandfather had explained that the sailors' greatest asset was the experience they had gained by their years on the water and the experience of their ancestors as well. Just as the storyteller passed along a historical narrative of his past, the sailor transferred orally everything he knew about the stars, ocean currents, prevailing winds, rocks, and shoals from one generation to the next.

Silas's grandfather had told him that most vessels now had two very useful navigational aids to determine the depth of water, a sounding pole and a sounding line. He said if they were used prudently, these devices would prevent the ship from foundering in shallow water. Silas hoped the ship they would leave Antioch on would have these modern devices.

When the three men met the next morning, Paul told Silas that he had sailed a few times before without encountering any trouble at all. "I found that the mind of an experienced sailor is filled with reliable navigation charts not yet committed to papyrus. Moreover, most sailors have at least a crude sense of geography and can often detect distant islands by the cloud formations over them. Of course, as an additional safety measure, all ships sail as close to the coast as possible and are never out of sight of land for very long."

These words were reassuring to Silas who well remembered the stories of storms on the Great Sea that had both thrilled and frightened him when he had heard them many years ago from his grandfather.

Just as Silas was beginning to relax, Barnabas began to speak. "If we don't start out very soon we will be in the season of storms. Before long harsh winter weather will close the Great Sea for the season and we won't be able to leave at all. But don't worry; I'll take care of you. I'll leave now to walk the fifteen miles to the port and be there before the end of the day. Ships leave Seleucia for Cyprus regularly. It won't take me long to arrange for passage."

Late the next day Barnabas returned to inform his friends that they would set sail in two days' time. The Christians at Antioch were excited when they heard this. They had been fasting and praying for the safety and success of the four men ever since they heard that their church would be sending out a mission to bring Christianity to the outside world.

Silas said good-bye to Rebekah and the children, not knowing where he was going beyond Cyprus or how long he would be away. Then, with the autumn sun warm on his back, he joined the other missionaries as they left Antioch to walk to Seleucia. They must be ready to board the ship early the next morning.[2]

The sea was unusually quiet for that time of the year and Silas felt quite at ease soon after they left the Orontes River. They had not sailed for long when Barnabas asked the others, "Where do you think we should go after Cyprus?"

Paul cut off the reply Silas was ready to make by saying, "There is no need to discuss that. We will be shown the way, step by step, as we go along." Silas noticed that Paul had a dreamy, faraway look on his face.

As they neared the end of their 120 miles on the water, Barnabas made another effort at conversation. "I've been thinking," he said. "We will spend many nights sleeping in the open under the stars or in the rain. I suggest that whenever we are in a city we attempt to procure proper lodgings. We can hope that this would be in a private home by invitation, but if not we should seek living quarters that we could rent at a nominal price. I realize that our funds are limited, but when they are gone I'm sure we could earn our keep somehow."

Paul made no reply, and the expression on his face seemed to say that lodgings should be the last thing on their minds.

The ship put in at the port of Salamis on the eastern coast of Cyprus. Barnabas had a big smile on his fierce face. Excitedly, he led his friends off the ship and onto the streets of his youth. Ignoring Paul's lack of response to his suggestion, he took them to a small inn that he remembered from long ago. After arranging for the absolute minimum of comfort, he suggested that they store their few belongings and go to the Jewish quarter. They had packed the bare necessities to ease the burden of travel: extra pairs of heavy sandals, warm cloaks, leather ground sheets, and containers for food and drink.

Barnabas led the way through streets he remembered from his younger years. He took his group to the Jewish section and the synagogue of his youth.[3] He introduced himself and the others to all those who were present, a few of whom he knew, but most of whom he did not. The synagogue now served the Jewish Christian community of Salamis.

Before long the missionaries were teaching regularly at the synagogue. Some of those present at the sessions had fled Jerusalem after the stoning of Stephen and had first brought the message of salvation through belief in Jesus Christ to the Jews of Salamis. Other early arrivals left Cyprus and took the message to Antioch, where they encouraged the acceptance of Gentiles into the church. It seemed strange to Silas that the group of Christians responsible for bringing Gentiles into the church at Antioch had not done the same at Salamis.

After the missionaries had spent several weeks with the Jews of Salamis, Barnabas abruptly announced, "Now we will take our mission to Paphos,[4] the capital city and center of the Roman government of Cyprus. It's located at the far western end of the island."

After preparing for a journey of eighty miles, the missionaries set out following the trail along the southern coast of Cyprus toward Paphos. Their leather pouches were filled with bread and cheese, and water skins filled with wine were slung over their shoulders.

The supplies had been provided by the members of the church at Salamis. Although the going was rough from time to time, on the whole the pleasant winter climate made the walk along the shore quite enjoyable. The travelers could see the mountainous part of the country far to the north. Barnabas said that was the region that supplied the timber for much of the shipbuilding activity of the countries surrounding the Great Sea.

As they walked along, Silas began to tell his companions some of what he had learned about Cyprus while studying at Alexandria. "Long before Cyprus became part of the Roman Empire, it was controlled by Egypt. The Egyptians wanted its copper supply. The beautiful red metal I saw so much of in Alexandria had come from Cyprus many, many years before."

"Unfortunately, the Egyptians were successful in their mining efforts," Barnabas said. "The island was depleted of its wealth of copper."

As the four men came closer to Paphos, Barnabas warned his companions they would confront a familiar obstacle when they arrived at the capital. "Paphos is well known for the worship of Venus, the goddess of sexual love. You know what this means. We will have to cope with prostitutes once more. But the church at Antioch continued to prosper in spite of the prostitute priestesses at the Temple of Daphne, so the church can grow at Paphos as well."

"Barnabas," Paul said, "we might as well get used to combating sexual sin, because no matter where we go in the Roman Empire we will surely encounter it. The emperor is responsible for the poor morality. As head of the state religion he encourages the worship of traditional gods to foster a bond of spiritual unity, and sexuality seems to be very much a part of their traditional worship.

"The worship of traditional gods, however, is not necessarily a handicap for delivering our message. It might even help our effort. I believe that religious paganism with all its many gods representing mysterious, supernatural forces that the people cannot understand causes a spiritual restlessness. That uncomfortable condition may open the door for the Christian way of life to enter.

"I believe that there is a spiritual hunger in the gentile world. We see evidence of this whenever serious-minded Gentiles attend our synagogues. They are intrigued by our morality and our belief in one God who is concerned with human life. I only regret that we were not successful in reaching many Gentiles at Salamis."

When the missionaries arrived at the capital, they were met by a messenger. He informed them word had been received that men who had been teaching at Salamis had left there to come to Paphos. He assumed they were the men, and if so they were to follow him to appear before the official representative of Rome in Cyprus.

They had no alternative but to accept and follow the messenger to the proconsul's palace. Once there they were introduced to Sergius Paulus. Silas knew he was responsible to the senate at Rome for both civil and military matters in Cyprus. Because of his position he was highly respected, and what he believed was what the general population was supposed to believe.

Silas soon realized that he was a very superstitious man. This was most evident when he introduced a Jewish member of his staff, Elymas, whom he proudly announced was his private wizard. Sergius explained that the wizard's specialties were the performance of magic tricks and foretelling the future.

Silas was surprised when the proconsul did not ask Elymas to demonstrate his talent, but ignored him after the introduction to address the missionaries. He said that he had heard a few things about their belief and wanted them to explain what it was all about. Barnabas responded, but he had not gone far before Elymas, obviously recognizing that what he was hearing might mean the end of his influence in the government, started to dispute almost everything Barnabas said.

Silas began to worry. He knew that if Sergius Paulus believed his own staff member and not Barnabas, their visit to Paphos would be a failure, possibly resulting in imprisonment for teaching false doctrine. Silas felt desperate. They might avoid a prison sentence, but if Elymas prevailed, their acceptance elsewhere would be more difficult or even impossible.

Just when the proconsul seemed to be responding to his wizard, Paul sprang into action. He stepped forward and, as if strengthened by the Holy Spirit, pointed his bony finger right in the wizard's face. He called him a child of the devil and the enemy of everything that is right. He told Elymas he was full of deceit and trickery and accused him of perverting the right ways of God.

Before the astonished wizard could recover Paul placed his hand on Elymas's head, and in the name of God declared him temporarily blind. When the proconsul could see that his wizard had lost his sight, he ordered him led away and greeted Paul with high praise. The missionaries had been guaranteed a successful stay at Paphos.[5]

Many meetings were held in the synagogue. They were well attended, and most of those present at each session were Gentiles. Silas was sure that the large gentile interest was due to Sergius Paulus's conversion.

A few Jews also came to the meetings. One of them was Elymas. His sight had been restored, and his new belief had regenerated him.

After four months, the missionaries were satisfied that a vigorous movement had begun in Paphos, so they decided that the time had come to leave Cyprus and move on to the next opportunity. After Paul's successful defiance of Elymas in the presence of Sergius Paulus, he had emerged as the undisputed leader of the group, so Paul announced their next destination. When he told the others that they would head for the mainland of Asia Minor and visit Perga, Barnabas left without comment to engage a ship. He soon returned to report that he had been able to book passage on a large vessel headed for the Roman coastal province of Pamphylia.

The winter storms had now passed. After a sea voyage of 150 miles over relatively calm water, Silas had convinced himself that he was a seasoned sailor. The four men left the ship at a harbor on the Bay of Attalia from where they made their way eight miles inland to Perga. Silas had been told that this city housed a temple honoring Artemis and that the goddess played a dual role as the protector of wild animals as well as the giver of fertility to humans.

Silas assumed there would be a synagogue in the city and that they would not have any trouble finding it, but before they even started to look for it, Paul shocked his companions with an unexpected and curt directive: "We will not be staying here, but will leave for another location early tomorrow morning," was all he said. Silas looked at Barnabas and John Mark and saw that they appeared to be as flabbergasted as he was.

Silas had no idea why Paul would suddenly change their itinerary. At first he feared that the health problem Paul suffered from had worsened and led him to decide that walking for a few days would be less stressful than teaching. Then he realized that if that were the case, he could have asked him or Barnabas to take over while he rested at Perga until he felt better. What Paul added after a short silence, however, assured Silas that his friend must be feeling reasonably well. "Our next stop will be Pisidian Antioch."

Paul had told the others earlier that the only road to that city in the Roman province of Galatia went over the Taurus mountain range. Because he had said that it was one of the most difficult and hazardous routes in the world, Silas knew Paul would understand that he would have to be physically fit to even try it. He would not want to risk becoming ill on the journey and be a burden to his companions. He must have another reason for the sudden change in plans. Paul seemed reluctant to talk about his decision, so Silas realized that he might never know the truth about it.

Silas had not recovered from the effect of Paul's sudden decision to bypass Perga when the next blow fell. This time it came from John Mark. He abruptly told the others that he had decided to leave the mission and return to Jerusalem.[6] Just as Paul had done, John Mark gave no explanation for his action, and once more those who were stunned by an unexpected announcement were too dazed to ask for one. Without saying anything more, John Mark rushed off.

After John Mark had passed out of sight, the missionaries discussed the reason for his sudden departure. Barnabas, anxious to make an excuse for his cousin, suggested that he missed the excitement of the important meetings of the Jerusalem church council which often took place in his mother's home. Paul guessed that because of his young age and lack of experience, John Mark was afraid to venture into new overwhelmingly gentile territories. Although Silas did not give his opinion, he wondered if John Mark might have left because his cousin was no longer in charge of the mission. He had noticed that his friend had lost much of his enthusiasm for the journey as soon as Paul became the leader.

As Silas continued to think about John Mark's departure, another possible reason for his decision came to mind. A few days earlier when Paul had described the hazardous route to Antioch, he noticed that John Mark had shuddered as if he thought anyone would be foolish to attempt such a perilous journey. Perhaps the thought of an exhausting trek through a mountain pass, and the fear of bandits who might be hiding along the way, had caused his friend to leave the mission.

Although Silas believed that Paul's decision was a strong indication that he felt up to a rigorous trek over a rugged mountain trail, he was still concerned about the effect it might have on him. As they were preparing to leave, Silas said, "Paul, why don't we delay our departure for a while? We could continue to work here and save our earnings until we have enough to buy a donkey that you could ride to Antioch."

"I will not ride a donkey to Antioch," Paul shouted. "Donkeys in this part of the world bring a very high price, and we can't spare the time it would take to earn what one would cost. The care of one would be expensive and time-consuming. We would be much better off if I walked with you and Barnabas as usual. In fact, I believe walking will be good for me."

The next morning Paul insisted that before they started out, they equip themselves with staffs, not only to assist them while they were walking on rough mountain roads, but to use for protection against wild animals and thieves.

"Paul, in my humble opinion the staffs will be useless in defending ourselves against well-armed, mountain-hardened criminals," Barnabas said with a grin.

"Well, they will certainly be better than nothing if we are attacked by robbers on the dangerous road, and they might turn out to be very useful if we pass through fields where sheep are grazing."

Barnabas, now comfortable with Paul's leadership, said, "You're right, Paul. I'm sure that I could drive off any ferocious sheep with my staff."

"I'm not trying to protect you from an attack by an angry sheep, Barnabas," Paul said, now smiling, "I'm worried about an attack in sheep country by hungry wolves or perhaps bears waiting to feast on a tender lamb. If the shepherd should manage to drive off the animals, they might decide to satisfy their hunger by dining on human flesh, and any man without a staff for protection would make an easy meal. Now, let's be on our way."

As the walkers trudged along away from the flat seacoast and closer to the towering mountain, the sun which had appeared earlier hid behind some heavy clouds. Before long the wind gathered enough strength to blow grit into the missionaries' faces. Then the first drops of rain fell and made tiny balls by mixing with the dust on the road.

The three men put their cloaks on over their robes and carried on. Soon the rain became heavier, and the wind began to blow stronger, driving what Paul said he hoped would be the final spring downpour hard into the men's faces. After a while the rain stopped, but they were already drenched. Silas was beginning to believe that John Mark had made a good decision. As they rounded a corner, the missionaries were suddenly stopped by a huge boulder. It blocked the road almost completely, and they had a difficult time getting around it.

"I'm glad we didn't meet that deadly obstacle during the rainstorm, because we would not have been able to see it. We would have crashed right into it," Silas said.

"I'm thankful it did not come crashing down on top of us during the storm. We are lucky to be alive," Barnabas replied.

Hours later, when they stopped for the day, they hung their garments up to dry on the trees at the side of the road. The three men, shivering from the cold because of the lack of cover, and fearful of being attacked by thieves or wild animals, spent a restless night.

The next morning welcomed the missionaries with warm sunshine but a difficult situation. The slope was steeper and the footing less friendly. The staffs were an absolute necessity. The missionaries' leather sandals gave little protection from the loose stones that covered the trail.

"Can you believe that this trail is supposed to be a road traveled by the Roman army and kept up by them?" Barnabas asked.

"I know that the Romans are good road builders," Silas answered. "They must avoid dangerous mountain trails. Perhaps they only clear them when soldiers are preparing to go through."

"That may be, but in my opinion what we are walking on now is not much more than a shepherd's track."

By dusk the three men were exhausted from exerting themselves in air that had become increasingly thin with the rising elevation. After the usual ration of food, sleep came easily in spite of the unfriendly terrain.

The next day brought a storm. The heavens exploded with thunder and lightning. By this time the missionaries had reached the beginning of the pass, and high walls began to stretch up on either side. The water from the downpour gathered on the ridges and then came cascading down in a series of waterfalls. Before long the trail they had been walking on had become a raging river, and they waded through it against the current.

The men were so exhausted by their ordeal they did not even have strength for conversation, so the long day seemed endless. Eventually, the rain stopped and the river bed dried up, but the skies did not clear. Then the day grew darker, not just from the black sky or approaching night but from the rock walls that were closing in on them with every step they took. Soon they were walking through a very narrow canyon.

Silas felt as if the walls would soon be compressing the air out of his lungs, but then the walls began to spread open, and soon sufficient level ground appeared to make an overnight stop possible. The men needed the little strength they had left to eat their daily allotment of food with a few sips of wine.

The fourth day began with rewarding sunshine that remained with the exhausted missionaries for the next three days. The final portion of their one-hundred-mile trek to the plateau of Pisidian Antioch was not nearly as rugged, nor was it as lonely. They met several travelers and wagonloads of marble destined for building projects in Rome.

When the city of their destination came into sight, Barnabas began to laugh. It was the most pleasant sound Silas had heard for many days, but Paul asked, "Are you thinking of something funny or have you finally gone completely mad?"

"I was just thinking how lucky we were that the weather was so bad when we were on the most dangerous part of the trail. Neither wild animals nor bandits were foolish enough to leave their lairs. Only missionaries dared to go out in such stormy weather. We should be thankful that we are arriving safely. The only attack we suffered was from the merciless rain."

Shortly after the missionaries entered the city, they discovered that marble mined in the area had been used to build a temple dedicated to the victories and achievements of Emperor Augustus, the adopted son of Julius Caesar. The senate had declared Augustus a god after his death. Tiberius had succeeded Augustus and had ruled until just nine years previously, but he had not yet been declared a god. Caligula had followed him, and now it was the sixth year of Emperor Claudius's reign. Of course he was hoping to be declared a god.

They soon located the Jewish quarter and the synagogue, which they visited on the first Sabbath. After the regular service was finished, the leader followed the usual procedure when guests were present and asked if new arrivals in the community wished to speak. Paul jumped up.

When Silas heard him address the congregation as Jews and God-fearers, he realized that Paul had recognized the presence of Gentiles so he was surprised to hear Paul deliver what had become his standard talk when he spoke to totally Jewish groups.

"You Jews are God's chosen people. After your ancestors suffered as slaves in Egypt for many generations, God brought them out of captivity. For forty years he led them as they wandered through the wilderness. Then he brought them to Canaan, their Promised Land. After they had lived there for 450 years he gave them judges to rule over them until they clamored for a king so they could be like other nations. To fulfill their wishes he gave them Saul whom he soon replaced with David.

"Then came the time when John the Baptizer told your people that God would very soon keep his promise and send the Messiah to them. He urged all who could hear to repent. Just as John had foretold, God gave you his chosen ones, a descendant of David, to be your Lord and Savior, and now I tell you that he is Jesus Christ.

"The Jews and their leaders in Jerusalem did not recognize Jesus as their Messiah when he appeared there. Then, fulfilling the prophecy read in your synagogue every Sabbath; they allowed him to be crucified.

"But wait, the history of your people does not end with the cruel death of Jesus. The final proof of his identity was yet to come. On the third day Jesus rose from his death by crucifixion. Then he lived on earth for forty days teaching his chosen disciples to be his apostles and take his truth to the world. Now we know that although following the Law unconditionally is impossible, the forgiveness of sins is not. Salvation is now given as a gift to Jews and Gentiles alike, if they believe in Jesus, repent, and ask with faith to be forgiven."

Paul's sermon stirred up a great deal of interest among many of the Jews and most of the Gentiles who heard and understood his message. Several people came up to Paul and urged him to return on the next Sabbath and tell them more.

When the missionaries arrived at the synagogue on the following Sabbath, Silas was overjoyed to see that it was filled to capacity with people eager to hear what Paul had to say. Many more Gentiles were present than at the first meeting at Pisidian Antioch.

Paul had not spoken many words, however, before several antagonistic Jews began rudely to dispute everything they heard. Searching his mind for an explanation of the unusual turn of events, Silas could only believe that the Jewish leaders of the city resented the presence of so many Gentiles in the synagogue and had stirred up their people encouraging them to confront Paul.

Paul said to the Jews who were protesting, "We had to speak the Word of God to you first. Since you reject it and do not consider yourselves worthy of eternal life, we now turn to the Gentiles."[7]

With these words Paul left the enraged Jews in the synagogue, but he was followed by thankful Gentiles. Silas was as disturbed with his unbelieving countrymen as Paul was; he longed for them to become Christians. He also believed that Gentiles should become Jews to be completely Christian, and they would have more difficulty accomplishing this if they were not allowed to return to the synagogue.

Because the anger of the Jews did not subside, the missionaries could not resume sessions in the synagogue, but this did not stop the new Gentile Christians from meeting. They gathered to hear the missionaries wherever space was available.

Unfortunately the Jewish protesters continued to spread their anger, and soon they had acquired sufficient support to force the three men out of the city. Although Silas was saddened that their own kind had rejected them, he was happy with the success they had enjoyed with the Gentiles, though he wished that somehow these new believers could consolidate their conversion by becoming Jews.

As they were leaving Antioch to continue their tour of Galatia, Paul announced that their next stop would be Iconium, ninety miles away.[8] To reach their destination, Silas, Paul, and Barnabas had to cross a fertile well-watered plain that was the source of much of the grain and fruit for Galatia and the neighboring Roman provinces. When they started out, Silas could feel the sharp snap of an autumn day and there was no threat of rain. The last of the grain crops had been harvested and the trees had been picked clean of fruit. The walk would take less than a week, and would be much more pleasant than their recent trek to Antioch.

The three men, buoyed by their recent success with the Gentiles at Antioch and the pleasant condition of the road they were traveling on, arrived at their next location in high spirits. They soon found the Jewish quarter and the synagogue where they would attend the Sabbath worship.

When the day came for Paul to deliver the sermon that had been successful elsewhere, many Jews and God-fearers became believers, and as usual Silas was kept busy with baptisms. As at Antioch, some Jews did not accept the message of Jesus and resented the presence of Gentiles in their synagogue. Silas was beginning to believe that this would be the condition wherever they went. The Gentiles who were not converted offered the missionaries no harm, but unlike them, the non-believing Jews stirred up their people in an attempt to gain enough support to drive the missionaries out of the city.

As the antagonistic Jews increased their number, the ranks of the Christians became swollen as well. Soon two large groups were opposed to each other, and as the church services continued, the non-Christian Jews became more antagonistic, while the mostly gentile believers became more defiant.

The missionaries were afraid that if they remained in Iconium any longer riots might develop, so to preserve the peace and their own lives they decided that they should be content with the progress they had made with the Gentiles and the few Jews who had become believers and leave for Lystra not more than twenty miles away.[9]

Lystra was an outpost of the Roman Empire with very little Jewish presence, so the missionaries would be entering a city with a mostly gentile heathen population, with no Jewish quarter and no synagogue. The absence of a synagogue in which to meet and teach did not stop the missionaries. They just took to the streets, teaching and healing everywhere they went.

Silas noticed that whenever they met in a certain area, one man, a cripple who could not walk, was always there eagerly waiting to hear Paul speak. One day as Silas watched he could see that the cripple seemed to have an even deeper interest than usual in what he was hearing. Paul must have noticed this also and interpreted the man's attention as an expression of great faith, because suddenly he said to him, "Stand up on your feet." Without hesitation the cripple responded by standing and walking for what he afterward said was the first time in his life.

A man in the crowd who had been watching closely shouted out, "The gods have come down to us in human form! Zeus and Hermes are here. Our patron gods have come down from heaven to favor us. The messenger god and the king of all gods, the ruler of heaven and earth, are right here with us. We must prepare a sacrifice to honor their visit and thank them for what they have done."

By this time the crowd was worked up into a frenzy, and the pagans began to shout out praises to their gods. Silas motioned to the mob that he wanted to speak, and eventually they calmed down. He was successful in making them understand that their visitors were only human, and because of that the sacrifices they proposed would be sinful. The crowd remained quiet.

Paul resumed speaking. He explained that he and his friends had come to the people of Lystra to bring them the Good News of salvation through belief in Jesus Christ and to turn them away from their pagan gods. Paul told them that only one true God existed. He made everything, and they must believe in him to be saved. God, who was with them in the form of the Holy Spirit, had healed the cripple. The crowd was swayed. They remained quiet and attentive for the rest of the service.[10]

A few weeks later Silas saw what looked like an angry crowd approaching the city as if they were prepared to storm it. When they came closer, he recognized several antagonistic Jews he had seen before either at Iconium or Antioch, he could not remember which.

The hostile mob directed their venom toward the missionaries with hateful denunciations. Their noisy presence and violent indictments soon convinced the Gentiles of Lystra that the three visitors to their city were there only to do them harm. The pagans who had worshiped the missionaries as gods a short time before were now ready to persecute them. The Jews then concentrated their verbal attack on Paul, telling the Gentiles that he was the ringleader of the interlopers.

In the total absence of Roman authority, mob rule was the law. Angry Gentiles seized and bound Silas and Barnabas and stoned Paul savagely. Hooting and yelling, they dragged him outside the city, where they left him for dead.

The Jews departed, however, and a compassionate Gentile released Silas and Barnabas who went out to find Paul. Battered and bleeding almost beyond belief, he was still breathing. After some time they were able to revive him and with great difficulty help him struggle back to the city.

As Paul limped along, supported by his two friends, Silas could see the look of utter disbelief on the faces of those who thought they had killed him. The crowd was too stunned and confused to make an attempt to attack Paul again, so the three men were left to freely make their way to the inn where they were staying.

The next morning the missionaries decided that to preserve their limbs and lives they would stay inside until Paul was well enough to walk and then they would leave Lystra.

Three days later Paul surprised his friends when he said, "Let's prepare to move on, I'm ready to start out."

"You're far from being well, Paul. You need more time to heal before we go."

"Silas, I'm well enough to leave this place, but to satisfy you, I agree to walk more slowly than usual. I'm anxious to visit Derbe next. Even at a slower pace we should cover the sixty miles in about a week's time."

"Well, if you insist on starting out, let's at least wait overnight."

The three men left Lystra early the next morning about an hour before daylight to avoid the possibility of another attack.[11]

Eight days later the men were safe at Derbe, where they were given a warm reception by the large Jewish population of the city. At the conclusion of each meeting in the synagogue one of the three was asked to speak. They preached sermons that were appropriate for Jewish groups, followed by messages that emphasized the Good News of salvation through belief and faith in Jesus Christ. As always, they reminded the congregation that salvation was impossible through the Law of Moses alone.

The missionaries enjoyed many rewarding sessions without opposition from those who did not believe as they did, but because the meetings were exhausting, especially for Paul, they decided to go no further, but to go home, stopping at each of the cities they had visited previously.

The three men first stopped at Lystra, the gentile city where Paul had been so viciously attacked. This time, however, the missionaries were treated with respect, and not just by those who had believed the message that Paul had delivered on their first visit. Others who did not believe may have still thought that the three were gods and left them alone for that reason. After all, they had seen Paul walk back into their city after they had been sure that he had been killed.

The missionaries spent much of their time strengthening the belief of those who had become Christians. To ensure a continuation of their faith they appointed elders to be leaders. They repeated this procedure at Iconium and Antioch. This time they established a church at Perga, also.

At each of these places, Silas baptized new converts.[12] In addition; Silas took his turn with the two older men to deliver the group's message.

At the Bay of Attalia, a vessel was bound for Syria, and Barnabas wasted no time in convincing the owner that he had space for three more passengers. As soon as the ship was on the open sea, Silas found a quiet spot where he was able to sit and relax for the first time in his recent memory. The soft breeze rocked the boat gently, massaging his tired body.

Silas now considered himself a seasoned sailor and he was also comfortable resting on the ship because for the first time since they left Antioch almost two years before, the three missionaries were not driving themselves toward the next challenge. Silas loved working for the church and was pleased with the success of their journey, but he longed to be reunited with his wife and children.

Silas thought about the wonderful years ahead when he would share the rest of his life with his family, working for a living in Antioch, doing whatever he could for the church there, and watching his children grow up to become ever stronger in their faith. He hoped they would be leaders in the Christian community, and that the stories he had in mind to tell them about the mission, both the successes and failures he had been part of, would be a learning experience that would help them.

Silas became uncomfortable when he thought about the friction between Christian Jews and unconverted Judaists, but he knew that he must tell the children all that happened because they would be exposed to this animosity as they grew older.

He had often asked himself, "Why can't these unconverted Jews accept what we tell them as the truth, and not treat what we say as fanciful stories? If only these doubters had received the same personal revelation that Paul and I had been given, they could not help but believe. Why can't they accept as the truth my experience at the cross and what happened to Paul on the road to Damascus? Why can't we make them understand that Jesus will be returning soon? Is it a failure on our part, or is it that only some have been chosen to believe?"

As Silas continued to reflect on their mission he realized that the great success they had with the Gentiles had alone made the journey worthwhile. He only hoped these new Christians understood that the belief they had accepted was a sect of Judaism and not a unique and independent religion. Silas told himself that this should be clear to them, because they acknowledge that the Israelites are God's chosen race and that Jesus Christ had come to them as their Messiah.

He thought also of the conversion of a few Pharisees. Because of their background and education, they would make great teachers, or *rabbis* as they were often called. Although he would welcome Sadducees into the fold, he feared most of them would prefer to just live the life of the rich and famous and remain collaborators of Rome.

A sudden fear struck Silas. When he left home almost two years ago, Martha was six and Joseph was five. Would they still remember him? If they did, would they feel that he had deserted them? If the children had become estranged, how would this affect his relationship with Rebekah? Had his devotion to the church destroyed his relationship with those he so deeply loved? Silas prayed that he would not return to his family as a stranger.

Chapter 17

Home Again

ON THE SEVENTH morning after leaving Perga, Silas gave thanks as the ship docked at Seleucia. He disembarked with the other missionaries and transferred to a small river boat to travel the last fifteen miles to Antioch. When they arrived at the city, they quickly made their way toward the Jewish quarter.

The early afternoon streets were crowded with people. They had not gone far when they were recognized by some of their Christian friends, who greeted them with loud shouts of welcome. Silas was stunned when Rebekah ran forward to throw herself into his arms. He knew then without a doubt that he was returning to the same love that he had left so long before, and he gave thanks that their marriage had been one of love and not one by arrangement, as was so often the case in their culture.

Silas knew that Rebekah had received no news from him for a few months and had not known whether he was dead or alive. He had sent letters from time to time, of course, but, because of the shortage of both papyrus and messengers traveling between Asia Minor and Syria, they were few and far between. The postal service of the Roman Empire did not handle personal letters. Rebekah told Silas that her only comfort had been the knowledge that he was engaged in what she considered to be the most important work possible, but now he was home and they were together again to become a whole family once more.

The greeting of love from Rebekah wiped away much of the anxiety Silas had brought with him, but one concern still troubled him. "Rebekah, I can't wait to see our children, but they're so young. I'm afraid that they might have forgotten me."

"Don't worry, Silas. We've talked about you every day. They will know you as soon as they see you, and they will be happy to have you back. They will want to hear all about your exciting adventures and the many strange places you've visited."

"You're a wonderful wife and mother, Rebekah. I couldn't be any happier than I am now."

Word of the men's arrival spread quickly and a crowd of Christians soon gathered. They gave thanks for the missionaries' safe return, but then they demanded a full account of their accomplishments. Paul invited the welcoming crowd to return to the public square early in the afternoon of the following day. He promised that he and his friends would give them a full report at that time.

As husband and wife walked off together hand in hand, Rebekah excitedly told Silas that she had some wonderful news for him.

"Your generous, loving father sent us enough money to buy a new, larger home. It is wonderful, and I can't wait for you to see it."

Silas was happy for his family, but he regretted that he had not been the one to provide the new home. He felt depressed, until he remembered what his father had told him when he left home as a fifteen year old.

Thomas had said that his son's role was to spread the Good News and that in doing so he would also fulfill the pledge he made to his grandfather. Then he had explained that it would be up to him to remain in Jerusalem and take care of his business. If he was successful, he would be able to provide the funds necessary to help the family survive and help the church grow.

The feeling of inadequacy that Silas was suffering disappeared with the memory of his father's words and he said, "Of course, I am most anxious to see our new home, but my first interest is our children."

Rebekah had left them in the care of a friend, so they set off for her home. After a hasty greeting, Silas rushed to his two children. He hugged them with the love he had saved for many months. They melted in his arms. Their genuine love made his worry about coming home disappear completely.

Rebekah's friend urged him to sit down, which he did, managing to hold one child on each knee. After a while, Rebekah begged him to tell them about his life as a missionary. He replied that as anxious as he was to tell them all about his adventures he must hear everything about her and the children first.

"Well, you missed a very interesting and, I believe, very important time in the lives of our children, but let me assure you they have been well taken care of. Our children enjoy a wonderful opportunity that neither one of us was able to have; and that is the good fortune to be raised in a Christian home.

"My most important consideration has been for their future, and I have been doing my best to prepare them for that. Joseph is fortunate because he will have you as a role model, but I'm also very excited about what is waiting for Martha in the years ahead, because I believe that the Christian world will provide her with opportunities denied women in the past.

"She will not have the same recognition that men will enjoy. In the synagogue she will still be subordinate to men and be forced to stand behind a partition during the service, and in the Temple she will not be allowed to go beyond the Court of Women. She will still hear that prayer many men say, 'Blessed be God that he did not make me a Gentile, a slave, or a woman.' Nevertheless, her role will not be restricted to taking care of the home and family. I believe that Jesus wanted women involved in spreading his message.

"Our children will have the best of our Jewish tradition enriched by our new faith. But enough about the children's future. Now I'll tell you a few things about their past and present.

"Not everything was well with us while you were away. Both children suffered illnesses, and I was worried about them several times, but we are fortunate here in Antioch to have a physician who is very competent and knowledgeable about medicinal herbs. He was a Jewish slave who purchased his freedom and received his professional training in Tarsus. His medical achievements earned him Roman citizenship.

"Because of our great faith in God and the skill of our doctor, Martha and Joseph survived those treacherous early years unlike so many other less fortunate children. In spite of periodic illness, our little family has been as happy as possible with an absent father. We are fortunate to be living in Antioch. We are generally free from persecution here. As you know, many of the Jews in the city are Christians who fled Jerusalem after the stoning of Stephen, and countless others have joined us since then.

"Just after you left, Joseph began his formal education. He now spends a half-day six days a week at the synagogue. I take him there early every morning and pick him up at midday. He is taught the Torah, reading, writing, and working with numbers. While Joseph is at the synagogue, I teach Martha everything she needs to know about home life while we do the many household chores that must be done. In the afternoon I spend time with both children teaching them about Jesus and his message. Then they go with me to do the shopping and help at the church.

"When he is older, Joseph will begin the study of a business or trade in the afternoon. I hope that he will be able to learn from a scholarly scribe as both you and Paul did. Of course, Joseph must have a Christian teacher."

Both children had been sitting contentedly on their father's lap, listening to everything, but they hopped down to go with their parents when Rebekah said, "Enough of that for the present. Now the children and I will take you to our new home and show you what your father has done for us all."

Now that he was back in Antioch, Silas hoped that he would be able to take care of his family in the home his father had provided. He knew that it would be quite modest, and because of the poor financial condition of the other Christians in Antioch, he and Rebekah would not want it any other way.

Their new home was the typical private dwelling of Israelites without wealth that Silas had become familiar with since leaving Alexandria. He had been told that such houses had undergone very little change over the past several centuries. A fieldstone wall enclosed a courtyard in one corner of the square-shaped property. The absence of windows in the house would keep the four rooms warmer in winter and cooler in summer, but also would make the interior dark and somewhat unpleasant.

Before inspecting the inside, Silas followed Rebekah and the children up a stairway on an outside wall to the second floor. Because it was without a roof, it was bright and would offer relief from the dreary interior. Next, Rebekah led her family back down into the courtyard where she pointed proudly to two ovens sunk into the ground and a cistern to collect rainwater. The ovens were in the eastern corner of the yard, where prevailing winds would tend to blow the smoke away from the house. A supply of friction sticks and a white broom plant for lighting the fire were kept next to the ovens.

When they went into the first ground-level room, they paused while Rebekah lit a lamp. Silas admired the floor because it was covered with limestone slabs that would make it much easier to keep clean than would be possible with a packed-mud floor. Even in the dim light from the single lamp, he could see wall niches in which he recognized their ceramic dishes and vessels and a hand mill for grinding grain. He immediately felt at home.

Rebekah usually bought bread from the baker, but if she did not have enough money, she would bake her own. Silas had seen her make bread countless times. She would start with the grain, selecting either barley or wheat, and removing weeds and other contaminating substances. Then she would grind the grain and collect the flour on a cloth below the mill. Rebekah's friend would come over often to help, taking turns doing the grinding. Rebekah would mix the flour with olive oil to make a dough, adding salt and leaven in the kneading trough that he saw hanging on the wall and then putting the risen dough into the oven to be baked to perfection.

Next to the kneading trough, he recognized the small wooden storage box which held their wooden bowls and their only bronze vessel. Of course, there was still no glassware; it was much too expensive for them.

The next room contained the familiar table set on short legs and surrounded by their couches so Silas and Rebekah could eat in a reclining position. The children would have to sit upright until they were older. Each of the two bedrooms had one chair, a storage chest, and a table for a lamp. The lamps, like those in the other rooms, were pottery vessels containing olive oil. The smaller of two openings on the top of each lamp was pinched to support the wick. Oil was added to the lamp through the larger opening. Simple, but new, rugs covered the floors of the bedrooms. The beds were the same rectangular wooden frames with crossbars extending from the rails to support the mattresses that Silas and Rebekah had acquired when they were first married. The walls and ceilings of all the rooms were smoothed with plaster. Silas knew that he could live happily in their new home forever.

With the tour finished, Rebekah prepared the evening meal. She had already placed a pot of vegetable soup with beans, green vegetables, and herbs over the open fire in the courtyard. She apologized. If she had only known that Silas would be home for dinner, she would have somehow obtained a bit of lamb to add to the soup, but she knew that he would be happy to share a meal with his family for the first time in many months, no matter how simple it was.

Silas was starving, just waiting to dip pieces of the good bread Rebekah had bought from the baker into the soup that was simmering on the fire. As he satisfied the children's curiosity with stories about faraway lands and strange people, he could see Rebekah preparing a salad of cucumbers, leeks, and onions. He was glad that he was back in an area where there would be no shortage of salt to season both the soup and salad. Local merchants had ample supplies of salt that had been collected from the evaporation of water blown up on the shore of the Dead Sea and brought to Antioch.

Thinking about family dinners of the past, Silas hoped there would still be fruit, perhaps figs, with the meal. He had not had figs for some time. He was quite sure that Rebekah would have cheese, and of course wine, because the water at Antioch was not safe to drink.

After they had dinner and the children were put to bed, Silas, as he had promised, told Rebekah about the mission journey with Paul, Barnabas, and John Mark. Then Silas and Rebekah retired to their new bedroom.

The following morning Silas and Rebekah ate a breakfast of bread, cheese, and dried fruit, and then they went their separate ways.

Silas intended to spend the morning trying to reorganize his business, and in the afternoon he planned to go to the public square where he would join Paul and Barnabas to give a full report of their mission.

Rebekah told him she wanted to devote her morning to a relaxing walk through the market areas where she could dream about all the things she would buy if she could afford them. Silas had been surprised when she explained that she had been working at the potter's wheel. She told him that because of what she earned to supplement the support received from his father, it had been unnecessary for the church to provide any help, but of course there was no money left over for luxury items.

Nevertheless, pretending to shop in the markets seemed like a proper celebration of her husband's homecoming. Silas agreed with her plan. He had chosen not to go with her, but in his mind's eye he would follow her wherever she went throughout the morning.

After she took Joseph to school and left Martha with her friend, he knew she would start by walking through the narrow streets of the Jewish market, stopping from time to time to get a good look at the stalls set up in front of merchants' homes to inspect whatever was offered for sale. She would see such delicacies as nuts, dates, olive oil, and even fish. Rebekah would return here later to buy what she needed for dinner, but first she would go outside the Jewish quarter into the agora where life would be crowded and exciting in the morning. Many in the market would be busy with their shopping and others would just be standing around waiting for someone with whom to gossip.

Silas could see her walking through the public square where the missionaries would give their report later to all who were interested, Jews and Gentiles, Christians and heathens. Passing into the main market area, Rebekah would surely recognize a few merchants who had reputations for being dishonest. One man was said to be able to manipulate the scales in his favor. He did not believe that "the Lord abhors dishonest scales, but accurate weights are his delight."[1] Another merchant had a reputation for withholding merchandise to force the price up. She would see that most of the merchandise displayed was not what she really wanted or could afford. Silas imagined the precious metals, pottery, jewels, cosmetics, dyed cloth, wool, spices, rugs, livestock and even slaves that were always offered for sale.

Further along she would come to the import area. Antioch's seaport at Seleucia enhanced the city's trading position. Cotton from warmer and more humid countries as well as fine ceramic ware from distant lands would be on sale. Phoenician blown-glass drinking bowls were vessels of choice for those who could afford them. A few glass-designer products signed by the artist would be available. She would see the natural color of local wool blended nicely with imported red, purple, and indigo blue dyes.

Passing this area, Rebekah would enter another section that offered better quality local products. One of them, linen from Syrian flax, was recognized as superior to the imported material. Other local fibers that had been spun, woven into fabrics, and made into tunics for both men and women that hung from the neck to the knees or lower would be on display. Loincloths for men made of linen or leather would be offered for sale. Mantles or cloaks for additional warmth would be available. These were in demand because they were often torn in times of sorrow or distress. There would be brightly colored head cloths that servant girls used as supports for carrying water pots. Storage jars for scrolls would be plentiful. Many tradesmen, including carpenters, metalworkers, potters, tentmakers, bankers, fullers, and laundrymen would wander through all sections of the market, hoping to get a contract with someone.

Finally, Rebekah would return to the Jewish quarter where she would buy the vegetables and bread she could afford and then pick up the children. She would be thankful that there were only two meals a day to plan and pay for. As Silas continued to make preparations for reopening his business he smiled as he pictured in his mind Rebekah's day in the market.

The three men gave the report of their mission. It was well received, and the missionaries were highly praised.[2] Many non-believers, both Jews and Gentiles, were in the crowd because they were very curious about the journey of the Christians and unable to understand why they would attempt such a dangerous and exhausting ordeal.

Rebekah brought the children just as Silas imagined she would. She thought it would be good for them to see their father honored and to better understand how important his contribution to the church had been. After the session was over, the family returned home to enjoy another dinner together.

In the months after the missionaries returned to Antioch, they worked with the leaders they had appointed as elders to take over while they were away, helping them with energy and enthusiasm. The missionaries were pleased to be home. The church continued to grow as new converts were admitted after confessing their faith in Christ as their savior and being baptized. It seemed that most of the new Christians were Gentiles. Realizing the need for organization within the growing church, Silas and the others persuaded the elders to form a governing council similar to the one the men were accustomed to in the synagogue.

Silas had reestablished his business, and Paul and Barnabas had returned to their trades. Nevertheless, all three still had time for the church, and Silas was with his family every evening. He was happy with his life and had begun to look forward to the future when Joseph would become active in the church. Silas had taken over the duty of teaching his son, which he loved doing, and of course this gave Rebekah more time to spend with Martha.

In spite of his satisfying life at Antioch, Silas was still disturbed because he did not know what the proper relationship of converted Gentiles with the Christian church should be. It seemed to him that because they were not Jews, they could not be complete Christians, so what were they? Also, the number of Gentiles in the church at Antioch was increasing rapidly. He knew that they would soon outnumber the Christian Jews and he feared that when this happened, their Christian church would become a gentile organization.

Silas was not the only one concerned about these problems. A group of Christian Pharisees in Jerusalem firmly believed that in order for Gentiles to become Christians the men must first become Jews by being circumcised as decreed by Moses.[3] When they learned of the large population of uncircumcised Christian Gentiles in Antioch, they set out for that city resolved to remedy the situation.

When the Jerusalem Jews arrived, they lost no time in telling the gentile men of the church that in order to be saved, they must be circumcised. Paul and Barnabas disputed this and argued vehemently with the newcomers. Silas did not know what to think. He had always believed that the Gentiles should become Jews, but he had never thought that being circumcised was essential for salvation. Before long the arguments became heated, and when there seemed to be no hope of resolving the issue at Antioch, Silas, Paul, Barnabas, and the Jews who had come from Jerusalem agreed to take the case to the apostles for a decision.[4]

Because of the urgency to receive a decision, the group went directly to the church council to request a meeting when they walked into Jerusalem three weeks later. The apostles agreed to see the Christians from Antioch the following morning.

While Paul and the others were looking for temporary living quarters, Silas went to visit his parents whom he had not seen for two years. His father was now fifty-three and his mother two years younger. Of course they were surprised and overjoyed to see their son. When Silas asked if there had been any word from his grandfather, Thomas replied that every time he went to answer a knock at the door he hoped it would be a messenger bringing good news from Alexandria, but so far that had never been the case.

When eventually the conversation turned to more pleasant subjects, Silas thanked his father for providing a fine home for his family and giving them additional financial support. Thomas replied that he was happy to have been able to do it and thankful that the demand for his services had made it possible. Then, in answer to his parents prodding, Silas told them about his missionary journey and the roles Rebekah and even the young children were playing in the church. When Silas finally confessed to the reason for his visit to Jerusalem, Thomas said he was sure that members of The Way everywhere would soon see no difference between Jews and Gentiles. Silas admitted that he, himself, was still having trouble giving them full acceptance. After sharing the evening meal with his parents, Silas left to seek Paul and the others from Antioch.

The next morning, the matter was presented to the church council. After a great deal of discussion for and against the necessity of circumcision to become a Christian, Peter, who had returned to the city after the death of Agrippa, got up to speak. He reminded all those present that several years previously he had accepted Cornelius, a Gentile, into the church without circumcision. He emphasized that the proof his action was proper was provided when the Holy Spirit descended on Cornelius and the other Gentiles just as the Holy Spirit had descended on the apostles. God had made no distinction between circumcised and uncircumcised.[5]

After these presentations had been made, Silas heard a new voice. James, the brother of Jesus, stood up to address the assembly. After Peter had fled to Caesarea to escape from Agrippa's men, James had become the leader of the church in Jerusalem and was now very influential.

He said, "I have been convinced by what I have heard that Gentiles should be accepted into the church without question just as they are. Nevertheless, if they become one with us and live as Jews, they must at least adhere to our code of proper conduct. They must abstain from food polluted by idols, from sexual immorality, from meat of strangled animals, and from blood."

The leaders agreed with all that James said and decided to send two of their own members to Antioch with Silas and the others as emissaries to certify that their report was approved by all the members of the church council.

Silas listened to all that had been said and finally he understood that in God's eyes all races are the same and the grace of God is a free gift for everyone and not something to be earned. He was at peace at last.

When the group returned to Antioch and gave their report, harmony was restored to the church. In the days that followed, Silas, Paul, and Barnabas went about their work of teaching with new vigor.[6]

Silas often told Rebekah that he could not be any happier than he was. He had a wonderful wife, fine children, a good home, and a beloved church. Now, eighteen years after leaving the city of his birth, he had the satisfaction of knowing he was fulfilling the pledge he had made in Alexandria when he was just a young boy.

His grandfather had fervently desired that he search for the truth, find it, and disseminate it among their people. This he was doing, although not as he had anticipated. Instead of finding the truth through study with learned rabbis in the greatest library in the world, Silas had found it in the teachings of Jesus and in his personal knowledge of the crucifixion and resurrection of the Messiah.

Instead of returning to Alexandria three years after he left to begin his advanced studies, he had gone to Damascus to spread the truth. He had accomplished his purpose by teaching there and later at Syrian Antioch and in the several countries he had visited with Paul and Barnabas. He felt confident that in each of those places he had contributed something further to the fulfillment of his promise.

Chapter 18

On the Road Again

ONE DAY AFTER a meeting at church, Paul came up to Silas with the surprising news that he and Barnabas had decided to go on another missionary journey.[1] He explained they believed that their role in the new Christian world was to continue to take the message to those who needed reinforcement, and especially to those who had not yet heard it.

Silas went home that evening and, as usual, told Rebekah all that had happened during the day. "Rebekah, Paul surprised me today when he told me that he and Barnabas had decided to start out on another missionary journey."

"Why, I think that's wonderful, Silas!"

"Yes, I do too. I understood Paul's compulsion to spread the Word, and I'm certainly in favor of him doing that, but I'm worried about his wellbeing. I'm afraid that his physical condition is not what it should be for such a grueling undertaking."

"I agree that Paul is not well. I've noticed that his health has deteriorated during the past few weeks, but I don't think you need to worry. Once Paul is doing the work he loves, he will feel much better, and, of course, he will have Barnabas to take care of him."

The next day Silas paid a visit to his friends as they were making plans for their second mission. When Silas arrived he heard Barnabas ask, "Paul, where do you think we should go this time?"

Before Paul could reply, Silas answered the question. "Why don't you stop at each of the churches you visited on your first mission?"

"That's a great idea, Silas. That's exactly what we'll do."

When Silas heard Paul agree excitedly with his suggestion he hoped his enthusiasm meant that he was not worried about his health.

Barnabas said, "I agree with Paul. Thanks for your suggestion, Silas. I can't wait to start out. I'm excited about the prospect of leaving on another mission and am anxious to leave as soon as possible." Then in his deep voice he called out, "I'll prepare to contact John Mark. We must have him on our team."

Silas was surprised when Paul jumped up, looking very much as he had when he confronted Elymas on the island of Cyprus, and pointed his finger directly at Barnabas. "I will not allow him to come with us," he shouted. "He deserted us once and he may well do it again. He is neither a devoted man nor a reliable helper."

There was no doubt in Silas's mind that Paul meant what he said, and that he had issued his last word on the subject.

Then it was Barnabas's turn. This time, as quietly as he was able to talk, he replied, "Paul, I'm very disturbed by your attitude. If you go without John Mark, you will go without me. He and I will go my way. I will lead our mission. You can go alone on yours." With that Barnabas stalked out.[2]

Because Silas could think of nothing that would ease Paul's pain, he said good-bye and left. On the way home he began to wonder if Paul's reaction to Barnabas's suggestion was a reflection of the sickness from which he was suffering, whatever it was. He was devastated by the thought of his two friends quarreling and separating. He could not bear the thought of Paul going on a mission by himself. When he reached home he began talking to Rebekah as he passed through the door.

"Now I am more worried than ever about Paul," he said. "I know those two men are stubborn, and neither one will change his mind. I also know that Paul will not cancel his plans for a mission journey. We have a real problem on our hands."

"Why don't you say what you are trying not to tell me?" Rebekah asked. "I know that you feel you have to go with him, and I am reconciled to that. Don't worry about us. The children and I will get along just as we did when you went on your first mission."

Silas was flabbergasted and relieved. He knew once more that he had a very special wife. "I'm glad you understand. I feel that I must go with Paul. Even if his health is better than we think it is, I will do all I can to make the journey physically easy for him, but I have a more important reason for joining Paul. I believe that I have been called to go with him, and that the time has come for me to assume more responsibility for the leadership of what has now become a two-man missionary team. I will be leaving you and the children once more with a heavy heart, but I know that I must go to spread the Word to the world."

"As much as I hate to see you leave, I understand that what you are about to do is vital to our faith. I am proud of you, and the children will be also."

Once Silas had received Rebekah's blessing he returned to Paul.

"I knew that you would come along. God bless you, Silas. Now we will make our plans for the mission. The church here is well established and no longer needs us."

During the next few weeks, Barnabas was nowhere to be seen, but he must have managed to contact John Mark and invite him to come along on a mission with him, because his cousin appeared one day apparently ready to leave for whatever destination Barnabas had in mind. John Mark had not been in Antioch long before Silas heard that Barnabas had arranged for sea passage to Cyprus.[3] He had decided to follow Silas's suggestion and start by repeating the successful tour he had made of his home country with Silas and Paul three years previously.

After Barnabas and John Mark sailed away to begin their journey, Paul came to Silas to discuss their mission. He made it clear that they must follow a completely different path from the one Silas had recommended, because Barnabas and John Mark had announced it was the one they were taking. Silas agreed, and said that he would be satisfied with whatever itinerary Paul planned to follow.

"Thank you, Silas. Instead of leaving by sea for Cyprus we will start off by walking overland toward Asia Minor[4]. Now let us go to meet with the elders and to receive their blessing."

Silas had mixed feelings about embarking on his second missionary journey. He was anxious to begin and reconciled to leaving his family again for a while, but he knew he would miss Barnabas and John Mark and the camaraderie the four of them had shared when they started out for Cyprus almost three years previously. On the other hand, he relished the opportunity of working more closely with Paul. Paul was like an older brother for whom Silas had the highest respect. Paul would be the leader of their expedition, not only because of his age, but because of his experience on the road to Damascus. Silas would be in the company of a true apostle.

Before dawn the next day Silas said good-bye to his brave family and joined Paul to walk toward Seleucid. The two men wore their standard travel garb, tunics over loin cloths, and sandals with heavy leather soles. Each of them took a wine bottle and enough food in a wicker container to last several days. They also carried a few silver denarii coins that they had saved over the past week. Early in the day they crossed the Orontes River on a small boat to begin their trek through the countryside of the Roman province of Syria.

Soon they were walking through the pleasant market garden area where the Antioch farmers grew the produce they offered for sale in either the agora or the Jewish quarter. A little further on, they passed through farmland where the grain crops would soon be ready for the fall harvest.

Because Paul realized that Silas had grown up in the city and was not familiar with farm practice, he explained what he had learned was about to take place. "The grain you see waving in the light wind will soon be ready to be cut with sickles. Then it will be bound into sheaves ready for threshing. If the farmer who owns this crop is wealthy enough to possess a cow, that step will be much easier. He will just drive the cow back and forth over the grain to crush it. Next his family members will come out and throw the grain up into the air, allowing the sea breeze to separate the light chaff. Silas, you became a seaman on our first journey; now you have become a farmer on this one."

"Thank you for the education, Paul. I may not be a farmer, but I'm looking at something ahead that I am familiar with. I can see olive groves and vineyards, and I know without being told that oil and wine presses will soon be put to use."

"Before that there will be fresh grapes for sale, and after that raisins will be plentiful."

Further on Silas and Paul passed through fields of flax, which would be used to make the fine linen Silas had often seen on sale in the agora. Then the flax stalks would be used to make baskets like the small ones that now contained their food. The first day's journey was indeed very pleasant. Silas was thankful he had not had to worry about a rough sea voyage.

When Silas and Paul left the farmland they soon reached the trade route along the narrow coastal plain. Then, for the first time, Paul told Silas where they were headed. "We will soon arrive at Tarsus, the city of my birth and younger years, and the refuge you selected for me when I was not accepted in Jerusalem." Silas thought it interesting that both Barnabas and Paul began the missions they were directing with a visit to their birthplace. By walking twenty to thirty miles each day the two missionaries arrived at the outskirts of Tarsus five days after leaving Antioch.

Silas could tell that Paul was happy to be back in the city where he had been born. He seemed to be more relaxed and even appeared to be in better health. Paul enjoyed showing Silas some of the more important sights, including the university and the school of philosophy, both of which he had attended before going to Jerusalem to study under Gamaliel.

As they walked through the market area, Silas saw many fine foods on display and was relieved that they would soon be eating appetizing meals. Merchants of stalls were selling milk, yogurt, cheese, wine, grape jelly, and fresh and salted fish. As they passed a street oven, Silas saw a woman hand her dough to the baker. He wondered whether she had chosen not to do her own baking, or whether she did not even own an oven. Paul pointed out a baking sheet the baker had just placed over an open fire. He had spread grains on it to prepare popped corn.

Silas was relieved to be in a city where they expected to find work and earn enough to at least enable them to buy some of the food they had just seen. He said he hoped to find a few people who would be looking for a scribe who could write a letter for them, and Paul replied that he hoped to find damaged goat-hair tents that needed repairs.

On the Sabbath the two men attended the service in the synagogue, where Paul addressed the congregation. Many of the people he was speaking to had listened to him previously and were anxious to hear him again. He reminded them that the only way to salvation was through acceptance of the free gift of the grace of God. He told them that belief in Jesus Christ would bring them the salvation they did not deserve, but he emphasized that grace did not give them the freedom to sin. Paul explained that by the grace of God, he had been converted from a persecutor of Christians to a believer who had devoted his life to Jesus Christ. He told them that as a young Pharisee he had sought in vain to get God's acceptance by trying to fulfill the Law.

After a successful ministry in Tarsus, Paul seemed to be much like his old self. He and Silas set off for the churches in southern Galatia that they had visited on their previous journey. They agreed that their first stop would be Derbe.[5]

Silas knew that their trek to that city would be more difficult than the coastal walk they had just made from Syrian Antioch to Tarsus, and he was concerned that Paul might lose the recent improvement in his health. Paul, however, assured Silas that if they took at least five days to reach Derbe he would have no problem.

When the two men left the Roman province of Cilicia they headed west following the great international trade route between Asia Minor and Syria. On the second day they reached the foothills of the Taurus Mountains. Once more the two missionaries would have to navigate a route through the peaks, but this time they would follow the less tortuous pass known as the Cilician Gates, and they would not be doing it in the rainy season. Just as Paul had anticipated, the two missionaries arrived at Derbe after five days on the road.

When they approached the city, Silas recalled the relief he felt when they had arrived there previously. After the treachery at the gentile city of Lystra, the friendly reception at the Jewish city of Derbe had been most welcome.

This time, however, their entry was much different. The first sight to greet their eyes was a funeral procession with, as was the custom, every able body of the Jewish quarter following the widow who led the way. Because it appeared that the entire Jewish community was participating in the service, Silas and Paul had no alternative but to join the gathering and walk along with the mourners.

As they fell in with the group, Silas recognized many Christians, among them the widow, whom he and Paul had met with on their previous visit. At the tomb they listened to a few memorial speeches, after which the family of the deceased man left to walk between two parallel lines of mourners.

Silas knew that, following local custom, a few friends and neighbors who were not part of the procession would have been busy at the grieving family's home during the funeral ceremony. They would have prepared food and then moved all the furniture, placing it so that it faced the wall. Because of this arrangement, the mourners, when they arrived, would have to eat the food while standing or sitting on the floor.

In the meantime the procession had reversed itself, with the widow leading it back to her home. On arrival the mourners would be served the standard funeral fare of bread, hard-boiled eggs, and lentils. Silas realized that this death in the Jewish city of Derbe would interfere with their plans for worship services, because deep mourning would go on for seven days, although weeping would be restricted to the first three days. During the seven-day period, the family members would not wash, wear shoes, or participate in study or business. The seven-day period would be followed by thirty days of lighter mourning.

When Silas and Paul entered the home of the deceased, sad notes from a solitary flute provided the only sound. Silas waited until the time was appropriate and then spoke to the widow and her family.

"I understand your grief but assure you that your present suffering is nothing compared to the happiness already enjoyed by your departed loved one. Death cannot separate your husband and father from Christ. Just as he lived with Christ, he died to be with him. Jesus said, 'I am the resurrection and the life. He who believes in me will live, even though he dies.'"[6]

Although Silas knew the mourners would continue to grieve, he felt assured that after hearing these words of the new Christian belief they would face life with renewed faith and hope. After the deep mourning period was over, Silas and Paul met with the Jews of Derbe before leaving for Lystra, a city sixty miles further west.[7]

Once more they made the five-day walk on a decent Roman road with very little trouble. As the two men drew closer to Lystra, and passed the spot where Paul had been left for dead, Silas hoped their reception by the Gentile Christians in the city would be as friendly as it had been on their return visit there two years before. He had no desire to encounter the hateful Judaizers again, or on the other hand to be worshiped as a pagan god come to earth.

He was relieved when the elders they appointed on their last visit rushed forward to receive him and Paul with open arms. They assured the two men that all was well. The church had prospered in the missionaries' absence.

One group of believers who gave Silas and Paul an especially warm welcome were Gentiles who long before the missionaries' first visit to Lystra had become disenchanted with their religion of cults and their assortment of gods. Their wavering belief had led them to consider the religion of the Jews. The higher standard of morality and the belief in one omnipotent God had attracted them, and what they found was what they thought they needed.

The God fearers had hesitated to become fully committed to the Jewish religion, however, and while they were still indecisive, a group of zealous evangelizing Pharisees had come along and persuaded them to convert to Judaism. They learned some of the fundamentals of the Jewish faith, such as the proper observance of the Sabbath and the Pharisaic dietary laws. Then the men were circumcised, both men and women were baptized to be ritually clean, and the Gentiles became Jewish proselytes.

A few years later when Silas and Paul arrived on their first mission and taught in the synagogue, many of these proselytes had come to listen. They had believed what they heard, took the final step, and became Christians. Now when the missionaries returned on their third visit the proselytes welcomed them and offered thanks for the blessing of Christianity.

Among the many newcomers to the church at Lystra was a young lad named Timothy. Timothy was even younger than Silas had been when he first joined Paul at Damascus. Silas spoke to Paul about him: "The elders have great praise for Timothy and predict a bright future for him in the church. I believe he would make a strong addition to our team and a wonderful replacement for John Mark."

"I agree, Silas. He could be a great help to us. You are closer to his age than I am, so why don't you invite him to come along with us?"

When Silas asked Timothy to become part of their mission team, he described some of the hardships they might face. These did not dissuade Timothy, and he accepted the invitation, interpreting it as a challenge.

During their conversation, Silas discovered that Timothy was the son of a mixed marriage. His mother was a good Christian Jew, and his father was a good Christian Greek. At one time, because of his strict Pharisaic background, Silas would not have recognized such a marriage. Now, of course, he had learned that in God's eyes there was neither Jew nor Gentile, but only Christian.

Nevertheless, when Silas discovered that Timothy had never been circumcised, he thought this might be causing some concern in the small Jewish community. Worried about this, in deference to the few Jews living in the community,[8] he urged Timothy to be circumcised to establish his identity.

After the missionaries had enjoyed two successful weeks in Lystra they left that city to continue their journey westward, and Timothy was with them when they paid visits to Iconium and Antioch of Pisidia. When Silas told Timothy about his first visit to Antioch as a member of a three-man team, he began to wonder why they had not encountered Barnabas and John Mark. He assumed they had either changed their route or spent more time in Cyprus on this journey.

Timothy was most anxious to learn all that he could about Christianity, and Silas and Paul answered the many questions he asked as they walked along. Silas was pleased that Paul did not seem at all bothered by the long walks. Rebekah had been right when she predicted that his health would recover when he returned to the work he loved.

The group's next destination was Troas, but when they arrived there, Paul informed Silas and Timothy that he had received a vision in which he was told not to stay at Troas but to cross the Aegean Sea and go to the Roman colony of Macedonia in Greece. Silas was not one to argue with Paul when he claimed to have had a vision, so he agreed that they should leave Asia Minor and make their first visit to Europe.[9]

The three men were soon able to arrange passage on a substantial seaworthy craft built locally. Silas found out that the shipwrights who created the unique vessel had used a new and superior method of joining the hull planks by dovetailing, and when the hull was completed they had reinforced it with framing and sealed it with pitch. After hearing all this, Silas felt quite comfortable when they sailed away from the harbor at Troas.

The first day's voyage was a short sail to the mountainous island of Samothrace, where the ship anchored for the night. The second day took them to Neapolis, the seaport of Philippi, where they went ashore. Once on land the missionaries began the ten-mile walk to one of the major cities of Macedonia. Philippi had been the site of the defeat of the army of Brutus and Cassius by the forces of Augustus Caesar and Antony. That battle sealed the fate of the Republic of Rome and led to the establishment of the Roman Empire.[10]

Silas soon found out that Philippi was the exception to the rule that wherever ten Jewish men lived there would be a synagogue, because he and Paul could not find one anywhere in the city in spite of the large Jewish population. Nevertheless, they knew that where Jews lived, a meeting place of some kind must exist, even if it wasn't a synagogue, and on the day after the Sabbath the three men found it.

When they noticed several Jewish women walking in the same direction, they knew that they were on their way to a place where they could meet to pray. They soon arrived at a spot along the bank of a small river. Once there, they realized that the site had been selected as a place of prayer for the devout Jewish women of the city.

When Silas asked permission to address the group, they gave it, probably curious to find out who the bold men were. After he and Paul delivered sermons of salvation through belief in Jesus Christ, one of the women, named Lydia, came up to speak to them. "Thank you for telling us about a new and different faith that offers us hope for salvation. I don't want to wait one more day before my family and I are given that baptism you told us about."[11]

Silas knew that Paul, as usual, would depend on him to perform the baptism so he started to prepare for the ritual, but Paul announced that before Silas baptized the family he would tell them what the ceremony meant.

He explained that Christian baptism was quite different from the baptism Jews used to ceremonially cleanse proselytes. Paul told them that Christian baptism followed repentance of sins and commitment to Jesus Christ. He said that just as Christ died on the cross, so their sins would die in the water, and just as Christ was resurrected, so they would be born again from the water into a new life in the church family. The immersion in water symbolized a complete change in the believer's life when that believer recognized that the death, burial, and resurrection of Jesus Christ had created the way to salvation.

After the baptisms had been performed, Lydia told Silas and Paul that she was a wealthy merchant from Thyatira, a city in the Lycus

River valley southeast of Troas, and that she sold Tyrian purple dye. She explained that it was obtained from tiny shellfish that were only found in the vicinity of Sidon and Tyre on the Phoenician coast.

When Silas heard this he realized why the country was known as Phoenicia: the name meant land of purple. Lydia said that a great many shells were required to obtain just a small quantity of dye, which was why it was very rare and expensive. Silas and Paul were well aware that only the wealthy wore garments dyed with Tyrian purple. Lydia said that although her home was at Thyatira she owned a place at Philippi, and she insisted that the three missionaries stay with her while they were in the city.

Timothy walked beside Silas talking to him as the group started out for Lydia's home. "Silas, I'm very thankful to have had heard the explanation of Christian baptism that Paul gave to Lydia's family. I've certainly learned a great deal in the short time since I joined you and Paul."

Silas realized from the size of Lydia's house that she indeed was a very wealthy woman. He knew that her home would make an excellent base for them, and that it would be more comfortable than any accommodation they had had previously.

The first meal at Lydia's confirmed his assessment. A servant girl ladled the lentil soup into ceramic bowls of a quality they had not seen before. Some of the utensils were silver. The bread was fresh and tasted good, whether it was used to wipe the serving bowls or dipped in honey.

During their time at Lydia's, the missionaries enjoyed smoked fish, dried fish, baked pigeon, goat cheese, dates, olives, dried fruits, nuts and, of course, mulled wines and occasionally beef. No wonder there was chatter and laughter at the evening meal, and more enthusiasm than usual the next day. The wealthy, as well as the destitute, unsuccessful, and defeated sought the new belief.

The riverbank meeting place soon became the site of frequent gatherings for the three missionaries and a large group of Christians. One day Lydia told Silas quietly that a girl they could see in the distance was a slave.[12]

Timothy was listening. "Silas, I don't know anything about slaves because there weren't any at Lystra where I lived. How did that girl come to be one?"

"Timothy, you are full of questions as usual. I assume that like most slaves she has been one from birth, although it is possible that she was sold into slavery or sentenced to slavery as a result of committing a crime of some sort. You might be surprised to know that slaves enjoy a great deal of freedom in daily affairs and can serve in any position, earn money for themselves, and own property. This slave girl doesn't look very prosperous, but in my opinion slaves are better off than many free persons and sometimes even receive a higher rate of pay. Some slaves are able to buy their freedom early in life, and most are freed after several years of service. Pharisees and Sadducees accept slavery, but for some reason Essenes do not."

"I've never heard of Essenes. Who are they? What kind of people are they?"

"I'll answer that one," Paul said. "The Essenes are a small political party, just as Pharisees and Sadducees are, but they are quite different in many ways. They are headquartered somewhere along the west shore of the Dead Sea. Believe me, they have some very strange beliefs. For example, they claim that they alone are true Israelites. Like us they believe in one God and hold Moses in very high esteem, but they embrace the sun with such reverence that some consider them to be idolatrous. They do not trust women, and most refuse to marry. Before you ask me how they perpetuate themselves, I'll tell you how it's accomplished. It's mostly done by adoption. That's the end of today's lessons. Now, I believe Lydia wants to speak to us."

"The slave girl seems to be coming closer," Lydia said. "Let's try to avoid her. She's insane. Timothy, I'll tell you something about pagan Philippians that you probably don't know. They believe that an insane person's mind has been destroyed and replaced with the mind of a god. Because of their strange belief, infidels of this city listen to the ravings that come out of the girl's mouth waiting for anything that might come from the mind of a god. They believe some of the things she says are prophetic messages from one of their heathen deities.

"I'm sorry to say that a group of dishonest men are manipulating that feebleminded girl by implanting ideas in her head. Then they force her to claim that she can foretell the future, which she will do for a fee. Any predictions she makes are bits and pieces of information cleverly concocted by her masters and imprinted in her mind. Of course, the money she collects goes directly into the pockets of those who control her."

Lydia had no sooner said this when the slave girl approached the missionaries offering to tell them what was waiting for them in the future. They ignored her and walked on.

After that day the slave girl would follow Silas, Paul, and Timothy and shout out, "These men are servants of the Most High God, who are telling you the way to be saved."

She had been coached to say this. The men who ruled her life thought this would flatter the missionaries and bring them some new business. One day, Paul, who had not been feeling well, became irritated with this daily annoyance and said, "In the name of Jesus Christ, I command you to come out of her."

With these words the slave girl's brain was wiped clean of the fraudulent stories she had been forced to tell. She realized at once how cruelly she had been manipulated and how adversely her advice might have affected some of the people who had been brought to her to have their fortunes told.

Of course she was very happy to be like other people, but her unscrupulous masters were frantic because of the loss of business they would suffer. Now that she was no longer insane, they could neither implant oracles in her brain nor convince the Philippians that she possessed the mind of a heathen god.[13] Furious with their loss of income, the dishonest men seized the three missionaries as enemies of the state, and took them to the city square to appear before the magistrates there.

When they were asked to present their charge they responded, "These men are Jews and are throwing our city into an uproar by advocating customs unlawful for us Romans to accept or practice." The crowd that had gathered in the market place to find out what all the excitement was about believed this charge. Without waiting for the magistrates to pass judgment, they attacked the three men.

Roman officials could not tolerate an outbreak of public violence, even when it was not created by Jews. With a desperate effort, the magistrates regained control. When the crowd was silenced, the chief magistrate motioned for the accusers to come forward.

Silas had no sooner uttered a prayer of thanks for being spared from the anger of the mob when he heard the voice of the chief magistrate. "We have discussed the charges with the accusers and agree with them that these foreigners have not conducted themselves according to Roman law and should be scourged. We will recess for a short time to determine what harm their offense has caused the citizens of Philippi. When we reconvene we will announce the sentence."

Beads of sweat had formed on Silas's brow and he was shaking with fear. The memory of seeing Jesus' body being torn apart sickened him. He knew that Paul could not survive the maximum sentence prescribed by Roman law. He would die well before the fortieth lash. He had no idea how many either he or young Timothy would be able to take before death took over. Then he looked over at the flogging post. Two lictors had been instructed to take up their positions, one on either side of the post.

Soon Silas heard the chief magistrate's voice once more. "We have determined that the accused men have not committed a crime serious enough to warrant the maximum sentence. Each of the two men will receive four lashes, two from each side. We have found no offense against the boy."

Silas could hear sounds of grumbling from the mob, disappointed because the maximum sentence was not given. He offered thanks that Timothy would be spared and a fervent prayer for the strength he and Paul would need to endure their beating. Four lashes would be sufficient for the nails and bits of scrap metal in the ends of the leather thongs to tear through their flesh and expose the bones of their backs.

Paul was the first to be ordered to the whipping post. He walked forward boldly without protest. He was stripped to his loincloth and his hands were tied around the post so his face was up against it. Silas gasped as the lictor on the right took a step back to give him space for a full-force blow. Then, with a horrible whistling sound, the whip raced through the air to strike Paul across the back. Silas shuddered realizing that excruciating pain was shooting through Paul's body. With the second stroke, this one from the lictor on the left, Silas could see Paul's body jerk with the agony the blow created.

With each lash the excited crowd roared with enjoyment. They were entertained by the flogging even though it was not the maximum they thought Paul deserved. Finally the fourth blow ended the severe punishment. The rope tying Paul's hands was cut and he fell to the ground. The lictors dragged his body out of the way and pointed to Timothy to come for it. Silas could not tell whether Paul was dead or alive. He saw that they were ready for the next victim, and he was the one.

Silas was ordered to take up his position. He walked to the post fearful, but determined to survive, although he was not sure that would be possible. The first two strokes brought him almost unbearable pain. The third stroke was so violent that it forced his head against the post, causing him to lose consciousness and to be mercifully released from the pain of the fourth stroke.

After the whipping was finished, Timothy was signaled forward to remove Silas's body. When the chief magistrate was informed that both men were still breathing, he ordered the three of them thrown into prison with their feet secured in stocks.[14]

Two strong soldiers tossed the unconscious bodies and Timothy onto a cart and hauled them away. They delivered their cargo to the prison along with the chief magistrate's instructions. The jailer, realizing that he was in charge of three very bad people, ordered the soldiers to throw the men into a tiny cell where they would be crowded together. The jailer locked their feet in stocks, bolted the door, and left his prisoners alone with their misery. Timothy was terrified. He had been spared the flogging, but he had no idea whether his friends and mentors were dying or struggling to live. The first glimmer of hope came when he saw Silas stir and then open his eyes to stare around the cell as if he was trying to determine where he was.

"Thanks be to God," Timothy cried. "You are in prison, but you are alive."

"How is Paul?" was Silas's response.

"He is breathing, but that is the only sign of life in him."

Timothy explained what had happened after Silas had lost consciousness. Just as he finished giving Silas the horrible details, they heard Paul's voice, almost as strong as ever.

"Thanks be to God, we are all alive. Don't despair. Our faith will keep us alive, just as my faith kept me alive when I was stoned at Lystra. God is well aware of what happened to us and the terrible pain we are suffering. We must ask for his help and believe that it will come and all will be well."

As soon as they were able, Silas and Paul put their robes back on over the horrible wounds. Then they prayed together and began to sing hymns. As the three men continued to praise God with song Silas was surprised to hear other voices joining in with them. Although they were in an isolated cell, their voices had been heard and the songs had been recognized by other prisoners locked up close by.[15]

The singing continued far into the night hours, until it was interrupted by a rumbling and shaking that Silas was sure was caused by a major earthquake. The very floor of the cell rocked and trembled. One big blast was so severe that the bar that kept the door locked was knocked out of its supporting slots, allowing the door to fly open. At the same time the pins that held the foot stocks shook free, and the prisoners were liberated.

The blast that released the prisoners also brought the jailer out of his quarters. According to Roman law, a jailer who allows a prisoner to escape inherits the prisoner's sentence. The jailer, apparently assuming that the three prisoners had been sentenced to death, threatened to kill himself. To prevent the man's suicide Silas shouted, "Don't harm yourself! We are all here!"

The jailer picked up his lamp and carried it to where the prisoners were standing. He looked into their faces, recognized the men who had been preaching a message of salvation and asked, "Sirs, what must I do to be saved?"

Paul answered. "Believe in the Lord Jesus, and you will be saved, you and your household."

"Leave the prison, come to my home, and tell me how this is done."

This was all the three men needed to hear. Without hesitating, they followed the jailer in the darkness of the night.

The jailer wakened his wife and children and asked for their help. While they washed the horrible wounds that covered the backs of the two men, he told his family about the terrible scourging and all that had happened since then. After they finished cleansing the exposed shredded flesh they applied healing ointment to ease the pain.

All the while the jailer and his family were tending their patients, Silas and Paul took turns telling them about the salvation that was possible through belief in Jesus Christ. By the time the wounds had been tended to, the jailer and his family had heard enough. They had become true believers and asked to be baptized. Once this was done, the unlikely group shared a common meal.

After the three men had given thanks that their lives had been spared, Paul surprised the jailer by asking him to escort his prisoners back to their prison cell.[16]

Then at the first hour of the day, the jailer came to the cell jubilant. A messenger had just arrived with an order from the magistrates for the prisoners' release. He knew that he had witnessed divine intervention once more.

Although the three men were puzzled by the short duration of their confinement, they did not waste any time leaving the prison to return to Lydia's home. During the next several days Silas and Paul's wounds began to heal.

Paul told Silas that in addition to the physical pain they had suffered, they had also been subjected to illegal treatment. The angry mob had attacked them before the magistrates had even offered an opinion, and then they had been scourged and thrown into prison without a fair trial.

Paul reached below his robe and pulled out what looked like a talisman. Silas knew that a good Christian like Paul would not have such a heathen adornment, and of course he had seen it before and knew what it was. Paul took the object in his hand and spread open the two hinged wooden pieces to expose his diptych. It contained the properly witnessed certification that he was a Roman citizen. If their case had been properly heard, the magistrates would have discovered that Paul had Roman citizenship, so he and his companions would have been protected.

Paul decided to send a formal complaint to the magistrates, and he asked Silas to help him compose it. In the letter which the two men drafted they emphasized Paul's Roman citizenship and reminded the magistrates that they had ordered him and his associate scourged. Next they pointed out that, although they were aware that the penalty for scourging a Roman citizen without a fair trial could warrant the death penalty, they had decided not to press charges.

They explained that in consideration for their leniency, they expected appropriate compensation from the magistrates. First, they wanted a formal apology for the illegal treatment of Paul and Silas. Second, they required a promise that the magistrates themselves would safely escort the three missionaries out of the city when they were ready to leave.

Two days later a formal apology and the required promise came in a return letter. Satisfied with this, Silas and Paul conducted a final service with a group of Christians at Lydia's home. Before leaving, the two missionaries appointed elders to oversee the work of the church after they left. The next day the three men were escorted out of Philippi as they had requested, Silas and Paul still suffering from painful back wounds but with heads held high.[17]

The missionaries trekked westward once more. They walked along the Egnatian Way, which was the Roman superhighway from the west coast of Macedonia to Asia Minor. This time they walked in miserable winter weather. They were not far enough from the sea to avoid the salty frigid wind, and the grey skies overhead did nothing to drive the dampness out of the air.

Shivering as they went, the missionaries passed through Amphipolis and Appollonia without stopping to get warm because they were anxious to reach Thessalonica as soon as possible.[18] Their aim was to start a Christian church in what they considered a most important city. They believed that because of the heavy traffic moving through Thessalonica on the Egnatian Way, the exposure of the church to travelers would bring many converts. All three men were aware of the importance of location for a church, and at Thessalonica they thought they had a good one.

Silas was relieved when they reached the capital city of Macedonia. He had been worried about Paul walking the cold, hundred-mile-long stretch of highway, but fortunately his friend arrived at Thessalonica without any serious signs of fatigue. The city was located on the Gulf of Thessalonica of the Aegean Sea.

Silas knew from his study of Alexander the Great during his school years that the city Alexander founded here boasted an excellent harbor and was the terminus of an important sea route. This, along with the effect of the Egnatian Way, made Thessalonica a great trade center. It was also a free city, which meant that it was without a Roman garrison.

Because they would be working in a busy commercial city, the missionaries would meet people from many different countries. Of course there was a Jewish presence, and therefore a synagogue in Thessalonica, along with plenty of evidence of both Greek and Roman gods.

The three men soon located the Jewish quarter, and Paul asked the first man they met if he knew where they could find a place to rent. Before the man could answer, Paul explained that he and his friends expected to stay in Thessalonica for some time to talk to the people about Christianity.

"My name is Jason, and I welcome you to Thessalonica. When I visited friends at Antioch a year ago, I heard some things about your belief and I would like to hear more. There is no need for you to rent a place to stay. Come to my home and live with me as my guests."

By the Sabbath they had recovered from the stress of the walk and the winter cold. They followed their custom of attending synagogue where Silas and Paul addressed the congregation on each of the first three Sabbaths.[19]

When they conducted a service for a Jewish congregation where there might be opposition from non-Christian members, Silas spoke first and Paul afterward. Their combined talk resulted in a very powerful message. They decided that this special presentation was needed on the third Sabbath at Thessalonica.

Silas spoke. "I came to Jerusalem from Alexandria as a young, proud, and haughty Pharisee almost twenty years ago. On the third day after I arrived I saw a man I was sure was an impostor, a false prophet, and a threat to my belief. His name was Jesus. Some days later fate intervened and took me to the trial where Jesus was accused of a crime he did not commit. At that trial I shared the blame for sentencing an innocent man to death.

"For some reason that I did not understand, I was drawn to the crucifixion site where I witnessed the unbelievably cruel torture of Jesus. There I first suspected that I had been a party to the death of the Messiah. The first clue came when I noticed that he reacted as if the cross was meant for him, and he refused pain medication as if he chose to suffer. Then, beaten, raw, and bleeding, he said, 'Father, forgive them, for they do not know what they are doing.'

"Next, at midday, I was terrified when all at once complete darkness hid the cross from view. It was only the sixth hour, and yet there was not a trace of light. After three hours of standing paralyzed by fear, I was brought back to reality when the darkness was swept away at the ninth hour by a voice from the cross that said, 'Father into your hands I commit my spirit.'

"These words brought me out of my three-hour trance and I left for the Temple to join my father. He told me that the curtain hiding the Holy of Holies had been torn from the top down at the ninth hour, the very same time that the cross reappeared out of the darkness.

"But this was not all. I found out later that on the third day Jesus was raised from the dead and lived on earth with his apostles for forty additional days. I personally spoke to many of those who had been with him. After he went to heaven to be with his heavenly Father, the Holy Spirit descended on those who believed in him and I was there."

Before the crowd could react to Silas's message, Paul stood and began to speak.

"I know that many of you are shaking your heads in disbelief at what Silas said and are calling him a fraud. I had the same reaction when I first heard that story. In fact I was so upset that I vowed to search out everyone who believed Silas's words and throw them into prison. I had so much success doing this that I soon ran out of victims in Jerusalem and received permission to go to Damascus and bring the sinners there back to Jerusalem for punishment.

"But on the road to that city, an extraordinary thing happened. I was blinded by lightning and a voice identified as Jesus instructed my companions to take me to the home of Judas in Damascus where a man by the name of Ananias would come and restore my sight, and bring me to believe Jesus was the Messiah, just as Silas has claimed. This happened exactly as I had been told. Now I do believe Silas's story, and I do know that the Messiah has come. There is still more. He will come again, and very soon. Believe me. Repent and prepare for him."

As always happened at these sessions, Silas and Paul's message was accepted by some, but rejected by others, and a great debate about the Torah followed. Many felt that this new branch of Judaism they had just heard about would destroy the Torah.

At this point Paul hastened to explain that Jesus had not come to destroy the Law of the Torah but to fulfill it. He told them Jesus emphasized that the two greatest parts of the law were love of God and love of neighbor. He was always careful to add that only faith in Jesus Christ and not the Law alone could bring salvation.

Silas saw once more that their message seemed to be more readily accepted by many of the Gentiles present than by most of the Jews who were in the congregation. Weeks later many of the Jews who had resented what he and Paul had said organized some of the riffraff of the agora into an angry mob and convinced them to storm the home of Jason. The non-believing Jews who were behind this intrigue assumed that the missionaries would be there.

When the ruffians found out that Silas and Paul were out teaching somewhere, they took their anger out on Jason, making a citizens' arrest of him and some of his friends and parading them off to appear before the magistrates. There, the organizers of the plot accused Jason and his associates of harboring the men who they claimed had been upsetting the civilized world and who were now busy raising havoc in Thessalonica. Not satisfied with this charge alone, they added that Silas and Paul were trying to replace Caesar with another emperor whom they called Jesus.

Although these accusations disturbed the magistrates and infuriated many in the crowd that had gathered, to avoid a possible riot, the accused were allowed to go free after just posting a bond. They were told they would be summoned to return for a hearing later.

Shortly after Jason and his supporters returned to his home, Silas, Paul, and Timothy arrived. Jason feared that the same treatment was waiting for the missionaries, so he persuaded them to leave Thessalonica that very night.[20]

Once more the three men headed west, this time without the benefit of daylight. Although Silas and Paul were unhappy about their final days at Thessalonica, they were hopeful that the first seeds of Christianity had been sown there. This time the early-morning breeze off the sea promised a balmy spring day.

Three days later they arrived at Beroea where they received a wonderful reception. The Jews had heard about the message that Silas and Paul had delivered on the third Sabbath at Thessalonica and wanted to hear more about the Christian belief. They had not been influenced by the non-believers of the capital city at all. The welcoming crowd encouraged the missionaries to go to the synagogue at once and speak to them.

Silas spoke to a sympathetic crowd, and then when Paul took over there was still no accusation that the two men were trying to destroy the Law. When Paul was through, many who had heard his reference to the Torah said that they were anxious to get a chance to study it to confirm what he had told them.

Silas felt that most of the Jews wanted to believe Jesus' life and sacrificial death was the fulfillment of their prophesies. They asked

Silas and Paul many questions and begged them to come back the following day.

When the missionaries returned, many Greeks were in the congregation. A few Jews had managed to obtain papyrus scrolls of the Scriptures, and they had been able to verify that what Paul had told them was true. Silas and Paul continued to meet daily with the people and the number of believers grew with each session.

Timothy continued to listen, as he attended every gathering. After one session he spoke to Silas. "Silas, I appreciate what you have taught me, answering all my questions patiently. I know I have much more to learn, but while I continue to learn, I would like to take a more active role in your mission. I look forward to the day when you and Paul will give me a full share of the workload."

Before long the daily meetings began to take a toll on Paul's health, because he insisted on making a living as well as preaching. Working as a tentmaker in the evenings gave him little time for rest. Finally he agreed to let Silas handle a larger portion of the teaching sessions.

After the missionaries had been in Beroea for several weeks, a group of the antagonistic Jews of Thessalonica arrived on the scene bent on making trouble.[21] Silas could hardly believe their hate could be so strong that they would walk sixty miles just to stir up the people of Beroea. He realized, though, that they must have had a strong belief they were actually doing God's will.

The protesters made it known soon after their arrival that they resented Paul's ready acceptance of Gentiles. Then they told Silas that they could not believe his message, because a Messiah would never allow himself to be crucified. They criticized him for not understanding that the Messiah would come as a military leader and not as an ineffective peacemaker. Then they accused Paul again, this time for worshipping a false emperor. Silas realized they could do this because the word Paul had used for *Messiah* also meant *emperor*.

Both Silas and Paul knew that this charge was a serious one, because Roman law made it illegal to predict a change of emperor and the protesters were accusing Paul of doing just that. They agreed that it was time to leave for Athens, the next stop on their journey.

After appointing elders, the missionaries started off. They realized it would be dark by the time they arrived at the coast twenty miles away, but feared that it would be too risky to wait until morning to leave Beroea.

They had not gone far when two desperate-looking strangers stopped them and asked where they were headed. When Paul answered, *Athens,* the men volunteered to escort them to the coast and arrange for sea transportation.

Silas thought the strangers resembled two agitators he had seen earlier among those who had come from Thessalonica, but before he could say anything Paul had accepted the offer. Several hours later they arrived at a small coastal town where the strangers arranged for their passage with two idle fishermen. Their escorts had said the sail, which would be less than two hundred miles, would follow along the coast of the Aegean Sea and be quite safe, even in the dark of night. The three men boarded, the small crew cast off, and the voyage began.

By the time the sails were hoisted, the ship was engulfed in a dense fog and the shoreline was no longer visible. When Silas asked if they should not wait until morning, one fisherman replied in a language he did not understand. Now he was really worried. Silas hoped they were headed southeast, but under a cloudy sky and in dense fog he could not verify this, and he feared they would never reach the great city of Athens.[22]

Chapter 11

Athens and Beyond

LATER IN THE night the fog gradually disappeared, the clouds parted, and Silas felt welcome relief. The shoreline had become visible and was exactly where it should be. The small fishing boat was on the right course!

He was thankful that he had not let either Paul or Timothy know about his fear in the dark of the night. The last of his anxiety disappeared when he discovered that the crew member who had previously remained silent spoke Greek. The man informed him they would reach Athens the next day.

The closer the small boat got to Athens, the more excited Timothy became. Silas listened as Timothy described the many famous sights he expected to see. Then he said, "I am anxious to hear what those most learned philosophers have to say about how we should conduct our lives."

Silas was shocked to hear that Timothy seemed to hold the wise men of Athens in reverence. He and Paul had never heard him talk about them before. Paul responded, "Timothy, their wisdom is of men and not of God. With God's help we will meet some of these philosophers you have heard about and confront them with the truth. Then you will discover that their knowledge is false and their intelligence is squandered." Timothy did not respond.

On their arrival in the city the missionaries were able to rent temporary living quarters near one of the many synagogues that Athens boasted of. They went to work immediately to bring the Good News of salvation through belief in Jesus Christ to as many Jews as would listen to them. Discouraged by the poor reception they received, the three men left the synagogue and went out onto the early summer hot city streets to take their message to the Gentiles.[1]

Athens was considered to be the intellectual capital of the world, but Silas and Paul were not to be intimidated by what Timothy or anyone else thought about the city. They stepped onto the streets with boldness, confident they had a message that should be heard, and they shared it with everyone they met whether they listened or not.

The ubiquitous idols troubled the missionaries as they went from one part of the city to another preaching the truth. At a corner crowded with marble gods, Paul said with a rare attempt at humor, "There must be as many idols as Greeks in Athens."

They soon discovered that the best place to reach the people was in the city square. Many others had messages, and they competed with the missionaries for time, space, and ears, but fortunately, the opposition that Paul and Silas encountered in the square was more civil than any other they had met before. They were challenged with sharp debate rather than threats of violence. Although some of the speakers referred to the missionaries as common know-nothings, they responded to Silas and Paul with argument, not hatred.

The reception they were given in the square was so much more civilized than the one they had encountered at Thessalonica that it made Timothy feel a little less embarrassed about his admiration for the wise men of Athens. Many who heard the message of the saving grace of Jesus concluded that there must be a god they had no knowledge of, but they didn't think one more god was anything to get excited about.

Most of those who frequented the city square were there for one reason only, to discuss new ideas, no matter what the subject was. Some who listened to Silas and Paul were the highly educated philosophers whom Timothy had heard so much about. They were curious about the strange belief of the two missionaries, and suggested that they present their philosophy to the Supreme Court of Greece, which they said was meeting on the Areopagus at the present time. They explained that this august body made decisions on religious beliefs as well as civil legal cases. When Silas and Paul said that they would welcome the opportunity to address the court, they were led away from the square.

The philosophers who escorted the missionaries to the Areopagus represented two quite different schools of thought. Those who were Epicureans stressed the intellectual pleasures of life. They believed that everything happened by chance, because the gods were too far away to have any effect on humans, and that there was no existence after death. The Stoics, on the other hand, worshiped their gods because they believed that there was life after death and that it was patterned on the morality of life before death.

Timothy walked along beside Silas and Paul on the long trek to the Areopagus as they planned their strategy. They knew that no one on the court would be familiar with the Jewish Scriptures, so they decided on a different approach. They chose a theme they thought would be suitable for the learned members of the court who would be intelligent enough to understand the existence of an omnipotent God. Then they decided that Paul should speak first.[2]

When the procession reached the Areopagus the missionaries could see that the dais on which the members of the court sat was a perch hundreds of feet above the city square they had just left. Directly across from where the two men would present their case to the most renowned court in the world, the Acropolis stood, a towering hill adorned with temples honoring the heathen gods of the Greeks.

When the three missionaries were introduced to the court, Paul said that he would be the first speaker. To get their attention he began by boldly criticizing the men of Athens.

"You Athenians are very superstitious and seem to need a god to protect you from every single misadventure, but in your city of hundreds of identified gods I was surprised to see one altar with the inscription *To An Unknown God.* I know who your unknown god is. It is the very one that I know as the one true God and the one I am going to talk about.

"My God made heaven and earth, and everything that is on or in the earth. My God is not an idol living in temples or on streets, and therefore is not to be worshiped as an idol. My God does not need anything from humans other than love. On the other hand, it is my God who provided everything good that you Athenians have and enjoy. My God wants mankind that he has created to search for him and understand and believe in him.

"One of your own poets said, 'In him we live and move and have our being. We are his offspring.' Whether your poet knew it or not, he was describing the one true God that I have been talking about. If, as your poet says, we are truly God's children, then manmade idols of stone or metal cannot represent him. My one true God, who is also your one true God, will forgive the sins of the past, for you who did not know him. With the revelation of the truth through the birth, life, death, and resurrection of Jesus Christ, the Son of God, all is changed, and everyone must now repent, ask to be forgiven, and be baptized, to be saved."

When Paul mentioned the resurrection, the Epicureans scoffed, but the Stoics asked to hear more. Paul knew that an argument was about to take place that would detract from his message, so he declined to say more about what he knew was a controversial subject. He concluded by emphasizing that only belief in the one true God, not the philosophy of either the Epicureans or the Stoics, would lead to the truth.

When Paul finished, dead silence fell. What he had said had made no impression on the court or the observers. Paul walked over to speak to Silas, who agreed that it would be useless to proceed further. The three men prepared to leave, when an elderly man stood up and began to speak in support of Paul's message. He surprised Silas when he announced that his name was Dionysius.

Silas recognized the name and knew that this was the same Greek who had studied at the library with his grandfather, but had left Alexandria for Athens just before he and his father had left for Jerusalem. He was impressed that Dionysius was now a member of the court of the Areopagus and therefore an intellectual and influential member of the aristocracy of Athens. When Dionysius finished his speech, he asked to be baptized. Silas told him how happy it made him to be able to bring a friend of his grandfather into the church.

With the baptism of Dionysius, however, came thoughts about his grandfather and worry that he probably had still not become a Christian. He prayed often that the letter he and his father had written would lead his grandfather to Jesus, but one thing Silas was sure of was that he was fulfilling the promise made to his grandfather more completely than either one had anticipated.

A second surprise came—and an even bigger one—when another supporter spoke on behalf of Paul. This time the speaker was a woman among the observers, named Damaris. Silas could not believe a woman was present at the Areopagus. Athenian women were regarded as inferior creatures with little more intelligence than children. They were thought to have strong emotions but weak minds. Usually their absence from the home was restricted to attendance at a funeral or special festival. Damaris said she believed Paul's message and thanked him for it. All she wanted now was to be baptized into the new faith.[3]

The members of the court and the observers were amused by what they had seen happen in front of them, but when the entertainment was over, the chairman closed the session and dismissed the crowd. As the three missionaries left the hill Timothy, overflowing with energy, strode ahead of the other two.

Paul said, "I'm certainly disappointed that there were only two converts, but I'm not discouraged. In fact, I believe we have received a blessing. The two new Christians in Athens are from different social levels. Their belief will expand into two groups of Christians that are widely separated in this great city, but will still be one under God. We will leave Athens in their good hands and move on to visit Corinth. It has become the political and commercial capital of

Greece, and more important to the economy of the country than Athens, the cultural capital."

"Paul," Silas said, "it just occurred to me that Athens will be one of the very few cities that we did not leave just to avoid persecution."

"Yes, that's true. I'm concerned about the Christians of Thessalonica. I'm afraid we left many of them with an incomplete understanding of the Gospel when we left them to avoid persecution."

"I have an idea, Paul. Our young friend walking down the hill there just a little ahead of us is anxious to be more active. Why don't we send him back to Thessalonica to investigate the condition of the church there?"

"He's just nineteen years old, Silas," Paul said, more than a little surprised. "That's a heavy assignment for one so young."

"But he's old beyond his years. He's matured greatly in the short time that he's been with us. He gets along well with people, and I believe the Thessalonians would confide in him. He is very perceptive, and I'm sure that he would return with a clear picture of conditions in Thessalonica. He recovered well from his experience at Philippi, and although he now knows what can happen to those who bring the Good News, he will not have to worry about being mistreated at Thessalonica. The non-believing Jews there will not harm one so young. He could meet us at Corinth to give his report."

"You've come up with an interesting idea, Silas. Shout at Timothy to wait for us and we will get his reaction to your plan."

Timothy was excited by the exceptional opportunity he was being offered and at the apparent confidence Silas and Paul had in him. He wasted no time in giving his thanks and accepting the challenge. Before the day was over, Timothy was on his way to Thessalonica and Silas and Paul were walking toward Corinth.

The road to Corinth was a busy one, and Silas and Paul spoke to everyone they met along the way, but their effort to stir up interest in their message was futile. Overnight they slept on their leather ground sheets under a tree in an olive grove, resolved not to worry about their lack of success.

They spent much of the time on the remainder of their two-day walk talking about the adventure waiting for them at Corinth. They knew they would face a challenge at what was known far and wide as *Sin City*. Silas and Paul realized that if they were to make much of an impact they would have to stay at Corinth for several months. Loose living, drunkenness, and lustful debauchery had made the city known throughout the world for its licentious life style.

The focal point of sinful living was the Temple of Aphrodite that sat boldly on the top of the fortress hill of the Acropolis. There, one thousand priestesses doubled as sacred prostitutes. At the end of the day, with their chores in the sanctuary finished, they descended to the streets of the city below to sell their bodies to the rich men of Corinth and the visitors from many other cities of the world who possessed the necessary coins. Aphrodite would present a bigger obstacle to their mission at Corinth than Daphne had at Antioch.

In Silas's opinion the explanation for the low level of morality of Corinth could be found in its history. He had learned at Alexandria that after the armies of Rome destroyed the city, Julius Caesar rebuilt it and populated it with freed slaves and destitute immoral people.

Silas and Paul were well aware that Corinth was also a very wealthy commercial city. It was situated on a narrow isthmus of land barely five miles wide between the Gulf of Corinth on the west and the Saronic Gulf on the east. Corinth took advantage of its location by enjoying a port on each coast—Lechaion on the Gulf of Corinth, and Cenchrae on the Saronic Gulf. A road through the center of their city connected the two, and substantial wealth was brought to the city by the four-wheel, oxen-drawn carts that traveled the road constantly.

The land link between the southern and northern sections of Greece also ran through Corinth and brought it additional business, and the prosperity of Corinth was increased by still another fact of geography. The two-hundred-mile sea route around Cape Malea at the southern end of the Greek peninsula was treacherous, but it could be avoided in one of two ways, both of which aided the commerce of the city. The first was to unload the ship at the Corinthian port on one coast and then transport the cargo across the isthmus to reload it on another ship at the port on the opposite one. The second way applied only to ships small enough to be hauled up out of the water and pulled across the isthmus on rollers. The transport of goods between north and south on land and east and west by sea passed through Corinth, making it the commercial center of Greece.

Of course Corinth's reputation for providing the fun of sinning encouraged many outsiders to spend their money in the city. Then, every two years a special event was responsible for the influx of wealthy visitors. They came to Corinth for the Isthmian Games, which were second in importance only to the Olympic Games.

The missionaries followed the Lechaion Road to Corinth, entering the walled city through the beautiful Propylaea gate where the road expanded into a twenty-foot-wide city street.

As much as Silas and Paul had heard about Corinth, they were not prepared for the hubbub that greeted them when they walked into the agora. Walks and shops lined each side of the street. The space between them was a noisy mass of confusion. Children cried, adults shouted, beggars begged, and dogs barked. Carts squeezing through any space wide enough for them were making their contribution to the turmoil as their wheels clattered on the stones of the street.

At the center of the agora was the Bema, a large elevated speakers' platform. When the two men saw this, they realized that it would be a perfect place to deliver their message to Gentiles because many of them would always be in the agora, but silencing the raucous crowd would be a real challenge for them.

Even though Corinth had become a Roman city, the Corinthians still worshiped Greek gods. Everywhere they walked, Silas could see temples, shrines to Apollo, Hermes, Heracles, Athena, and Poseidon. The temple of Asclepius, the god of healing, was surrounded by hospitals. Many who had been healed left replicas of their affected body parts on display at the temple.

When the two men had seen enough of the city to satisfy their curiosity, they sought and soon located the Jewish quarter. As was their custom, the missionaries were determined to bring their message to the Jewish community first, and they would begin as soon as they found a suitable place to live. They had barely started in their search when a young man walked up to Paul with a big smile on his face.

"I am Aquila, and this is my wife, Priscilla," he said.

"I am Paul, and this is my associate, Silas," was Paul's reply to the friendly greeting.

"Yes, we know. We recognized you from the description we have been given. We have heard many good things about you, and had hoped to meet you some time, but until an hour ago we had no idea when that would be. A friend of ours saw you enter the city. He told us you were here and that you would undoubtedly be coming to the Jewish quarter. We have been waiting here to welcome you."

"We're happy you did that. We don't always get such a warm greeting when we enter a city for the first time. Tell us something about yourselves."

"We are Christians who came here recently from Rome," Aquila replied.

"Why would you do that?" Silas asked.

"Perhaps you haven't heard. Emperor Claudius finally tired of the perpetual problems he said were caused by argumentative Jews, so to solve his dilemma he ordered every last one of us to leave, Christians and Judaists alike. We had no alternative. For some reason we do not understand, we chose to come to Corinth. We have lived here happily for quite some time now."

"Then you must be familiar with the Jewish section of the city," Paul said. "Do you happen to know of an inexpensive place we could rent?"

Now it was Priscilla's turn to talk. "While we were waiting for you, we had an idea. We have extra space in the building where we live. The rent is reasonable, and divided by three it would be quite inexpensive."

"That would be wonderful, but we do not want to impose," Paul said.

"You would not be imposing," Aquila said. "There's more to our offer than Priscilla explained. We were told that you, Paul, are a tentmaker, as we are. There is more than enough room in our shop for three tentmakers, and the company would be wonderful. Of course we would take advantage of having two great teachers living with us."

"But I'm not a tentmaker," Silas said, wondering what his fate would be.

"We know," Priscilla said, laughing. "You are a scribe, and there is a corner big enough to hold your ink pot and pen. I hope you can earn enough to pay your portion of the rent."

The four new friends walked off together. Corinth had suddenly become a wonderful place to live, work, teach, and learn. Silas and Paul were soon settled in their new home and teaching in the synagogue at least once every Sabbath.[4]

Meeting Aquila and Priscilla was not the only surprise the missionaries received. They had not lived with their new friends very long when Timothy returned from Macedonia. He announced that he had made a brief visit to Philippi before coming to Corinth, and the Philippians had given him an honorarium for Paul.

Neither he nor Silas had ever accepted a contribution of any kind for their service to the church, and Paul had no intention of keeping this one, but then Timothy explained that the Christians who sent it would be offended if he did not accept it. He said it was their wish that this small token of their love for him would mean that he would work less at his trade and spend more time at God's work. Paul could see no alternative but to accede to their wishes and accept the gift.[5]

"Now that we have settled that, Timothy," Paul said, "tell us about your visit with the Thessalonians. Silas and I are concerned because we were forced to leave Thessalonica prematurely to prevent bloodshed. We did not have sufficient time during the few weeks we were with the new Christians to build a strong and lasting belief."

"Your concern is well founded, Paul. I soon discovered that many of them had forgotten much of what you taught about the imminent return of Christ.

"One group is ignoring the necessities of everyday living, waiting for him to appear. Others are afraid that their belief and faith are not strong enough to ensure their salvation, and some poor souls who are ill agonize about what will happen to them if they die before the second coming.

"There are other problems, also, that must be addressed. There are a few believers who resent those in superior positions, especially when they are admonished.

"Another one concerns some of the new, weaker Christians who, I fear, may soon begin to backslide into the immorality that existed before we arrived.

"Paul, it pains me to report that there are a few who believe that your main interest is in yourself, and that you are inclined to be dictatorial. Unfortunately, this has led to a partial division in the church."

"Timothy, much of what you have told us so far is grievous, especially the Thessalonians' complaint that the demands I made as an apostle were interpreted as being dictatorial. The beginning of a division in the infant church is very disturbing, and I deeply regret that a misinterpretation of my teaching seems to have been the cause. Silas and I will listen to the rest of your report in the morning."

After Timothy finished his report the next day, Paul spoke to him as his mentor, while Silas listened. "Timothy, you have done a magnificent job portraying conditions as you found them at Thessalonica. Silas and I have a great task facing us, but thanks to your perception we know what we must do. Silas and I will write a letter which you can take back with you.

"We will admonish the Christians of Thessalonica, but we will also attempt to comfort and encourage them. We must restore their faith, and help them understand the second coming."

Paul and Silas worked diligently on a letter to the Thessalonians over the next two days, and when they were satisfied, Paul summoned Timothy. "Timothy, Silas and I give you this letter to take to Thessalonica. On your recent visit you functioned as an observer. Now with the help of this letter, you will return as a teacher."[6]

After Timothy left, Silas and Paul returned to their work at Corinth. Because of Paul's honorarium, he was able to spend much more of his time teaching and much less at his trade. This increased activity resulted in more conversions than they otherwise would have had.

Although a few of the new believers were Jews, most were Gentiles, but all was not peaceful. Many Jews, like their brothers elsewhere, did not believe the missionaries' message that Jesus Christ was the same Messiah foretold by many Jewish prophets and did everything possible to interfere with the missionaries' teaching.

Eventually Silas and Paul became so frustrated that they told the Jews they would leave the synagogue and concentrate on the Gentiles. They would spend more time teaching from the Bema, but it was with sadness that the two missionaries left the Jewish quarter and the pleasant home they had shared with Aquila and Priscilla.[7]

Soon, however, a Roman citizen stopped to greet Silas and Paul. He introduced himself as Titius Justus, and said that he had heard much about them. When he found out they were looking for a place to stay, he invited them to come home with him. He would be happy to give them lodging in exchange for the opportunity to learn more about their belief. Silas and Paul were thankful for the offer, and the arrangement worked out well.[8]

The two men continued to be upset by their lack of success with their own race, but one prominent Jew had become a believer. He was Crispus, the president of the synagogue, no less. Silas and Paul had hoped that his status would bring a few more Jews into the fold, but that was not to be, because he resigned his position soon after his conversion and was replaced by a man named Sosthenese. He too became a believer, but he was not active in spreading the Word, probably because he wanted to keep his position in the synagogue.

Although Silas often became discouraged by their lack of progress with the Jews, the two missionaries would not give up.

The majority of the Jews of Corinth not only refused to come into the fold, they resented the few who did. They protested the only way they knew how, by bringing a charge before Gallio, the proconsul of the Roman province of Achaia, in the absence of Silas and Paul, accusing them of advocating an unlawful religion. Gallio had a reputation for being very wise and knowledgeable about the Jews, and he sensed that there was no legal basis for the Judaists' action. He told the accusers he could not see that their charge included a legitimate crime, so he would not hear the case because he had no intention of getting involved in internal Jewish affairs.

Their lack of success in court enraged the Jews, so they physically attacked Sosthenese, who happened to be present at the hearing. They suspected him of being a Christian, even though he had not supported the missionaries in public. They continued to beat Crispus's successor in Gallio's presence, but because the proconsul did not think a riot would develop, he made no attempt to stop them. He considered their action was their way of solving another Jewish problem.[9]

When Silas and Paul heard about the attack on Sosthenese, they decided that they should leave Corinth to protect the few Jewish Christians of the city. Just before they were ready to start out, their good friend Titus arrived unexpectedly from Pisidian Antioch. Silas and Paul had met Titus at Iconium and he had become one of their most reliable helpers in all of Galatia. After greeting the two missionaries, Titus spoke further.

"It grieves me to report that there are serious problems in southern Galatia, among both the Jewish and gentile converts of the cities you visited. When you, Silas and Paul, left the Christians of these cities, they believed your message that salvation was possible only through faith in Jesus Christ.

"Then a number of Jewish Christians arrived from Jerusalem, taking a different message to one church after another. They claimed that what you had given the Galatians was only a partial understanding of the belief of what they called the Christian sect of Judaism. They told the Galatians that they would give them a complete and proper understanding of Christianity and introduced a new and different teaching that contradicted the true Gospel that you had brought.

"They taught that works and full observance of the Law were both necessary for the salvation of Jews and Gentiles alike. These new missionaries, like both of you, were raised as Pharisees, but they still believe that all who desire to be Christians must be circumcised, and must adhere to the hundreds of minor laws prescribed by the Torah as well, in order to be acceptable to God. Although they are Christians, they just cannot grasp the fact that justification through faith and justification through the Law are beliefs that cannot coexist. They disputed your teaching that salvation was something that came through faith alone and was not possible through works and the Law alone."

"Titus," Paul said, "before you say anything more, let me assure you that after we hear you out, Silas and I will send a letter to the churches of Galatia responding to all of the issues you bring up. Because we cannot be with them in person, writing to them is the best we can do.

"I'm amazed that the Galatians have abandoned what we told them. They have suffered too much for the truth to throw it away now. They will apparently have to be told about the true Gospel over and over. They must understand that although Judaism is a true faith, its purpose is only to lead us to the true Gospel."

"Paul, in an attempt to convince the people of Derbe, Lystra, Iconium, and Antioch that your message was not true, the new arrivals disputed the authority that you claim for yourself. They declared that you were not a true apostle because you were not one of the original Jerusalem twelve. They emphasized the contribution of Peter, James, and John in an attempt to dwarf your role. Many of the fickle Christians, Jews and Gentiles alike, believed everything the new teachers told them."

"Titus, the roles of Peter, James, and John must never be minimized, but the accomplishments of these great leaders of the church take nothing from me. In fact, I was fully recognized as an apostle by the Jerusalem church council and given their complete support and authority to go to the Gentiles.

"Your report is very discouraging. Silas and I have barely had time to recover from the bad news we received from Thessalonica, and now we have this. I'm beginning to wonder just how successful we have been.

"Titus, after we hear your full report, we will compose a letter to the Galatians in which we will emphasize that justification comes through faith in Jesus Christ only and not through works. We will explain that faith in Jesus meant faith in the cross, and that faith eliminates any difference between the circumcised and uncircumcised. Jews and Gentiles, free men, and slaves all are one in Christ. We will remind the Galatians once more that they became Christians when they received the Holy Spirit, which had come to them because of their faith and not because of the Law."[10]

The day after the two missionaries finished the letter, and it was on its way to Galatia, they left Corinth with Titus, Aquila, Priscilla, and Timothy. Timothy had just returned from Thessalonica to report that the letter he had delivered there had been well received. They sailed from Cenchrae, and made their first stop on the way home at Ephesus. Silas and Paul found the local synagogue there, entered into a debate with the Jews concerning their belief, and made such an impact that they were asked to prolong their visit and continue the discussions. Paul said that Aquila and Priscilla would stay on and lead the discussions. He explained that he and Silas had been on the road for three years, and the time had come to return to their home at Antioch, but they would be starting out on another missionary journey before long and Ephesus would be one of their stops.[11]

Silas, Paul, Titus, and Timothy returned to the vessel and sailed across the Great Sea to Caesarea, the Roman capital of Judea. Paul had stopped there for a few days after he had been forced to leave Jerusalem and was on his way to Tarsus. He had converted many during his short stay and had been looking forward for some time to visit the city once more and look up old friends.

After the four men had enjoyed a short stay, Paul left to take Timothy and Titus to Jerusalem for their first visit to the holy city, after which they would backtrack to Syria and Antioch.

Silas went his own way, anxious to get home and be reunited with family and friends.

Chapter 20

Home, Then Off Again

EARLY AFTERNOON HAD come when Silas walked up to the door of the house his father had built for him and his family. Silas was very thankful for the success of his father's business. He realized that devoting his life to the church meant that he would always need financial help from others just to provide his family with their absolute needs, but his poverty could neither diminish the satisfaction of his accomplishment nor spoil the joy of his reunion with Rebekah and the children.

When Silas walked through the open door, Rebekah and the children let loose with thankful shouts. The children understood that Silas was engaged in very important Christian work, but they were too young to fully grasp the significance of what he was doing. Nevertheless, they were very proud of him. Travel to faraway shores made for an exciting story, and they begged their father to tell it.

"First of all," Silas said, "let me ask you a question. Do you know how long a mile is?" They both nodded. "Then you know that if you walked one of them you would feel as if you had gone quite a distance. Well would you believe that Paul and I probably walked one thousand of them? Even though we traveled that great distance, we only saw a tiny bit of the vast Roman Empire!" He recounted some of their adventures in words they could understand, until their bedtime.

As soon as Joseph and Martha were asleep, Rebekah told her tale of being alone with the children for almost three years. When she had finished her story, she told Silas she had learned to accept the truth of their married life. "I know you will not be with us long before you feel the call to go off for a third time," she said. "I know your work as a Christian leader is more important to both of us than anything else we do. I know too that Paul's health continues to fail, and because you are ten years younger you may soon have to take over for him. You have worked closely with him for many years and by now probably think and act exactly as he does."

Silas thanked her for her understanding and support. Then, after giving her a detailed account of the mission, he admitted his fears. "I'm troubled by the direction the church seems to be heading. This is not because of our lack of success, but because of where our success seems to come from. As you know, I believe Christianity, as you have named it, is really the new Judaism, but wherever we preach to our own Jews, as many or more oppose what we say as agree with it. Often, after we leave an area, non-believing Jews persuade the Christian Jews to abandon their new belief. But with the Gentiles we make converts with little opposition from either non-believing Jews or heathen Gentiles. I worry that with time the Jews will abandon Christianity and leave it to become the religion of the Gentiles."

"Silas, I can understand how you feel about the future of our church, but I'm afraid that you will not feel any better when you hear what has happened right here at Antioch.

"We begin by attending the synagogue on the Sabbath for our traditional worship service. Then when the Sabbath ends at sundown and the next day begins, we gather at homes of the believers for the Agape meal. Because that is the day when Jesus rose from the dead, we have begun calling it the *Lord's Day*. Every family brings as much food to the common meal as it can afford. Unfortunately, some can only bring very little, and others are not always ready to share, and this disturbs me. At The Lord's Supper we celebrate with the bread and wine as the Lord commanded at the Passover meal. A worship service follows. The Torah is still a very important part of the worship service.

"In most cases the Lord's Day meal and service are held at a home that has a rather large open-air upper room which we refer to as the church—as if the church was a building as well as what we call our belief. The upper-room church is arranged in the form of the synagogue as much as possible. There is usually an altar at the far end, and if the location is really favorable, the view over the altar is to the rising sun in the east. The service still includes prayers, confession, readings from the Torah, teaching, and the benediction.

"What worries me is this. I have noticed several Gentile Christians ignoring the synagogue service and attending only the Lord's Day service. In my mind they are only partial Christians. As you know, we have a large number of Gentiles in our church here, and if this trend continues, the synagogue may disappear from their religious experience, leaving the church service the only form of worship for the majority of them. After what you said about the churches in Asia Minor and Macedonia, I am worried more than ever about our future.

"If, as you say, the Jews abandon Christianity and if, as I believe, the Gentiles abandon the synagogue, our church will become a gentile organization that ignores the Sabbath service in the synagogue and holds its only service on the Lord's Day."

"I believe that what you predict will happen, Rebekah," Silas replied. "We have been living in constantly changing times in this modern world ever since the crucifixion, and I have been very much part of what is happening. I am a Christian, but I still consider myself a Pharisee. A day never goes by that I don't shed some little part of my previous identity, and I can't deny that I'm better off each time this happens. I constantly strive to be a better Christian, but I am still a Jew and will always be one. All that I can do is preach and teach what I believe, with the guidance of the Holy Spirit."

A week later Silas went with his family to the city square where he and Paul took turns relating every detail of their second missionary journey. Occasionally, they called on Timothy to give his youthful version of a specific event.

In the months after the meeting, the Jewish quarter of Antioch carried on as before, the church in its midst slowly becoming more like a gentile organization and Silas and Rebekah becoming more reconciled to the change. After Silas had enjoyed close to a full year with his family and friends, the inevitable occurred. He and Paul decided that the time had come to begin their third missionary journey.

Early one late spring morning, Silas said good-bye to Rebekah and the children and then left, not knowing how long he would be gone or if he would ever see his family again. He met Paul, Timothy, and Titus and they walked together to the river bank where they persuaded a boat owner to ferry them across the Orontes to a spot near the coast. From there they began their long trek to Asia Minor to visit again some of the churches that they had been to on their previous mission. As the days became weeks and the footsteps became miles, the rough road ate away at their sandals. In one long walk the missionaries visited Tarsus, Derbe, Lystra, Iconium, and Pisidian Antioch, spending a short time with the Christians at each city. The missionaries gave thanks that no trace of a false gospel appeared anywhere in Galatia. Then six months after leaving home, they arrived at Ephesus to fulfill the promise made to its people the previous year.

Ephesus was on the Cayster River in western Asia Minor. The excellent harbors at nearby Miletus made it a commercial seaport. It was also a political and pagan religious center and capital of the Roman province of Asia. In size it was ranked next after Rome, Alexandria, and Antioch so it was one of the most populous cities of the world. The Pan-Ionian Games that were held there helped to make the city famous, as did the monumental Temple of Artemis.

This temple, which had been built to honor the Greek goddess of the moon, ranked as one of the wonders of the world, but the temple had a dark side. It provided asylum for criminals, which meant that the missionaries could be exposed to danger.

The missionaries met their first challenge as they entered the city gate. They were approached by one of the many souvenir vendors who made a living selling Artemis magic amulets to superstitious pagan visitors. Paul politely refused the offer that came, informing the man that their God did a much better job of protecting them from evil spirits and disease than his trinkets did.

As they left the area, Paul said, "Silas, we must explain the futility of these gadgets at the first opportunity we have to speak in the synagogue."

The missionaries again leased a temporary home in the Jewish quarter, and spent their first night there.

"I know that we are anxious to visit all those we met with a year ago," Paul said early the next morning, "but I think first we should look for Aquila and Priscilla. I'm sure you're as eager as I am to find out from them what happened here while we were away."

A few minutes later they found their friends, and after a heartfelt greeting they were deep in conversation.

"I'm happy to tell you that although the large heathen population remains a challenge, the church at Ephesus began to grow after you left, and the Christians' faith is strong," Priscilla said.

Paul answered, "Silas and I were confident that you and Aquila would provide the vigorous leadership needed for success."

Silas spoke seriously to them, "When we left you last year, those we had met with in the synagogue were Jews. I'm sure that by now many Gentiles have shown an interest in your message, and of course this is as it should be. Our experience elsewhere has been that the proportion of Gentiles in the church continues to grow as the church ages.

"My opinion is that gentile believers will soon become the majority and the Christian church will eventually become a gentile organization. When that happens, I believe we will see a change in the order of worship for most Christians. They will no longer attend the synagogue on the Sabbath, but will conduct their only worship away from the synagogue and hold it on the Lord's Day. Do you think this is likely to happen here at Ephesus?"

Aquila replied. "I believe it is inevitable that it will happen here and everywhere else that there is a Christian church. It is something we will have to accept and learn to live with. Nevertheless, I believe the trend toward the church becoming a gentile organization will be slower at Ephesus than elsewhere, because of the work of a man named Apollos."

"That's interesting," Paul said, "tell us about him."

"He is a very learned Christian who arrived here from Jerusalem shortly after you two left a year ago. He is an expert on the Scriptures and lectures on them frequently in the synagogue. He can cite many references that foretold the coming of the Messiah. Both Jews and Gentiles find the background he provides to be very helpful in linking the Torah with the new belief. The result of this is that the Jews have fewer tendencies to drift back away from Christianity, and the Gentiles have more interest in the Torah and attending the synagogue on the Sabbath."

Silas and Paul were impressed by all that they heard about Apollos, and they received a warm reception when they went to his door and introduced themselves. An interesting discussion continued for quite some time.

Silas was astonished, however, to find out that Apollos's knowledge of some things was superficial. He was an incomplete Christian. He had never been baptized in the name of Jesus Christ or received the Holy Spirit. Although he believed Jesus to be the Messiah foretold by the Scriptures, he did not recognize him as his savior. They spent the rest of the day bringing the truth to Apollos, and before they left him he had been baptized in the name of Jesus Christ, received the Holy Spirit, and become a complete Christian.[1]

The next time Silas talked to Apollos, he was surprised to discover that he had come to Jerusalem from the epsilon district, one of the two Jewish wards of Alexandria. Although Silas had come from the delta district, the two men had much in common, and they enjoyed several hours talking about their city.

Silas learned that Apollos had not only known his grandfather, but had worked with him in the library. He had, however, left

Alexandria shortly before Silas did and had no knowledge of his grandfather since then.

When Apollos first mentioned the world-famous library where Silas had expected to spend his days formulating Pharisaic rules and regulations, the pain of losing his dream came back to him. But a moment later the joy of living the life that was meant for him returned. Silas was embarrassed when his thoughts of the city where he was born and spent his younger days reminded him of his arrogant youth and false pride. He thought he had been living a perfect life in a perfect city, when he didn't know what the word *perfect* meant.

After Apollos was baptized and had learned more about the Good News of salvation, he became an even more effective teacher and did a great deal to help the two missionaries with their work. Eventually, he became so competent that they asked him to travel to Achaia to minister to the Christians living there.[2] Silas and Paul appreciated the help of Apollos. When he left them, they began to wonder who else might be responding to the great commission as he had and was working elsewhere in the world.

They had been told that Luke, their gentile friend and physician, was in Philippi. They had not heard from Barnabas since he left them at Antioch to go on a mission with John Mark. A rumor had arisen that John Mark had gone to Alexandria. Silas hoped that this was true, and that he would help his grandfather find the way of the cross.

As usual, Silas and Paul had begun their mission with the Jews, teaching them in the synagogue. All went well through the winter months, but in the spring the familiar opposition from non-Christian Jews appeared once more in the meetings.

Before long most of those whom Aquila and Priscilla had been so proud of had been convinced by newcomers that God's Chosen One would not come to die on a cross. When it seemed useless to continue, Silas and Paul decided to abandon the synagogue, look for another meeting place, and restrict their efforts to the Gentiles.

They found a hall belonging to the philosopher Tyrannus. The missionaries were given permission to use the facility during the heat of the day in the middle of summer when the high temperature made the building too hot for the owner to give lectures.[3]

Silas often said that only the most sincere believers would continue to worship under those terrible conditions. In the few months of the year that Tyrannus wanted to use his hall throughout the day, the two missionaries conducted their meetings wherever they could find space.

Before and after the sessions in the superheated meeting place, Silas and Paul busied themselves earning their living. Silas had to compete with the established scribes. Nevertheless, he managed to find enough business to support himself.

Because Aquila and Priscilla could not take care of the demand for their leather service, Paul started to work immediately, assisting the customers they were turning away. He began his working day early in the morning, cutting leather to whatever pattern he was following, then punching holes and stitching the pieces together.

He did not hesitate to interrupt his work to take care of miscellaneous emergency repairs. One of the most common requests was for mending a broken belt or strap. Paul would shave the two ends of the item before joining them. Then he would restore the leather by softening it with oil, and while he was doing this, his mouth was as busy as his hands. He lost no opportunity to spread the Word.

One day, as Silas and Paul were leaving the lecture hall, they were surprised to see Apollos standing nearby waiting for them. He said he had just returned from Corinth and must speak to them privately. When they found a secluded spot, he began, "You will be shocked by what I'm about to tell you. The conduct of both Jews and Gentiles in the Christian community of the city I just left has deteriorated almost beyond belief.

"Paul, you told me that when you left Corinth with Aquila and Priscilla, the few Jews who had become Christians had retained the morality of their new belief in spite of the heckling by antagonistic Jews, and that the Gentile Christians had completely abandoned their previous sinful ways. The church I saw bore little resemblance to the one you described. Many Corinthians have returned to their habits of loose living, drunkenness, and debauchery in their beloved city of Aphrodite. Sexual immorality is as prevalent as it was before you and Silas went to Corinth.

"I know that you would find their sexual behavior to be absolutely disgusting. Husbands and wives are no longer faithful to one another and frequently have sexual relations outside of marriage. Some are returning to the worship of idols. I'm sorry that I bring you such dreadful news, Paul, but you must hear it."

"Have they forgotten already that those who sin as they are doing will not inherit the kingdom of God? Don't they know that their bodies are temples of the Holy Spirit within themselves? Do they desire the same evil their forefathers pursued? The return to living in sin after we leave a city is beginning to become a familiar occurrence. First it was Thessalonica, then Galatia, and now Corinth. Let's hope that Ephesus won't be next.

"When it becomes possible I will go to Corinth, not to punish, but with love. Love is greater than even faith or hope, but I cannot leave Ephesus just now, nor can Silas. We've been told that the letters we sent to the other wayward cities seemed to have restored at least some semblance of Christian order. Silas, I don't know what else we can do but write to our friends in Corinth. I believe that we should admonish the Corinthians as our beloved children. But what do you think?"

"Sending a letter is definitely the answer, and let's get a start on it as soon as we've heard the rest of Apollos's story. Now, Apollos, what else should we know?"

"Well, I must tell you that the congregation has split up into four factions, each one pledging loyalty to a different leader. They have forgotten that all have the same leader in God. Paul, some have deserted you for Peter. I think that is because they do not believe you are a true apostle. The church is in a sorry state because of this division. They are constantly arguing with one another. To settle some of the many disputes that have developed, angry members are taking legal action in the heathen courts."

Paul held up his hand. "From what you have told me so far, it's clear that they have forgotten they are all one through Jesus Christ and that he, and not some heathen court, is the true judge the evil spirit, had left them. Silas and Paul were appalled by what they heard, and looked forward to the day when they could meet and expose these fake healers.

A week after the letter had been written to the Corinthians, the missionaries got their opportunity. Seven sons of a Jewish chief priest had arrived at Ephesus earlier. They had found out that Silas and Paul were in the city also and were teaching about the great power available through belief in Jesus Christ.

When the exorcists were told that many who heard the missionaries believed in this heavenly power, they decided to take advantage of the faith of any of the sick who believed. They were sure that if they used Jesus' name to identify their super spirit, rather than the one they had concocted, it would be easier to sell their fake cure.

Just as they began their first session of fraudulent healing, using the name of Jesus, the two missionaries appeared on the scene. Once more Silas witnessed Paul at his best. In the name of the Holy Spirit he accused the exorcists of sinful treachery and ordered them to leave the city at once. The priest's sons beat a hasty retreat out of Ephesus, and Silas and Paul explained to those who had gathered to be healed that the exorcists had used the name of Jesus only to take their money, making them believe in magic they did not possess. They explained that healing was possible only through the individual's faith in Jesus Christ and not through belief in a fraudulent magician. Many of those present who had believed in witchcraft vowed to turn away from the use of magic.[5]

Bad news came from Corinth that immorality had become rampant again after Apollos left. After Silas read the most depressing letter, he suggested that he and Paul split up so one of them would handle the problems at Ephesus for a short time, while the other would be free to go to Corinth for a brief visit. Paul offered to go to Corinth, because Apollos had reported that some Corinthians did not accept him as an apostle, and he would like to convince them of the truth.

Silas agreed because he believed the Corinthians' recognition of Paul as a true apostle chosen by Jesus Christ was essential to the acceptance of their message. So Paul went to Corinth and again told the congregations the story of his experience on the road to Damascus. Before long he returned to Ephesus disappointed. Regardless of whether or not they now accepted him as an apostle, his visit had done nothing to improve the morality of the Corinthians.

Not willing to accept failure, Silas and Paul decided to do something different. They would send Timothy to Corinth, hoping that a young, new voice would help. The next day the lad was on his way, but before long he, too, returned with a story of continued failure and harsher words spoken against Paul.

For several days neither Silas nor Paul knew what to try next, but because letters to other troubled areas had been successful, they decided to write once more. This letter would be brief, and for the first time it would be sharply critical.

"Let's send Titus to Corinth with our letter," Paul said.

"I agree, Paul. I believe he could help the Corinthians understand our message, and he can meet us at Troas to report their reaction. We will be stopping there soon on our way to Macedonia."

Before the day was over Titus was on his way to Corinth and Silas and Paul were back in the lecture hall busy teaching all those who would listen. The amulets that Silas and Paul had encountered when they first arrived at Ephesus were not the only good-luck charms sold in the city. The silver models of the revered Artemis were more elaborate and expensive, crafted by skilled silversmiths and sold to pilgrims who came to Ephesus to worship the goddess. Silas and Paul taught that these manmade articles were not deities at all, and so many people paid attention to the missionaries' words that the silversmiths began to suffer a loss of business.

The dynamic recognized leader of the silversmiths, a man named Demetrius, summoned all those engaged in making the sacred shrines to a meeting. He told them that unless they took action to stop Silas and Paul from preaching, they would soon lose their only source of income.

"If the two men are allowed to continue their mission, pilgrims will stop coming to worship their beloved Artemis. The entire civilized world will be deprived of her greatness, and Ephesus will lose its revered place among men!"

Demetrius was a powerful speaker, and the craftsmen were soon convinced that unless they took his advice, a great tragedy would descend on them. Full of anger, and of one voice, they began to shout, "Great is Artemis of the Ephesians."

Demetrius had achieved the response that he wanted. He stormed out of the meeting place leading the enraged mob shouting the war cry, "Great is Artemis of the Ephesians." Many citizens joined the rabble without knowing what all the excitement was about and added their protests to those of the silversmiths.

Demetrius led the angry group to the theater where performances usually began with a sacrifice to Artemis. Along the way, one of the craftsmen recognized two men, Gaius and Aristarchus, whom he had seen working with Silas and Paul.

"Grab them," he shouted, as he pointed at the Christians. "They belong to the group that wants to ruin us."

Without hesitating, several excited men rushed at Gaius and Aristarchus, easily subduing them and dragging them along as hostages. Another Christian who witnessed his friends' predicament ran to the lecture hall where he knew Silas and Paul would be teaching.

When they heard what had happened, they left their meeting place to rescue their friends. They had not gone far when sympathetic city leaders intercepted them and held them, fearing they might be killed if they tried to rescue the two men.

When the mob reached the theater, they caused mass confusion, even though no one there had any idea what the protest was all about. A few supporters of Silas and Paul were present, however. When they saw that Gaius and Aristarchus were being held against their will, they persuaded one of their number, a convincing individual named Alexander, to appeal to the crowd for the release of the two men.

As soon as Alexander called for attention, one of the silversmiths recognized him as an assistant to Silas and Paul. His shout of "Great is Artemis of the Ephesians" stirred up the crowd again, and they made so much noise no one could hear what Alexander was trying to say.

The crowd's raucous protest made Alexander's plea successful, because by this time the disturbance was very close to becoming a riot, and a riot was something the Roman rulers would not tolerate. One of the officials of the local government who was present went to the stage and signaled the crowd to give him their attention so he could speak to them.

When the people recognized him as a man of authority, they began to calm down. As soon as they became quiet enough to hear him he said he understood that they had a grievance but they were not addressing it properly. He was able to convince the angry crowd that only by taking their case before the proconsuls would they avoid the heavy hand of Rome descending on them.

"Furthermore," he said, "you must release the two men you are holding. I have been told that they are not leaders of the sect you oppose, but merely followers, and the proper place to confront them is in court, not in the open."

The crowd dispersed.[6] It was not compassion, but fear of Rome that saved Silas and Paul from the unruly mob. For some reason Silas and Paul were never ordered to appear before the proconsuls. In spite of the fact that they continued to teach against the worship of false gods, no charges were brought against them by the authorities.

Silas and Paul were satisfied with the progress that had been made at Ephesus. Before they left to meet Titus at Troas on their way to Macedonia, they returned the responsibility for leading the Christians of Ephesus to Aquila, Priscilla, and the elders of the church. Timothy had already gone on ahead with Erastus,[7] one of their new assistants, to return to Thessalonica and make preparations for Silas and Paul, who would visit there soon.

During their long walk to Troas, Silas said, "Paul, I've told you more than once about my father's decision to leave Alexandria. For quite a while now I have been convinced that the same force that drew my father away from Alexandria is now tugging at me. For some reason I do not understand, I feel that I am being drawn to Rome. Of course, because I am a Jew, I know that it will be impossible for me to go there as long as Claudius is alive."

"Silas, I'm glad to hear about your interest in Rome. I long to visit there also. Claudius will not live forever, but we have no assurance that Jewish Christians will be allowed in after his death. Of course, Claudius might outlive both of us. Nevertheless, I hope to visit Rome on our fourth journey, and Spain on our fifth.[8]

"But before we start out on any more missions, I want to raise funds to send to the mother church in Jerusalem.[9] As you know, we have heard that in spite of the financial help your father provides, the Christians who are still living in Jerusalem need help desperately."

Silas and Paul had much more to discuss on their eight-day walk, including the recent harsh letter to Corinth. Paul said that soon after sending the letter he regretted what they had done, because he feared the Corinthians would think it was in retaliation for their personal attack on him and that was not the case.[10] He said he would be glad to reach Troas and receive the report from Titus describing the conditions at Corinth.

When they reached their destination, however, they were greeted by the disappointing news that Titus was not there waiting for them. Paul decided to delay their departure for Macedonia for two weeks, hoping that Titus would arrive during that time. While they waited, the two missionaries conducted daily meetings.

At the end of the two weeks, when Silas and Paul left for Macedonia by ship, Titus had still not arrived. A day later the ship docked at Neapolis. The two men made the ten mile walk to Philippi, where they were given a very warm welcome at the home of Lydia.

Even on short notice, their hostess was able to conjure up a meal worthy to be called a banquet. They dined on tender lamb, freshly-baked bread, cheeses of different varieties, dates and figs, and the best of the area's wine. Lydia insisted that the missionaries stay in her home while they were in Philippi. Although Silas and Paul considered their previous visit successful, they could not forget the terrible scourging they had received while they were there. Even the recollection of their escape from prison and the conversion of the jailer and his family could not wipe out the memory of the torture.

While the missionaries were at Philippi, a messenger arrived from Rome to report that Emperor Claudius had been fatally poisoned by his wife and that Jews were once more being allowed to enter the city. A short time later Silas and Paul received a letter from Aquila and Priscilla. They had heard the news and had decided to leave for Rome to serve the Gentile Christians living there and the Jewish Christians they knew would be going back to the city. They felt there would be a great need for them at Rome, and they were confident that the elders at Ephesus were capable of carrying on.

Before leaving Philippi, Silas and Paul collected funds from grateful Christians for the church at Jerusalem. Lydia was a substantial contributor. When they resumed their trek through Macedonia, they were pleased to discover that this same willingness to help other believers was present wherever they stopped.

Several weeks after leaving Ephesus, the two men arrived at Thessalonica. They went directly to the home of their faithful friend, Jason, where they met Timothy and Ersatus.

There Jason said, "Your letter was well received and we are much better off because of it. Most Christians here now have a proper understanding about the second coming and go about their daily work with faith and thanksgiving. They have established a better relationship with their leaders and have a deeper love and respect for you, Paul. Now listen to this. My hearing before the magistrates was decided in my favor, and all is now well with me."

Just as Jason finished, Silas saw Titus coming through the open door. He knew by the grin on Titus's face that he was bringing good news from Corinth.

Titus said, "There has been a remarkable improvement in the Corinthians' behavior and I delayed my departure until I was reasonably sure that it would not decline after I left. Yes, the latest letter did upset some people when it was first read, but as the days went by, most Corinthians began to respond favorably and lead better lives."

Silas knew that Titus must have played a role in this great accomplishment, and that their confidence in him was well-founded.

"Of course, there are still a few problems remaining at Corinth that have not been cleared up," Titus said. "Unfortunately, the most important among them is the lack of recognition of you, Paul, as an apostle."

Paul interrupted Titus at this point. "In spite of the disappointment your last words bring, I am still rejuvenated by the change in conditions at Corinth and am ready to take the next step, which of course must be still another letter. This one will discuss the problem you just mentioned, and all the others that we have not yet heard about. Because you, Titus, have developed such a good relationship with the Corinthians, you should be the one to deliver the letter to them.

"I realize that some of the Corinthians still deny that I am truly an apostle because I was not one of the original twelve with Jesus, but that does not mean that I'm inferior to them in any way. I was chosen by God to be an apostle to minister to Jews and Gentiles alike. Since then, I have become rich in knowledge and I intend to tell them so.

"Titus, Silas and I did not deliver our previous letters personally because I thought my presence would only cause more trouble. But now I believe that after you give them our next message and study it with them, they will be ready to receive me once more. You can tell them that Silas and I will come to them for the third time very soon."

Titus smiled. "I'm happy to hear that you say that, Paul. When I meet with the Corinthians, I will prepare them for your visit. I will explain that you are using your God-given authority to build them up and not to tear them down. I will tell them that you know they are God's concern as well as your own, and your aim is to reconcile them to him."

"Titus," Paul said, "we appreciate your insight into the remaining problems at Corinth. I know your help will bring us success.

"I would like to tell the Corinthians about the money we have raised for the stricken Jerusalem Christians. The churches of Macedonia gave funds from their poverty through the grace of God. We must ask the Corinthians to do the same."

The next morning Silas and Paul sat down to compose the letter. Before the day was over, Titus left to deliver the letter to Corinth, leaving the two missionaries with high hopes for a still better relationship with the Christians there.[11]

A few days after Titus's departure for Corinth, Luke arrived from Philippi, which he now considered his home, having moved there from Antioch. He came to Thessalonica to see Silas and Paul because he had been away from Philippi at the time of their recent visit. The three men had met at Antioch, soon after Silas and Paul had returned from their first missionary journey, when Luke became a Christian, and they quickly became close friends.

Silas had his own reason for welcoming their physician friend. He believed that Paul should have constant medical attention, and he was resolved to convince Luke to join their mission so Paul would receive the care he needed.

A few weeks after Luke's arrival, Silas, Paul, Timothy, and Erastus left for Achaia. Luke was with them. Silas had persuaded him to come along, at least as far as Corinth. As they walked the road south, they made several brief stops, including Beroea and Larissa, before reaching Corinth.

They entered the city through the Propylea Gate and walked through the Agora. Gaius, the Gentile who had suffered for being a Christian while visiting Ephesus, rushed toward them. "Welcome to Corinth," he shouted. "I'm living here now, and I'm so happy to see you. I have so much to thank you for. Your letter was most rewarding, and Titus, the man you sent with it, is loved by all the Christians here. I was honored when he agreed to live with me while he is in Corinth. And now I insist that all of you join him and me and stay at my home."[12]

They were soon reunited with Titus, who confirmed that their third letter had been well received by the Corinthians, both Jews and Gentiles. Their recent good fortune seemed to be continuing.

Silas and Paul accepted the first invitation they received to speak to a mixed group of interested Corinthians. Because of their previous rejection of him, Paul was anxious to take advantage of the friendly reception the letter had generated. He spoke first and spent considerable time on the subject of grace. He told the Christians once more that only by the grace of God had he been converted from a persecutor of Christians to a fervent missionary. He added that his apostleship and ministry were the direct result of that divine grace.

He told them that as a Pharisee and non-believer he had tried to earn God's acceptance by fulfilling the Law, which was impossible, but then he learned that only through God's grace could he receive unearned salvation. He reminded the Jews in the congregation that a true Jew is one who believes that Jesus Christ is the Messiah.

After the meeting was over, the two men left together. As they walked along Paul said, "Silas, my longing to go to Rome and Spain has become a burning desire. We have brought the Good News to the lands east of the great city, so our next mission must be to head further west. With the death of Emperor Claudius, Rome is a safe place for Jews once more, even those who are Christians. Aquila and Priscilla have already gone back as have countless others and Titus has told me that he plans to leave for there soon.

"There was an infant church there, in which we played no part, before Claudius drove it out. I know that Aquila and Priscilla will do all they can to restore it as more and more Jews return, but they will have taken on a very difficult assignment, and they would appreciate our help.

"I have a concern about my health. I'm worried that I might not survive to be part of the mission and that you will have to carry on without me. It's a miracle that I have lasted fifty years in this dangerous world with my poor physical condition, but I pray that I will live long enough to help you and Timothy get started, and we should plan accordingly. I hope we will be able to leave for Rome immediately after we deliver the gift of the churches we served to the needy Christians of Jerusalem.

"In the meantime, we can do something to prepare the Christians of Rome for our arrival. We have recently been encouraged by the good that has come from our letters. Our written word is sometimes more effective than our spoken word. Let us write to the Christians in Rome to bolster their faith before we visit them. If I don't make it there, at least I will die with the satisfaction that I was part of the message they received.

"This letter will also give us an opportunity to send personal greetings to Aquila and Priscilla. We owe them our thanks, because the little we know about the Christians in Rome we learned from them.

"What we write will be somewhat different from what we wrote to churches that we were very familiar with. The scribe Tertius has offered to give us more help, so I would suggest that we dictate our thoughts to him. For once you will not have to do double duty."

"That sounds good to me, but it will be a major venture. I will do all I can to help, and if Timothy joins us, I know he will too, but I have a suggestion to make. I appreciate your effort to make me be more of a contributor and less of a scribe when we compose the letter, but I believe it should be entirely yours, Paul, because of what you told me earlier about the burning desire you have to bring the Word to Rome."

"Thank you, Silas, but I do want both you and Timothy with me to ask questions and make comments. I want our letter to be the complete story of the Good News. We must tell the Romans exactly what we believe and why we believe it. Let's talk more about this when we meet tomorrow."

The next morning Silas was the first to speak. "Paul, you invited us to ask questions. I would like to ask my first question right now before you begin. You mentioned earlier that there was an infant church in Rome before Emperor Claudius drove the Jews out. What do you think the source of their belief was?"

"Before I answer that, let me say that because of all that I have heard recently, I believe that when Aquila and Priscilla left the city, the Roman Christians lacked a good understanding of our faith and the situation is probably no better now. I believe that those who brought the Word to Rome were not well informed and were poor teachers.

"There are three possible sources from which the Romans could have learned a limited amount of the Gospel, and although each source had good intentions, none of them would have been properly qualified. One or more Roman soldiers who had become believers while stationed in a Christian community might have been sent back to Rome and brought part of our message with them. Some of the early Jewish Christians who were forced to flee Judea might have passed along what little they knew about our belief. Some of the pilgrims who came to Jerusalem for the Passover and experienced Pentecost before returning to Rome could have told about the experience they had.

"We don't know for sure who taught the Romans or what they taught them, but we do know from what we heard from Aquila and Priscilla that the development of the Christian belief in Rome was at a very elementary stage and that there were many misconceptions. In my letter I will try to right all that has been wrong.

"I will do my best to correct any improper interpretation of Christianity they may have. They may have heard about something one of us said, and misunderstood it. I want the Romans to hear the true message.

"I want the Romans to understand the righteousness of God and enjoy the proper relationship with God that will come to them if they have faith and trust him, realizing all that he has done for them, none of which they earned or deserved. Their belief in Jesus Christ will bring them salvation.

"I will tell those in Rome not to let their lives conform to the modern world they live in, but to present their lives to God as a sacrifice. I must tell them not to pass judgment on their fellow men, but to have respect for them. Jew and Gentile are serving the same God.

"I must give them a list of rules they should follow to live a proper life with one another. How different these rules will be from those we had as Pharisees, before Christ!

"I should explain that because we have been so busy bringing the Good News from Jerusalem throughout Asia Minor and Greece, we have found it necessary to delay our visit to Rome. But now our work elsewhere is done, and after we deliver the offering of the churches in Macedonia and Achaia to Jerusalem, we will come to Rome. I should ask for their prayers for our success at Jerusalem."

"I have a question, Paul," Timothy said. "Who do you think will read your letter?"

"Timothy, I pray that the letter will be delivered to Aquila and Priscilla and that they will enlist the help of scribes who will make enough copies so that everyone who yearns to learn more about our belief will get the opportunity to read what I have written. Though the letter is addressed to the Christians in Rome, both Jews and Gentiles, I will give thanks for any curious nonbeliever who reads a copy and becomes one of us."

After many hours of work over the next two days, the three men finished Paul's letter, satisfied with what they had done and it was on its way. Phoebe, one of the stalwarts of the church at Corinth, had volunteered to deliver it to Rome.[13]

When Silas began to think about Paul's comment in the letter about going to Rome, he realized that if they delivered the collected funds to Jerusalem first, as Paul had suggested, he might have an opportunity to visit his family. That would be wonderful. Nevertheless, he knew that taking the mission to Rome should be given top priority. For that reason he suggested that they split up. He and Paul could leave for Rome at once, and the others could deliver the purse to Jerusalem.

Paul, however, was insistent that he and Silas be with the group that delivered the churches' contribution. Silas could not understand why Paul would not designate someone else to take the purse to Jerusalem. He thought Paul acted as if he had been directed by God to do it himself, but as usual Silas submitted to his friend.

Then Paul surprised Silas when he said that although there was an urgency to get to Jerusalem, he wanted to visit the church at Antioch on the way. This was Paul's final decision and so an arrangement was made to sail from the Corinthian port of Cenchrae directly to Antioch of Syria just as soon as winter released its hold on the shipping routes. Although Silas was disappointed with the delay of the mission to Rome, he was thankful that he would have an opportunity to see his family for the first time in almost four years.

Chapter 21

On the Road Back

THE CAPTAIN OF the ship the missionaries had booked passage on sent word that the weather was suitable for sailing at last, and he would be ready to leave for Antioch the following morning. Silas, Paul, and their companions thanked Gaius for his hospitality and left his home at once to walk the five miles to Cenchrae to board the waiting ship.

Just as Paul was about to lead the others up the gangplank, a man ran to the ship.

"Stop," he shouted. "You must not board that ship. You are in great danger."

Paul stopped as if someone had grabbed him. Then he turned to see who it was that was crying so frantically. When he recognized the man as a Christian from Corinth and a friend of Gaius, he asked, "What are you talking about?"

"Believe me. I overheard three men plotting to kill your whole missionary team while you are on the ship and throw the bodies overboard so that no one would ever know what happened to you. They plan to board the ship as soon as they are sure you are on it. They are probably watching us now."

"I do believe you, and give thanks for your courage. We will do as you say, but you must be off because you, too, will now be in danger. Return to Gaius at once and remain with the other Christians for protection."

Paul turned to the others. "We should get out of here as quickly as we can. I don't believe that it would be safe to try to leave for home from this port on any ship. I suggest that we work our way by land and water to Patara. Sooner or later a ship will be leaving there for Antioch. Let's hurry and hope that we are not being followed by those desperate men."

The missionaries walked to Philippi instead of sailing to their doom, thankful that they had not sent their food supply to the ship prior to boarding as they sometimes did before a long voyage. After two weeks on the road, the group arrived safely at Neapolis, the seaport of the city of Philippi. The next morning they were on a small vessel that took them to Troas.[1]

While the missionaries waited there for a ship that would take them to Patara, or at least a little further along the way, they spent their time meeting with the Christians of the city. One week later, just as the Sabbath had come to an end, they received an offer to leave on a packet the next morning. The small ship was headed for Patara, with many ports of call along the way, the first one at Assos. This arrangement appealed to the missionaries because they would have an opportunity to spread the Word at each stop, so they accepted the offer.

Once the decision was made, the missionaries began their last worship service at Troas. After celebrating the Lord's Supper the teaching session continued in an upper-room meeting place into the late hours of the evening. Paul was still speaking at midnight, and although he was exhausted he continued to tell the eager ones what he knew they should hear. One young man, who sat by the window, dozed off and fell through the opening down to the courtyard.

Paul heard him scream in pain as he landed on the hard surface below. He rushed down the outside steps, followed by Luke. They ran over to where Eutychus was lying on the ground, battered and bruised, and gasping for breath. Luke knelt over him to inspect his wounds while Paul prayed that he might be healed.

Soon Eutychus's breathing became easier and then his eyes opened. When he looked up at the concerned and compassionate expression on Paul's face, he smiled and said that he was all right and only needed someone to help him home. Paul left Luke with the boy and returned to the meeting, where Silas had remained to console the weary gathering. Paul resumed teaching as if the accident had never happened.[2]

When the first rays of the morning sun beamed into the upper room, Paul closed the session with a final prayer. Then, as was his custom, he sent the believers off with these words, "The God of peace be with you all." The new Christians answered, "Thanks be unto God."

Once more Silas was astonished at his friend's endurance. He was sure that Paul, in spite of his poor health, could have carried on with the work he loved several hours longer. He had told Silas earlier that he expected the service would last until morning and that the group should be prepared to leave the meeting place directly after the final prayer and board the ship for Assos.

Now, however, because of his concern for Eutychus, Paul decided to delay his departure. He asked Silas to remain at Troas with him until they were assured that Eutychus's condition was improving, but he convinced Timothy, Luke, and Erastus to leave on the ship they had engaged to take them on the next stage of their journey. He told them that he and Silas would set out on foot and meet them at Assos where the ship would be docked at its first stop.

Silas knew that Paul was concerned about Eutychus, but he assumed his friend had another reason for choosing to walk. He believed that Paul wanted time for the two of them to be separated from the others so they could meditate alone and seek guidance from the Holy Spirit through prayer.[3]

The next morning, the two men were relieved to discover that Eutychus appeared to be well on the way to recovery from his fall. The Christian community, thankful for the visit of the missionaries, wished them well as they walked south toward Assos.

Silas had been told that because both that city and Troas were seaports, the road between the two places followed the coastline of the Gulf of Adramyttium, and this was welcome news. Silas knew that a coastal road would be easy to walk, and in spite of Paul's poor health, the two men negotiated the twenty miles in less than a full day.

Luke greeted them. "Welcome to Assos. It's wonderful to see you, but I'm surprised you're here so soon. If you had arrived an hour or two earlier you would have been here before our ship docked."

"I can't believe that," Silas said. "What took you so long?"

"The water route from Troas to here is much longer than the land route, and we had trouble getting around the treacherous Cape Lectum. But how is Eutychus?"

Paul answered Luke. "He was much better after a good night's rest, and because he was getting good care we decided it was safe to leave him."

"That is good news," Luke said.

"Yes, now we have one more thing to be thankful for," Paul said. "Before we do anything else, let's talk about the rest of our voyage to Patara. A visit with the Ephesians is most important, and the packet will stop at Miletus which is only twenty-eight miles from Ephesus. I suggest that we send a messenger ahead to request the church leaders to meet us at the dock." A messenger left a short time later.

As the five men got on board, Paul said, "In spite of all the stops we will make, if all goes well we will arrive at Jerusalem long before the observance of Pentecost." This was most important to all of them. Those who were Jews had believed the Pentecost celebration was one of the most important observances of the year, but now it was a Christian festival, celebrating the arrival of the Holy Spirit.

Because they were sailing so early in the season, the ship hugged the Aegean Sea coast of Asia Minor as it began the voyage that would eventually take them as far as Patara. On the first day the ship docked briefly at Mitylene, the chief port of the island of Lesbos. On the second morning they made a quick visit to the island of Chios. The following day they stopped at Samos for just a few hours. Silas and Paul regretted that the time spent at these places had to be brief, but they were confident that they had sown seeds at each location, and that others would soon come to water them. On the third day after leaving Assos, they arrived at Miletus and there waiting for them at the dock was a delegation from the church at Ephesus, just as Paul had requested.

Silas and Paul were not surprised at the warm reception they received from the elders of the church. They had spent more time at Ephesus than anywhere else and had enjoyed great success there in spite of opposition. After the five missionaries had circulated through the crowd and greeted everyone, Paul stood up on a rock ready to speak. Silas knew that Paul felt a very close relationship to the Ephesians. He feared that this would be Paul's last meeting with them and that he was about to hear a very emotional farewell address. Paul began by reminiscing.

"I know that you all remember very clearly the severe treatment we received from the hands of the unbelieving Jews on our previous visit. Their cruel interference forced us to abandon the synagogue of our ancestors. Fortunately, a Gentile came to our rescue. We were given the use of the hall of a philosopher where we were allowed to conduct our meetings. We continued to serve the Lord day after day in the almost unbearable heat of the summer months with tears and humility, but without fear of our enemies.

"During our three-year stay at Ephesus, we constantly taught repentance and faith in Jesus Christ in spite of opposition from both Jews and Gentiles, and this we did without financial help from those we ministered to. We labored to pay our expenses, did everything possible to help others in need, and encouraged all believers to do the same.

"Now, I regret to inform you that you will not see us again after this very short visit. We are on our way to Jerusalem to take the contribution from the churches in Macedonia and Achaia to the mother church, which is experiencing a very troubled existence. I fear that my reception at the holy city may be as unkind as it was twenty years ago. Although God has forgiven me for my past sins, my Christian brothers may not have. Nevertheless, we will proceed as we believe the Holy Spirit has directed us, without concern for our personal wellbeing. While we are in Jerusalem, we will attempt to add to the number of believers regardless of the consequences to us. If we survive persecution we will proceed on to Rome, and hopefully Spain, where so much waits to be done.

"But enough about Silas and myself. The burden of caring for the church at Ephesus now rests squarely on your shoulders, and we all know that you are up to the task. We realize that you did not ask to take over the leadership of the church when the time came for us to go elsewhere, but the Holy Spirit chose you to do it.

"We must warn you to beware of the human wolves who will attempt to destroy your human flock with false gospel. You must be vigilant to make sure some of your own number do not rise up against you and defect, taking others with them. Now, after three years in your service, we are giving you over to God and the unearned grace you will receive from him. We have done everything possible to bring the Word of God to Ephesus, and now it is up to you to carry on and move forward. Silas and I are confident that with the firm foundation we have given you, your deep belief will carry you without outside help and that your church will serve as a model for others."

When Silas heard this last remark of Paul's, he envisioned a Christian church of the future which would be self-sufficient and not dependent on traveling missionaries for survival.

Paul's speech affected the listeners greatly, especially his announcement that he and Silas would not see them again. Silas decided that Paul's words had said it all, so he only offered the final prayer and said his personal farewell to the Ephesians.

The missionaries, escorted by the elders of the church at Ephesus, boarded the ship and it set sail at once. As long as they remained in sight of the shore, Silas and Paul could see their supporters waving a sad good-bye.[4]

The next stop was at the island of Cos. After just a few hours there they sailed on. The following day they arrived at the island of Rhodes and stayed long enough for a very short meeting before docking at Patara, the main port for the province of Lydia and the last stop for the ship that had brought them from Troas.

Soon after they disembarked, Silas and Paul found the harbormaster and told him they wanted to go to Jerusalem by way of Antioch.

"I'm sorry, but you're out of luck. A ship left for Antioch three days ago, and the next one is not expected for three weeks, but there is a ship at the dock ready to leave for the Phoenician port of Tyre before going on to Caesarea, and it will get you to Jerusalem much sooner than a boat headed for Antioch that isn't even here yet"

"Thank you for your suggestion," Paul said, "but we want to visit Antioch. Silas, I believe we should wait for the later ship even if that means we will miss the celebration of Pentecost in Jerusalem. It's important to me that you get to Antioch and be reunited with your family, even if only for a few days."

"Thank you, Paul. Yes, I desperately want to see them, and I pray that we will arrive in Jerusalem for Pentecost."

Nothing more was said for several minutes, and then Paul spoke again. "Silas, I apologize, but I've changed my mind. I believe my Christian obligation is to get to Jerusalem as soon as possible. I'll tell the harbormaster we will take the ship bound for Tyre."

Silas knew Paul well enough to know that this would be his final decision. He would not see his family after all.

Silas's life was controlled by his dedication to the church, so he followed the Jerusalem-bound group to board the vessel that would take them on an uneventful four-hundred-mile voyage across the Great Sea, not to Antioch but to Tyre and then Caesarea. After five days on the water, the ship arrived at its first stop where it spent seven days to unload and reload before going on.[5]

The missionaries were welcomed by the Christians of Tyre. They had received the Gospel from Jews who had fled Jerusalem after the persecution of Stephen. One of them came over to speak to Silas. After introducing himself he asked, "Do you see that large ship tied up at the dock over there?"

"Yes, I was just looking at it. It is a big one, isn't it? Do you know what its cargo is?"

"It isn't carrying anything yet, but when it does it will be a very special ship. I was talking to one of the crewmen a short time ago. He said the owner had just received a lucrative contract from the Roman government. It will be leaving Tyre in about an hour from now. First it will head north to Antioch to pick up supplies for the army, and then it will return south to deliver them to the Roman garrison at Caesarea."

Silas rushed away from the startled man he had been talking to without a word. If he could arrange for passage on the ship ready to depart for Antioch, he could visit his family while the ship was loading there and then go on to Caesarea to meet Paul and the other missionaries when it was set to sail again. Minutes later, Silas had made the necessary arrangements with the captain and was ready to board the ship.

"Silas, that's wonderful news," Paul said. "I'm very happy that you have been blessed in this way. You have received a gift that you richly deserve. Don't worry if the rest of us have to wait for you at Caesarea for a few days. Because of the excellent time we made on the journey home, I no longer have any fear of being late for the Pentecost festival, and we will be safe at the Roman capital of Judea while we wait."

Less than an hour later Silas was on board the government ship, and after a week on the water he was at Seleucia. It was not yet daylight when Silas went ashore. He was told that if he wanted to be taken to Caesarea he must be back early in the morning of the fourth day. Alone and on a good road, Silas was able to walk much more rapidly than usual. He would be home by midday.

As he thought about Antioch and the home his father had provided, he wondered what changes four years had brought to his wife and children. Martha would be seventeen now, and Joseph would be sixteen. He knew from the last of the infrequent letters he had received from Rebekah that both children had done well. Martha had grown into a beautiful young lady and was very active in the church.

When Silas recalled that Rebekah had written that Joseph had finished his education and was dedicated to the spread of

Christianity, he realized at once what his mission was going to be while he was home. At sixteen Joseph was already one year older than he had been at the time of the crucifixion and the beginning of his life as a missionary. Silas knew now that Joseph must join their group to train for replacing either himself or Paul. He was elated by the thought.

Rebekah was home alone. She and Silas would have a precious hour or two together before Martha and Joseph would join them. Silas could hardly wait to let Rebekah know about his great plan for Joseph. He knew that she would be as excited as he was. He thought that the best way to introduce the subject was by asking if their son was making the best of every opportunity that came along.

Rebekah spoke with pride, "Yes, Joseph certainly has made the most of every opportunity offered him. He had the good fortune to study with the most learned rabbi at Antioch, and he did extremely well. Joseph has now finished his education and has grown up to be a fine young man. He recognized the challenge of doing a man's job and he accepted it.

"He has worked his way into a leading role in the church, and he has done a great deal to increase the number of believers in Antioch. He also worked diligently to become a scribe and to follow in your footsteps. Now he earns enough at his trade to keep our family alive. We really need his income because, for some unknown reason, we no longer receive help from your father, and of course the church cannot look after everyone. I don't know how our family would have survived without him.

"You will be very proud of him when you hear more of the details of all that he has done. He has become the man of the house in your absence, and because of what he is doing for your family it will be possible for you to continue your work away from us."

Silas's dream of taking his son away with him disappeared, just as the dream of studying in Alexandria with his grandfather had evaporated twenty-seven years earlier. He knew he must leave Joseph at home as the man of the house.

Fortunately, his disappointment was soon softened by two more joyful reunions, when first Martha and then Joseph returned home. Once they were all together they began an almost non-stop conversation for three days, and then the time came for another good-bye.

In the meantime, Paul was meeting with the Christians of Tyre. After he had finished speaking, one member of the gathering rose. "Paul, you must not leave here and go to Jerusalem. Nothing but disaster waits for you there. We have been informed that some Jewish Christians from Asia Minor somehow found out quite a while ago that you were going to Jerusalem. They are there now, waiting for your arrival. Our informants told us that once your antagonists find out that you and your associates are in the city they will place charges with the council of the church. We were told that although complaints will be made against all the missionaries, the formal accusation to be brought before the council will be against you alone. They plan to charge you with attempting to destroy Judaism."

Paul listened respectfully to all they said, but he was not to be deterred. "Thank you for your love and attempt to protect me, but I am confident that I am being led by the Holy Spirit. I must go to Jerusalem."

The local Christians could do nothing more. When the ship was ready to leave, they prayed with the missionaries and then sadly escorted them to the dock. Paul and his companions were no sooner on board when the vessel set sail. At the end of the first day they stopped at Ptolemais, twenty-seven miles to the south. The next day they sailed thirty-two miles further south to Caesarea where their sea voyage came to an end.

Philip the evangelist, who was one of the seven first deacons of the church at Jerusalem, now lived at Caesarea. He greeted Paul and invited him and his companions to stay at his home while they waited for Silas.

Philip had four daughters who professed to be prophets. Like the Christians at Tyre, they urged Paul not to go to Jerusalem. Once more Paul chose to ignore the warning. Persecution or the threat of it was nothing new for the missionaries. They had suffered dearly for spreading the Word in many places during their journeys.

Then Agabus, a prophet whom Paul had heard about at Antioch, arrived at Philip's home. He had come from Judea and was well aware of the tension in Jerusalem. Speaking dramatically, as was the custom of Jewish prophets, Agabus predicted that Paul would be bound by the Jews who were against him and handed over to the Romans for persecution. Despite the pleas from all who were present, Paul replied that he was determined to proceed and willing to die for his faith.

When those assembled understood that nothing would prevent Paul from going to Jerusalem, they said, "The Lord's will be done."

The next day the ship bringing supplies to the soldiers stationed at Caesarea arrived. When Silas disembarked, he was surprised to be greeted by Philip. The two men who had served together in Samaria twenty-five years earlier were happily reunited.

The following morning Silas joined Paul and his other companions as well as some of the believers of Caesarea, and together they started off to walk the fifty-five miles to Jerusalem.[6]

Early on the three-day walk, one of the Christians from Caesarea came to speak to Silas. "I feel that I must tell you that Paul has received multiple warnings to stay out of Jerusalem, but he has ignored them all. We know for sure that a group of Christian Jews from Asia Minor are prepared to take a charge to the church council that Paul is determined to destroy Judaism."

"I appreciate you telling me this, but I know Paul is determined to go on, and nothing any of us can do will stop him. The charges that will be made are false. They are only a subterfuge to hide their plan for revenge. These people have just never forgiven Paul for following the directive of the Sanhedrin and persecuting their friends and family members.

"What you've told me sends shivers through my body. Anyone who continues to carry their hate for so many years and walk so many miles for revenge will not give up. Regardless of what decision the church council reaches, the Christian Jews from Asia Minor will not rest as long as Paul remains alive."

Chapter 22

Trouble at Jerusalem

SILAS WAS OVERWHELMED by the magnificent reception they received at Jerusalem. The poverty of the diminished mother church had done nothing to dampen the enthusiasm of its members, and the missionaries had no opposition from any quarter. The Christians welcomed the opportunity to express their gratitude for everything the missionaries had accomplished. The high point of the celebration occurred when Paul handed over the contributions he had received for the needy to the elders of the mother church, a gift from the many congregations the missionaries had visited.

Although most of the Christians in the city were Jews, a few gentile believers were among those who had come out to show their support. One of these was Trophimus, a friend from Ephesus, who had just settled in Jerusalem and was happy to be able to see Silas and Paul again.

All except Silas decided to spend their first day greeting old friends and making new ones. He was eager to visit his parents, who were in their early sixties, and he was anxious to know if they had heard from his grandfather.

As Silas walked away from the small crowd of still cheering well-wishers, he saw a detached group of desperate-looking men who were not celebrating with the others and appeared not to approve of what was going on. The warnings Paul had been given crossed his mind as he passed them.

When he arrived at the home his family had lived in since the day they moved into Jerusalem, he was shocked to be greeted at the door by a complete stranger.

"My name is Silas, and I lived here with my parents until I moved away over twenty-five years ago," he said to the young lady standing in the opening.

"My name is Rhoda. I'm sorry to tell you that both your parents died less than two months ago. I moved in when I found out that the house was available. I was told that your father had been ill for years and had been unable to carry on his business for some time before his death. I also heard that your mother died a few days after your father, heart-broken and exhausted from nursing him."

Silas thanked Rhoda for giving him the sad news, and as he turned away from the family home he realized that his parents' deaths might have occurred while he was crossing the Great Sea. If the missionaries had only been able to get passage on the ship out of Cenchrae, as they had originally planned, he might have seen his parents once more before they died.

He was surprised that word of his parents' death had not gotten to Rebekah, but perhaps because of the undercover nature of his father's life, he had been isolated from the church and had no friends who knew where Rebekah lived.

With a heavy heart, Silas walked on to join Paul and the others at the home of Mnason,[1] a Christian from Cyprus, who had invited them to stay with him while they were in Jerusalem.

The following day had scarcely begun when a messenger arrived to request the missionaries to appear before the council of the mother church. No reason was given for the summons, but Silas assumed that the members wished to express their thanks to the contributing churches for the generous gift they had sent.

When they arrived at the appointed hour, the council had already assembled. James, the brother of Jesus, presided as usual, and he began to speak.

"Welcome back to the holy city, and thank you for the generous gift you gave the elders which is so badly needed. It is heartwarming to know that many Christians from countless churches throughout Macedonia and Achaia contributed to help their needy brothers in Jerusalem. The council members have also been hoping for some time that you would come here and report on your activities. To give the council members a better understanding of the teachings of your missionary group, I suggest, for reasons that will be clear later, that Paul act as the spokesman and give a full and truthful account of your mission."

Silas could not help but think that Paul was somehow playing a defensive role as he addressed the stern council of the Jerusalem church. The setting seemed so different from the recent one at Miletus where he spoke to the sympathetic elders of the Ephesian church.

Without being the least bit boastful, Paul described the missions in full detail including successes and failures, hardships and good times. When he had finished, Silas could tell from the reaction of the council members that they were more than satisfied with Paul's report. Regardless of what opinions they might have held before the session, Silas was confident that the mother church would now give the missionaries their full support.

When James rose to praise God and give thanks for the success the missionaries had achieved, Silas thought that the meeting was over. He knew the satisfaction he was experiencing would be felt by the other members of their group as well. Now he was anxious to congratulate Paul on his great accomplishment, but before he could reach him, James began to speak again.

"We have heard your report and I'm sure the entire council will agree that we are satisfied with what you have done. Unfortunately, others will disagree with us, and we know they are prepared to take action against you. These protesters have come to Jerusalem from some of the countries you have visited. They are here for the Pentecost celebration, but they are also here to place charges against you, Paul.

"The men I speak of are not from among the Gentiles you have had so much success with, but from our own kind. Although they are Christians, they have kept a strict Judaistic devotion to the Law. They have heard and they believe, although they have no proof, that you have deserted your heritage. They claim that you have persuaded Jews in some of the communities where you served to discard the Law of Moses. They also accuse you of instructing Jews in gentile regions to stop circumcising their sons and to abandon other ancestral customs.

"Because you are the only missionary so accused, we think these men have personal reasons for bringing their charges before the council. Of course, we do not believe that what they say is true. Nevertheless, we, and especially you, have a serious problem which must be addressed at once because your enemies will already know that you have arrived here, and they will not waste any time before taking action in an attempt to drive you out of the church."

Silas listened to Paul explaining that the very fact he had come to Jerusalem for Pentecost was evidence enough that he had not abandoned his ancestral faith, but was still very much a Jew. James countered that although his supporters would accept this as a valid argument, his opponents would not, and something else must be done to convince them.

"And we have a plan," James explained, "which, if you follow it to the letter, will prove your innocence of the charges. First, let me explain that there are four Nazarites in the process of taking their vows as prescribed in the Scriptures to verify their devotion to God and to give thanks for special blessings they have received.

"As you no doubt know, it is customary for some devout Jew to demonstrate his deep devotion to Judaism by reimbursing Nazarites, whenever they celebrate the rite, for their loss of income during their thirty-day confinement. Our plan is that you are to be that devout Jew. To further demonstrate that you have not abandoned your faith, you will also join the Nazarites for the last four days of the rite."

Silas knew that Paul would understand the rationale of the plan, and that if he followed it his adversaries would no longer be able to openly accuse him of forsaking Judaism. But he also knew Paul well enough to realize that his friend would be troubled by one thing in James's proposal. Paul would have to follow certain dictates of the rite which had lost their relevancy to both of them because they were no longer just Jews, they were now Christian Jews.

Silas knew that the one custom that would bother Paul the most would take place at the very end of the ceremony. At that time the Nazarites' hair, which had not been trimmed for thirty days, would be shorn and burned at the altar along with a prescribed sacrifice that Paul would have to supply. This procedure was no part of their new belief.

Nevertheless, as Silas knew would happen, Paul, because he was bound and determined to demonstrate to the doubters that he had not turned his back on his heritage, consented to the plan of the council. Paul joined the Nazarites in the Temple for the last four days of the ritual.

On the final day of the purification rite, word of what Paul was doing reached the ears of the Jews from Asia Minor. They rushed excitedly into the streets in large numbers, mingling with the overflowing crowd of local Jews and visitors to Jerusalem who had come for the Pentecost celebration, shouting, and making false charges against Paul.

"There is a heathen in the Temple preaching against the Law, the Temple, and even against us Jews," their leader proclaimed. When he shouted, "This man's sinful behavior in the Temple is making a mockery of the purification rite we all respect," many of the non-Christian Jews joined the protesting crowd.

Then one of the local Jews said in a loud voice, "I saw the man you're talking about walking toward the Temple earlier with Trophimus, a Gentile from Ephesus. I'm sure that the guilty man took his gentile companion into the Temple and even beyond the gentile barrier."

This was a crime punishable by death. When the street crowd heard what the man said, the Jews from Asia Minor immediately lost control. Paul's fate was no longer a matter to be handled by them before the church council. The mob of Judaists would take care of the heretic their way, and this they did by rushing to the Temple and dragging Paul out, determined to beat him to death. He would not be in the Temple to participate in the Nazarite sacrifice.

The frantic shouts of the angry Jews as they rushed to punish Paul created such an uproar that it was heard at the headquarters of the battalion stationed nearby. Although troops were always quartered at sites where an uprising might be expected to occur during a festival such as Pentecost, a larger force was always at the Temple because that was where trouble was most likely to erupt, and one thing that Rome would not tolerate in its provinces was civil unrest.

Any disturbance that could possibly evolve into something more serious would have to be suppressed at once or there would be trouble for those responsible for preventing turmoil. Authorities who did not take the proper action faced removal from office and grave punishment. When the noise generated by the shouting of the angry dissidents reached the ears of the battalion commander, he ordered his men to respond immediately to prevent the situation from getting out of hand.

The soldiers rushed to rescue Paul, and then, followed by the enraged crowd, they marched him off to appear before the commander.

When calm was restored, he asked what all the fuss was about. The Judaists were determined to punish Paul for defiling the Temple, but because they knew the commander would not be concerned by that, they shouted out a host of false accusations of crimes they said Paul had committed against Rome. Afraid that the Jews would become wild again, the commander ordered Paul arrested and taken away. The mob cheered, believing Paul was about to be punished.

Once the commander had Paul inside the barracks, he began to wonder about the identity of his prisoner. He thought that he was most likely some notorious character. Perhaps he was even one of those who were desperately sought by Rome and deserved severe punishment. Then he recalled a report he had seen some time ago concerning an Egyptian fugitive—he believed his name was Numar—who had organized four thousand known assassins into a makeshift army. He trained them just outside Jerusalem, preparing to storm the city.

Of course, when the time came to attack they were no match for the Roman army that had been brought in to defend Jerusalem. Most of them were killed or captured and imprisoned. But, as the officer remembered well, the leader had escaped and become one of the most wanted criminals in the empire. He knew that if the man he had in chains turned out to be that Egyptian, he would be in line for a grand promotion, but first he had to prove that his prisoner was Numar.

The commander would use the simple procedure that he had been successful with often in the past. He would boldly accuse his prisoner of being Numar. Then, based on his many years of experience, he would know from the way the prisoner responded with the expected denial whether or not that was the prisoner's name. The commander looked directly at Paul, eye to eye, pointed his finger in his face, and shouted, "I know now that you are Numar."

His hope for advancement vanished immediately when he heard Paul's response. "I am not Numar. I am an innocent Jew from Tarsus." The denial itself did not destroy the commander's dream, but the way it was delivered did. He heard not the voice of a common criminal, but that of a cultured Greek-speaking Jew.

Paul asked to speak to the mob that had just attacked him. The commander, flustered by his error in falsely accusing Paul, agreed to the strange request. When Paul appeared outside the barracks, apparently a free man, the hateful crowd began to protest in disbelief. Paul signaled for silence in the manner of one in a position of superiority. Immediately a hush fell over those gathered below him. They were overawed by Paul's unexpected release and his apparent authority.

By this time Silas, along with Paul's other friends, had heard what had happened and was standing nervously at the front of the now quiet but still angry crowd. As Silas looked around at the faces of those present, he was reminded of a similar scene he had witnessed twenty-seven years previously in front of Pontius Pilate.

He also recognized a group that he had seen before. They had been present at the joyful reception the missionaries received on their arrival at Jerusalem, but they had been huddled together in a corner not cheering, but just observing what was going on. Silas was now sure that they were the leaders of the dissident Christian Jews from Asia Minor who had never forgiven Paul for his persecution of them and were determined to get revenge.

Paul spoke in Hebrew, the native language of those who were attempting to persecute him. "I am a Jew, proud of my heritage," he told them. "I was born and educated in Tarsus. Then as a young man I came to Jerusalem to study the Law with the learned Pharisee Gamaliel. Because of my zeal for the Law, I wrongly persecuted the early believers.

"While I was on my way to Damascus to arrest as many Christians as possible, I was blinded by a great light. As I fell to the ground I heard the voice of Jesus. Those with me heard the voice, but saw no one. The Jesus who was to become my savior was talking to me.

"He told me that my companions should be instructed to lead me to the home of Judas in Damascus. After three days there, my sight was restored by Ananias, a pious man of Damascus known by all Jews as one who truly loved the Law. Then I was instructed to repent, be baptized, and prepare to be a witness for the God of our father by going out and telling his people all that had happened to me."

Silas had been watching the mixed crowd while Paul spoke to them and was relieved to observe that both Christian Jews and Judaists seemed to be receptive to his message. He hoped that they were beginning to believe Paul had not defiled the Temple or abandoned his ancestral faith and should be forgiven for persecuting the early Christians.

"Then I heard the voice of Jesus once more," Paul said. "This time I was told not to go to Jerusalem because I would not be believed there, but to go to the Gentiles instead. Although I did not want to leave my own, I knew it was God's will that I minister to others."

Silas was stunned to see the reaction of the Jews when they heard what Paul had said. In an instant the crowd had become an unruly mob again, just from hearing those last few words. The Judaists were now sure Paul had taken a Gentile into the Temple, and the Jews from Asia Minor saw an opportunity if they gave their support to the Judaists. Both groups had heard enough; they were determined to kill Paul.

Once more the battalion commander came to his rescue by ordering him returned to the barracks. The officer did not understand what Paul had said to inflame the crowd, and he must know what it was in order to handle the situation properly. A standard procedure was in place for this situation. To find out what Paul had said to create such an uproar, he would have him flogged until he explained exactly what it was. He believed that it had something to do with the statement he made about being ordered not to come to Jerusalem.

Just as the horrible beating was about to begin, Paul cautioned the centurion attending him by informing him that he had not been condemned, and that moreover he was a Roman citizen, showing the wooden diptych that confirmed his citizenry. The centurion passed this information on to the commander, who was horrified by what he had almost done. Scourging a Roman citizen was forbidden, and if it had taken place, the commander would have been severely punished.

Of course he realized that Paul could have murdered a Roman citizen and stolen his diptych, but the commander did not think that Paul was capable of such a violent act. Also, he realized that if he did not believe Paul's claim of citizenship and had him flogged, a messenger might be sent to Tarsus where, if Paul's Roman citizenship were authentic, it would be so registered in the census. The commander did not want to chance his career coming to a sudden end, so without hesitating, he rescinded the order to have Paul flogged.

The commander conceived a plan. He appeared before the crowd and said that both those protesting and the man under arrest were obviously deeply troubled about a difference in their religious beliefs, but before any charge against Roman law could be considered, any offense committed against a Jewish law would have to be handled by the Sanhedrin. The crowd had to accept the ruling.

Although the commander's decision would ease his burden, it would also produce a very complex state of affairs in the Jewish High Court:

The Christian Jews from Asia Minor, instead of placing charges against Paul before the Christian church council, would now be supporting charges of the Judaists against Paul in the Supreme Court, and it was hostile to those of the Christian faith.

Paul would be appearing as a Christian Jew before the same court that had commissioned him twenty-four years earlier to persecute Christian Jews.

Later Paul had defied this same court when he was converted to Christianity and joined those he had sworn to destroy.

His change of heart, however, had not appeased all those whom he had persecuted. The Jews of Asia Minor were some of those who had never forgiven Paul for persecuting their loved ones, and standing before the Sanhedrin, they would not be in a favorable position to obtain satisfaction.

Paul would be pleading his case before the court that had unsuccessfully ordered his arrest at Damascus many years before. In the eyes of the Sanhedrin, Paul was a fugitive from justice.

The Supreme Court agreed to hear the case, and at the appointed hour the commander led the military detachment that marched Paul off to defend himself against whatever charges that would be made. The commander was legally responsible for his prisoner even in the Jewish High Court, although it was not mandatory for him to personally accompany the accused man. Silas was able to slip into the court just before the proceedings were to begin.

When the session began, the Judaists, who were now in control, referred only to Jewish law. They had no need here to claim that Paul had broken the law of Rome. They attempted to win the favor of the court by accusing Paul of destroying the heritage of the Jews and diminishing Judaism, the religion the Supreme Court was pledged to protect. They said that the ruckus he caused outside the military barracks was a result of his heresy.

Then Paul was called to be interrogated by the court that considered him one of their most wanted, although there was no way they could legally charge him. When Paul was asked to explain why he had caused such a disturbance on the streets of Jerusalem, Silas was startled by the words he heard coming from Paul's mouth.

First of all he did not use the prescribed form of address when he began to talk to the august body, but spoke to them as equals. Silas knew that this obvious lack of respect would not go well with the high priest, so he was not surprised when Ananias ordered the court attendant to strike Paul for his indiscretion.

Then it was Paul's turn again. Silas was shocked to hear Paul declare that striking him was illegal. This remark brought Sadducee members of the court into action. They accused Paul of insulting the high priest. Paul replied to this accusation by saying he was unaware that the man who gave the order to strike him was the high priest.

At this point the Sadducees returned to their places and the court suddenly became quiet, everyone waiting anxiously for what would happen next. Silas smiled to himself at Paul's response, because he knew his friend well enough to understand that he meant the man he had addressed was not worthy of being the high priest. Ananias had a very questionable moral standing.

Paul broke the apprehensive silence. He shouted out, "I am not on trial for attempting to destroy my heritage and cause a ruckus. I am a Pharisee and am on trial because I believe in the resurrection of the dead." The Sadducees, who did not believe in life after death, jumped up at once to protest what Paul had said.

Immediately, a great argument that had taken place between the two parties many times before broke out once more. Paul's strategy had succeeded. Now the commander began to worry again about a riot. Even an argument in the Sanhedrin could develop into an uprising in the streets. To put an end to something that might escalate into another difficult situation, he ordered the high priest to dismiss the court and marched Paul back to the barracks. Relieved that Paul would be safe, Silas slipped away unobserved.

That night as Paul slept in prison, he was told in a dream that the time had come to take The Way to Rome. As he pondered on this the next afternoon, his nephew came to give him valuable information about a meeting held earlier that same day.

After their failure, the Christian Jews from Asia Minor were more desperate than ever to do away with Paul. They selected the forty most determined of their number to go to the Hall of Hewn Stone. They would appear before the court as faithful Judaists and not as Christian Jews.

They would demonstrate that they were righteous and justify their proposed action by registering their vow to neither eat nor drink until they had killed Paul, the heretic, who they would claim was determined to destroy Judaism.

The Jews from Asia Minor knew that the Supreme Court was just as anxious as they were to get rid of Paul. They wanted Paul punished for killing Christians. The Sanhedrin wanted Paul punished for not killing Christians. The Jews knew that without Paul present to set the members of the court against each other, they could obtain the court's recognition of their devotion to Judaism and then ask for help to eliminate their common enemy.

Soon after the forty men arrived at the court they were granted an audience.

Once they received the blessing for what they proposed to do, they disclosed their plan. "We respectfully ask you to contact the battalion commander and request Paul's presence before you for further questioning. Explain that because this time the hearing will be informal, and without any of the accusing parties present, it should not be necessary for the commander to be there. Tell the commander that a small detachment to escort Paul to the court and return him to prison will be sufficient, and there will be no need for a further waste of his valuable time.

"The commander prefers not to appear before the court, so it is likely that a hearing he does not have to attend would please him. After the arrangement has been completed, some of our group of devoted Jews will hide along the chosen route. When Paul comes to meet with you, they will kill him.

"It is not likely that his small escort of soldiers will interfere. They will realize that Paul's mysterious disappearance would mean just one less potential problem for their commander. All of us will be rid of the traitor, and there will be no evidence to implicate any of you."

Members of the court, Pharisees as well as Sadducees, saw nothing wrong with this plan and agreed to carry it out.

Paul's nephew, a worker in the court, was within hearing distance during the entire meeting, and as soon as it became possible the young man left the Hall of Hewn Stone and walked calmly through the adjacent Temple to the street outside. Once there he hurried to the barracks where he knew his uncle was imprisoned. He was granted permission to visit Paul, and as soon as they were alone, he told him all that he had heard.

Paul, appreciating the risk his nephew had taken, thanked him for what he had done, but then asked him for even more help. "If I am to escape from those who would murder me," he said, "I need the help of the battalion commander. This means that you must tell him your story. To get to his quarters you must be escorted there by the guard on duty. He has been treating me kindly and I believe he will cooperate. I now ask you to go to his station and request that he come to me."

Of course the boy agreed to do this, and before long he returned with the guard. Paul told the guard that his nephew had an important message for the battalion commander and requested that he be taken to him. With just a little hesitation, the guard made it known that he would do his best to get the boy an audience. After some time the guard and Paul's nephew returned.

When the boy was alone with Paul, he explained what had happened. "Not only was the guard successful in convincing the commander to see me," he began, "but the officer believed my story and was incensed that the Jewish High Court would attempt to dupe him and allow a murder to be committed. He told me to say nothing to anyone about the situation and not to worry because he would send you to Caesarea where you would be protected and treated fairly."

A short time later the commander began a letter to Felix, the governor of the Roman province of Judea. In it he described Paul's appearance before the Jewish Supreme Court. He explained that he had taken him there because he believed there were charges against him for some infringement of one of the many strange Jewish laws that should be disposed of before charges against Roman law could be considered.

He wrote that when the hearing ended in an argument between rival Jewish political parties, he had Paul taken to prison to protect him from his antagonists and prevent the possibility of an uprising.

Then he told the governor that a young informant whom he considered reliable had come to his office a day later to report what he had just overheard while working in the Sanhedrin. He repeated the boy's story about the attempt of the Jewish High Court to bypass him and allow a group of dissidents to murder Paul. The commander told the governor that because of this development he believed the case should be tried by Rome and not the Jewish court, and because of the unusual circumstances surrounding it, the defendant should be sent to the capital to be tried in the higher court there.

He said he was positive that as soon as it was discovered that Paul had been taken to Caesarea, one of the parties involved would send a delegation there to charge him with some violation of the Roman law. He finished the letter by explaining that Paul would be escorted to the capital by troops for his protection and would have already arrived there when the governor read the letter. Then he respectfully asked for a fair trial.

Late that night the commander sent for a centurion and ordered him to assemble a large detachment and prepare to escort Paul out of Jerusalem under the cover of darkness. When the troops were ready to leave, the commander gave the centurion the letter with the instruction to deliver it personally to the governor immediately on arrival at Caesarea. Then the small army started out.

Paul mounted one of the baggage animals and rode in the midst of the seventy-man cavalry. A heavy rearguard of foot soldiers followed behind. By morning the horsemen and Paul had reached Antipatris, forty miles away from Jerusalem and twenty-five miles from Caesarea. When the foot soldiers arrived the next day and confirmed that Paul had come to no harm, they returned to Jerusalem. Paul then proceeded with the cavalry and arrived at Caesarea later the same day.

The governor sent for Paul and promised him a fair trial if someone arrived to present charges. In the meantime, he explained, because Paul had been accused of crimes against Rome, he would be kept in prison.

About the time Paul arrived at the capital, Silas learned that a small delegation from the group of forty assassins was on its way to visit the Sanhedrin and request an audience with the chief priests. The plotters were anxious to receive confirmation that their plan was working. While they were on their way to the court, the remaining assassins were busy searching for a suitable hiding place.

When the members of the delegation arrived at the Hall of Hewn Stone, they were informed that the battalion commander had been contacted and the request of the faithful forty for Paul to be returned to the Sanhedrin for questioning had been made, but the message received back was that it would be impossible for Paul to appear before the Supreme Court again because he was on his way to the provincial capital.

Then the chief priests said that the commander had told them if anyone wished to prosecute Paul, it would have to be for an infringement of Roman law, and the trial would have to take place at Caesarea.

The Jews from Asia Minor were devastated, but then the high priest spoke. "Do not despair; I intend to go to Caesarea myself to make sure that the heretic Paul receives the death sentence he deserves."[2]

Chapter 23

Caesarea

ALONE IN HIS cell at the praetorium built by Herod, Paul gave no thought to the possibility that his antagonists might come to Caesarea and convince the governor that he was guilty of a crime bearing the death sentence. He was not concerned about the wonders of Caesarea-on-the-Sea either. He had no interest in the magnificent double aqueduct that brought water from the springs at the foot of nearby Mount Carmel. Of course it was on Mount Carmel that Elijah had challenged and defeated the prophets of Baal;[1] but that was long ago and Paul's concerns were not about the past. He had no interest either in the huge theater or the cleverly engineered harbor; both built by Herod the Great. His mind was only on the future. He knew the time would soon come when he and Silas would take The Way to Rome.

After Paul had been in Herod's praetorium for several days, and Pentecost had come and gone, word came that a group of notables had just arrived from Jerusalem prepared to charge him with crimes against the government. A day later, when he was led into the courtroom, he was relieved to see Silas, his faithful friend of a quarter century, and an empty seat next to him where he could sit.

Paul barely had time to greet Silas when he saw Ananias, the unscrupulous high priest. He was surprised to see him in a civil courtroom where officially he had no authority, but Paul knew that the cunning man wouldn't be present unless he was confident that he could use his influence to get the verdict he wanted.

Felix entered and the room became silent as the governor began to speak. "The court will now come to order; I am ready to hear the charges. So we can begin, will the group from Jerusalem please introduce themselves."

Ananias jumped up in response. "I am at Caesarea for that exact purpose. For those who might not know, I am the high priest. However, because I am in a civilian court, I am present here only as an interested observer and not in my official capacity."

Silas whispered to Paul, "He certainly lies with ease. I'm sure that his disguised role today will be that of chief prosecutor. Fortunately, he will not be as dangerous here as when he sits as judge in the Jewish Supreme Court."

"That's enough about me," Ananias continued. "We have several respected members here of a righteous group dedicated to the task of bringing justice to Judea. You will meet most of them as we proceed. First I would like to introduce Tertullus, a very learned man and the official lawyer of the group. He will present the facts that will prove that the accused man, Paul, is the leader of a sect dedicated to eliminating the Roman presence in Judea."

"Now that you have introduced your official lawyer, may I suggest that you let him present his case," Felix said.

"Thank you," Tertullus said as he jumped up. "I will begin. But there is one matter to bring up that may be more important even than the evidence we will present. Before I make a single accusation, I must make use of this opportunity to offer our deepest gratitude to you, our most worthy governor, for the many improvements you have made that have benefited most of us here today. We will be forever grateful to you, our country's great leader, for the peace we enjoy and all the wonderful things you have done for all Judeans." When Tertullus paused and glanced at Ananias, he received an encouraging nod from the high priest.

"Did you ever hear such sickening rubbish, Paul?" Silas whispered. "How long is he going to babble on like this?"

"Now to get down to the business before us. Let me tell you, honorable governor, this man Paul has initiated unrest among Jews everywhere. He has traveled throughout the world, and most recently he caused a serious ruckus in Jerusalem. I believe his goal is to start a major disturbance that will develop into a riot."

Tertullus could see that Ananias was well pleased. "Now hear this. He is the leader of the Nazarenes, a notorious group known to be a rebel sect. I'm sure you know better than I that sects of one kind or another have caused the authorities of the Roman government elsewhere a great deal of trouble in the past and are a continual source of anxiety for leaders like yourself. They are often led by a fiery leader, such as Paul is, who encourages public protest. I believe Paul intends to drive the Romans out of Judea."

Assisted by several silent consultations with Ananias, Tertullus presented a host of additional falsified but harmless charges against Paul. Then he introduced other members of the group from Jerusalem, who of course confirmed that everything their lawyer had said was absolutely true. Tertullus rested his case and sat down next to Ananias.

"Now, Paul, let the court hear how you will defend yourself," Felix said.

Silas sat nervously waiting to hear what his friend would say.

"First let me point out, your honor, that I have only been in Jerusalem for a very few days, so it would be easy for one of your staff to determine exactly where I have been and what I have done, and to confirm that I have caused no trouble at all and that all accusations made against me are false and contrived.

"Tertullus said something about what he termed a rebel sect. I know nothing of any rebel sect. The gathering of truly righteous men that I am part of is the Christian outgrowth of Judaism, which is the faith of both Tertullus and the court observer Ananias. The Way, as our Christian belief is often called, has neither the desire nor the ability to eliminate the Roman presence in Judea.

"Now I will tell you what really caused the ruckus in Jerusalem that Tertullus referred to. I returned to Jerusalem after many years of absence for the express purpose of bringing a gift of money to the impoverished and forgotten Jews of the city. After presenting the purse to those so desperately in need of help, I went to the Temple—not to cause a disturbance, but to sponsor a group of devout Jews performing the purification rite.

"While I was participating in this most holy ritual, I was seized by a mob of misinformed Jews. Perhaps they were members of the rebel sect Tertullus referred to. They dragged me out onto the street shouting and yelling and threatening to kill me. I was arrested, but only for my own protection. This was the ruckus Tertullus brought to your attention. None of those who caused it are here at Caesarea today.

"Neither Tertullus, the observer Ananias, nor anyone else has reason to suspect that I have committed an offense against Rome. The only legitimate accusation that this group from Jerusalem could make against me would be my refusal to follow the high priest's order several years ago to murder members of The Way in Damascus, but my action at that time did nothing to eliminate the Roman presence in Judea."

Paul could see that he had the full attention of the governor as he began his closing statement, "Now I will tell you what this trial is really all about. I'm sure you can see that the group Tertullus represents is none other than the Sanhedrin. That body is controlled by Ananias, who is determined to eliminate me for personal reasons. That is why he is here in Caesarea today. I believe the high priest should be asked what his motive was to take the trouble to assemble a legal team and travel a great distance with them to charge me with a civil offense, knowing he did not have a shred of evidence that I was guilty. That is all I have to say."

Felix was visibly impressed by Paul's presentation, but he was in an awkward position. After hesitating briefly he said, "Because the testimony is very confusing, I want to hear the background of the case from the battalion commander when he pays his next visit to Caesarea, before I proceed to a decision. The court is now adjourned. I will give ample notice before reconvening."

The accusing party was dismissed and Paul was returned to prison, but this time he was given the privilege of receiving visitors.

A day later Timothy and Luke arrived to join Silas and be near Paul. As the weeks passed, Silas discovered that he and his friends were not the only ones to take counsel with Paul. Felix often sent for Paul, requesting him to be brought to the governor's residence and meet with him and Drusilla, his Jewish wife.

Whenever Felix asked about Paul's faith in Jesus Christ and Paul answered by talking about righteousness and judgment, Felix became visibly nervous, but the governor's apparent sense of guilt did not prevent him from hinting that a bribe might bring Paul complete freedom. Paul, of course, paid no attention to this and time passed slowly on. After he had been held for two years and the battalion commander had still not put in an appearance, Felix was recalled to Rome.

Felix had been gone less than a week when Nero appointed Porcius Festus to succeed him. Just three days after the new governor arrived at Caesarea, he went to Jerusalem to meet the Jewish authorities and explain his policies to Ananias.

Silas was relieved when he heard that although Festus had agreed with Ananias that Paul's trial should be delayed no longer, he had insisted that it be reconvened at Caesarea, and not at Jerusalem as Ananias had suggested. The high priest could not object to the governor's decision. Festus returned to the capital after spending several days with the Roman authorities of Jerusalem, and a delegation from the Sanhedrin, led by Ananias, followed soon after.

As soon as Paul's adversaries arrived and made their presence known, the governor convened the court. Festus took his seat and summoned both parties to enter. The high priest was asked to speak first, then several members of his party were invited to have their say. Silas stood with his friends, and together they listened to a long list of unsubstantiated charges against Paul.

When Paul got his chance to speak, he denied the charges, one by one, rightfully claiming that he had never committed any offense against the Law, the Temple, or Rome.

Festus seemed to be sympathetic with Paul, but he had to consider his favorable position with the Jews of Jerusalem.

"I believe we have heard enough for today," he said. "A great deal has been accomplished and one more session should be sufficient. Because most of the alleged offenses were committed in Jerusalem, we will conduct the remainder of the case there in one week's time. Of course, I will be present to insure a just and fair verdict."

Silas was not surprised to hear Paul object to that trip to disaster. Murder on the road to Jerusalem would be the way the trial would be concluded.

"Because I have committed no offense against my own people, there is no reason why I should go to Jerusalem and be tried in the Jewish Supreme Court. I have committed no crime, but if there is one, it can only be against Rome. I am a Roman citizen and demand to be taken to Rome to be tried by Caesar."

Festus was stunned, but he could not refuse this request. Paul was informed that he would be taken to Rome as soon as transportation could be arranged.

While Paul was waiting in the praetorium, Herod Agrippa II, king of Galilee and son of Agrippa I, murderer of James, the brother of John, arrived at Caesarea. He had come with his wife Bernice who was the sister of Drusilla, the wife of Felix. Agrippa had come, as was his custom, to pay homage to the Roman governor.

Once the governor had disposed of the mandatory greeting and preliminary business discussion, he told Agrippa about Paul's trial and his demand to be tried by Caesar. He explained that he did not understand the offense Paul had been charged with and asked Agrippa to listen to the prisoner's story in a formal court session so he could give his interpretation. Agrippa agreed to do this.

When the day of the hearing arrived, the governor and the king entered the crowded court dressed in all their finery. Festus opened the session by explaining to everyone that he believed if Paul was guilty of any offense, it was against some Jewish law he was not familiar with, and the purpose of the hearing was to determine what the proper charge would be to send to Rome. Then he introduced King Agrippa and explained that because he was a Jew, he was well qualified to make this determination.

After this introduction, Paul was asked to speak. He began to tell the story of his life beginning with his birth in Tarsus. Paul talked on and on, fully intending to continue the tale up to the present day. Festus finally became impatient, and when he could take no more of what he considered to be absolute nonsense, he jumped up and shouted, "Paul, you're mad, stop your raving and sit down."

"I am not mad. Ask Agrippa whether I'm sane or not. He will have understood all that I have said."

By now Agrippa was getting tired of Paul's talk also, and he replied sarcastically, "Are you trying to carry on long enough to convince me to become one of those Christians, too?"

"King Agrippa, I pray that not only you, but everyone else in this room will eventually believe as I do."

"Paul, stop talking at once. I've had enough. The court is dismissed."

As Festus and Agrippa rushed out, Silas heard the king say to Festus, "This man should not have to face the possibility of imprisonment and even death in Rome. He could have been freed if he had not appealed to Caesar."

Festus was left with no alternative but to send Paul off to Rome, even without a clear charge against him. He ordered Paul to be returned to prison, this time under the custody of Julius, a Roman centurion of a force that served as a liaison between the provinces and Caesar. He would be responsible for Paul until he was imprisoned in Rome.

Silas, Timothy, and Luke had to accept the fact that Paul was going to Rome, not as a missionary, but as a prisoner. Of course they had no intention of deserting him. One way or another they would follow him, although they had no idea how they could do it.

As time went by, Julius became very friendly, first with Paul, and then with those who came to visit him. Eventually this friendship became strong enough that it gave Silas a bold idea. He asked Julius if he, the other two missionaries, and Aristarchus, a faithful friend, could accompany Paul to Rome. With just a slight hesitation, Julius agreed.

The next day Silas stopped to talk with one of the soldiers assigned to the praetorium and shared the good news with him.

"He's a crafty one, that centurion," the soldier replied.

"What do you mean?"

"Paul's not the only prisoner going to Rome, but he's probably the only harmless one. The others are hardened criminals. If they manage to break loose from their shackles, which they probably will, Julius, a handful of soldiers, and the crew together would not be able to subdue them. The centurion was pleased to have the opportunity to increase the size of his force. Of course, I don't think the help the four of you will provide is likely to change the outcome of any outbreak on board."

Silas descended rapidly from the height of happiness to the depth of depression, worried that he had invited his friends to join him in a watery grave. They would probably never reach Rome.[2]

Chapter 24

A Perilous Voyage

ROME HAD HUNDREDS of galleys serving as warships, but the government would seldom make one of them available as a prison ship. After Julius and the others had waited several days for commercial passage, a ship going to Asia Minor stopped at Caesarea. A day later the mixed group marched on board, and the first lap of the voyage began.

They had not sailed far when Silas realized that conditions on board, at least for Paul and his friends, bore little resemblance to those he had anticipated they would encounter on a prison ship. He could see that Julius continued to treat Paul with kindness and courtesy. He heard him tell Paul that he could meet with his friends whenever he wanted to. The prisoners, other than Paul, were confined and guarded by the soldiers, leaving Julius free to listen to what the missionaries were discussing.

Silas only hoped that the water would treat them as kindly as Julius was doing. It would soon be that time of the year when the sea sometimes became violent and the threat of winter storms made sailing too risky to chance. If they should encounter severe weather on their way to Rome, Silas hoped that the ship they were on had been as well built as that specially-constructed vessel that took them from Troas to Macedonia ten years before.

After two days sailing north close to the coast on a calm sea, the ship put in at Sidon, an important Phoenician trading center. Taking Paul on the first part of his journey to appeal to Caesar was not the captain's only concern. He had freight cargo to unload at Sidon, as well as other ports along the coast of Asia Minor.

Because of the late-autumn prevailing western winds, the next leg of the voyage was more difficult. They sailed first north and then west, making use of the protection afforded by the island of Cyprus. Then they spent the next few days tacking along the shore of Asia Minor before receiving help, from both land breezes and currents running along the coast, which brought them to Myra, a port and city of the territory of Lydia. This was as far as the ship would carry them.

Julius was lucky. Before long he had located and leased a ship loaded with Egyptian corn tied up at Myra and ready to leave for Rome.[1]

Silas had a personal interest in the ship, because it hailed from Alexandria, the city of his birth and youth. When he talked to members of the crew, he was amazed to be told about the circuitous route the ship had been forced to take to avoid the treacherous fall weather they would have encountered if they sailed northwest from Alexandria directly to Rome.

The Alexandrian ship, forced to follow a course dictated by the weather, left port with great difficulty. Each day's sail seemed to be more formidable than the previous one. The fear of the sea, that Silas thought was a thing of his past, began to return.

With considerable effort the ship made its way along the coast of Asia Minor before turning southwest into deep water. It was headed toward the island of Crete, a Roman province known to have a Jewish presence and a Christian following. Silas surmised that the Good News had been introduced to the Cretans by a few pilgrims returning from the Pentecost experience at Jerusalem.

The ship dodged the dangerous lee shore of the north coast of Crete, but it could not avoid the treacherous water of the Cape of Salmone as it rounded the eastern end of the island. From there it managed to fight its way along the southern shore where it found some protection from the northwest winds.

Eventually the ship docked at the small harbor of Fair Havens. The unfavorable weather had made the voyage to this point very slow and put it even further into the season of dangerous sailing. Silas had not been comforted by the realization that he had not seen any other ships on the water for several days, but the vessel made it to a port, and he joined the other missionaries to give thanks for surviving the treacherous sea.

Silas walked over to where Julius was standing staring at the not-too-distant, still-churning sea. "Julius, I think we experienced a miracle these last few days. I don't believe there could be any other explanation for our survival. We're very fortunate to have made it here to a harbor that is protected by small islands surrounding it. It's the ideal place to remain over the winter."

"I'm not so sure that's what the captain plans to do, Silas."

"What are you talking about? We would risk death if we left here now. I'm sure that we are long past the safe sailing season. I'll be glad when we're allowed to go on shore. It would be insane to leave Fair Havens before the favorable spring weather."

"Silas, it will be a business decision the captain makes. He will probably be influenced more by greed than by safety."

"I don't understand."

"Well, as you know this ship is heavily loaded with corn for Rome. You also know that it started out late in the season when sailing would soon become risky, but what you don't know is this is just the way the owner planned it. The later the corn arrives in Rome, the higher the price will be, and therefore the greater the owner's profit and the captain's commission will be. If the ship winters here and delivers the corn in spring, its value will have shrunk considerably, and the captain's bonus will have disappeared. But, I agree with you that we should stay right where we are now until the weather is more suitable for sailing, so I will go to the captain and see what I can do. I wish I had the authority to offer him a higher fee for remaining at Fair Havens, but unfortunately I don't."

Before long Julius returned. "Well, I had partial success. The captain said that neither he nor his crew had any intention of spending lonely months in an isolated town on the deserted coast of Crete. If they were to winter anywhere other than Rome it would be at the larger port of Phoenix, further along the southern shore of the island. He and many others were at Phoenix on a previous voyage. They know they would have a lively time there. The captain agreed to delay his decision on whether or not to attempt to go to Rome before winter until we arrive at Phoenix."

And so, to the dismay of Silas and the others, the captain announced that they were preparing to leave Fair Havens. Then, just after they left the port, a light southerly wind came up. Conditions had suddenly become ideal to carry them toward Phoenix, eighty miles further up the coast of Crete. The missionaries began to relax.

Soon, however, the gentle breeze began to strengthen, and before long it had grown into a tempestuous storm out of the northeast. Then it became so strong and unmanageable that the captain had no choice but to yield to it and run before the gale, letting the wild wind take him where it would—further out to sea. With the sail trimmed, the ship passed into some protection on the sheltered side of a small island that the captain recognized as Cauda.

Here he decided to bring the dinghy on board. He had been towing it behind and was anxious to get it out of the water before the waves dashed it to pieces against the ship. The crew members assigned needed every bit of their strength to bring the small boat on the deck.

By now the storm was so severe that the captain feared the ship might be broken apart. The sailors encircled it with ropes to hold it together. By this time they were being blown in the direction of the deadly Syrtis Sands, a site off the coast of Africa, that had been the burial ground of many ships. The captain ordered the crew to lower the mainsail, and begin to lighten the load by throwing any gear not needed overboard.

For several more dark days and darker nights the ship was tossed about in a violent storm. Without sun or stars the crew had no way to determine the course by day or by night and no way to control where the ship was headed. Miles of angry waves propelled by gale force winds were throwing the ship wherever they pleased. Faces were raw from stinging rain driven by the unrelenting wind. During the long nights the roar of the thunder seemed louder and the streaks of lightning more terrifying. The momentary light the fireworks gave only exaggerated the darkness that followed.

Because of the dwindling supplies, no one had been allowed food for several days. Only the missionaries, of all those on board, truly had any hope of surviving the storm. They were confident that their faith would see them through one more crisis.

Although Paul, like Silas and others, had objected to the captain's decision to leave Fair Havens, he still felt responsibility for the plight of his companions because of his insistence to take his case to Caesar. Because of that responsibility, he knew that it was time for him to assume authority over the centurion, the captain, and the owner of the cargo.

He knew that he had no right to do so, but he also knew that he alone could save all those on board, so he called everyone to gather together. When they had assembled, he began by criticizing the captain for not remaining in Fair Havens. Then he told them that the time had come to listen to him.

"Although I am just a prisoner on this ship, I have the advantage of a relationship with the one true God. I told many of you about the revelation I received on the road to Damascus. Now I will tell you that I received another revelation during last night's darkness. An angel of God appeared to me and assured me that I was destined to reach Rome. He told me that although our ship will be lost, everyone's life will be spared. We will be stranded, but left unharmed on an island somewhere in the midst of the Great Sea. We will all be saved. You must get rid of your fear."

Calm was immediately restored to the ship, but not to the sea.

Silas was aware that the non-ending battering the merciless sea gave the ship was dulling his mind, but he did his best to keep a count of the days. If his reckoning was correct, it was during the fourteenth terrible night since the ship had left Fair Havens that a storm-piercing shout reminded him of Paul's words that all would be saved. “Land! Land! We’re close to land. I know we are. I can hear waves exploding on the shore.” Silas’s faith told him that the sailor knew what he was shouting about.

Then the voice of a second seaman cried out, “Twenty fathoms.” And minutes later, “Fifteen fathoms. We’re being driven to shore. Do something, quick. The ship will be demolished if that’s a rocky coast waiting for us.”

Paul rushed up to the captain and said, “We must hold away from land until morning. I believe the torrential rain is letting up, and if this is so we may be able to see what we have to cope with at daybreak.”

The captain responded immediately, shouting, “Drop four anchors off the stern,”

As soon as the stern anchors grabbed hold, three sailors began to lower the dinghy, announcing that they would put out anchors from the bow. Paul knew that their real intent was to abandon ship and make for shore in the small boat, which would be a suicidal act. Before the sailors could get into the dinghy, Paul told Julius that he must keep them on board for their own safety. Without hesitating, the centurion ordered one of his men to cut the boat loose, and it was carried away by the waves.

Paul’s message about the divine help he was receiving gained him the respect of the crew. Then, when Julius ordered the dinghy cut free just as Paul had directed, they knew their fate was in the hands of Paul and were ready to listen when he spoke.

“I want everyone to take a bit of food from the little that we have left. You have not eaten for many days. You must have some nourishment in order to survive the ordeal that I know lies ahead of you. And now the time has come to lighten the ship further. The corn must be thrown overboard.”

No protest came from the owner when he heard Paul’s order. He had realized some days ago that his ship was doomed. Financial loss no longer mattered. His life was more important to him than any amount of wealth.

The driving and blinding rain subsided with the first hint of daylight, and all those on board the ship had a glimpse of land for the first time in two weeks. Paul told the captain the time had come to beach the ship. He replied by giving the order to cut the anchors loose and set the sail.

After consulting with Paul, Julius issued orders for the prisoners to be freed and everyone to abandon ship as soon as it was grounded. The soldiers were well aware that they would have to suffer the punishment the prisoners had been sentenced to if any of them escaped after leaving the ship. To prevent this from happening they were preparing to follow the standard procedure and kill every one of them. Paul's life was in Julius's hands.

Before the soldiers could make their first move, he ordered them to drop their weapons. They hesitated, amazed at the unusual order. Then the ship hit bottom with a jolt, and the centurion ordered everyone to jump into the foaming sea. Fearful for their own lives, the soldiers sheathed their weapons and followed the others into the water.

Some of the prisoners—gripped by fear—had refused to move, so Julius repeated his order, telling them to grab one of the floating planks that had been ripped away from the ship while it was being tossed about by the waves. He assured them that if they held on to a plank it would keep them afloat until they reached the beach.

The sea had retained enough strength to rock the beached ship, making it difficult to maneuver on deck, but Silas was able to work his way to the edge. He said a prayer and leaped into the churning waves. When he hit the water, he discovered that it was possible to be even colder than he had been on board the ship.

After the first few strokes toward land, he felt a sharp pain. The waves had tossed a large loose plank against his left arm. He grabbed one side of the plank with his right hand and somehow managed to get his left hand onto the other side in spite of the pain he still felt. Unable to swim easily with just one arm, he decided to ride the waves to shore holding on to the board.

Waves crashed over Silas, forcing stinging salt water into his eyes. After what seemed like hours Silas could see dozens of figures ahead of him in the water, but they were walking not swimming. Then, when he pushed one foot down, he was able to feel bottom.

Letting go of the plank he stood and began to walk through the crashing surf. Even the pain in his arm subsided as he walked up onto dry land where he joined his joyful friends and Julius.

As Silas looked around at the men on the sandy beach, he wondered how many would not make it to safety. Then he remembered Paul's words and the promise of the angel.

When no one was left struggling in the water, Julius counted the number of survivors on the beach. When he finished, he announced that everyone, including the prisoners, had made it to shore. Then he confirmed that his men, assisted by the crew, had been able to confine all the prisoners, except for Paul of course. The prisoners were so thankful to be alive they had not resisted.

Paul asked everyone to gather while he gave thanks that they had been saved. Silas was sure that it was clear to everyone, including Julius, that the hand of God had been with them. Before long the captain of the ship announced that he believed they had landed on the island of Malta.[2] Soon natives of the island who had observed the ship being abandoned came down to the sandy beach. They looked dangerous, and Silas began to fear that the survivors had escaped death on the water only to receive it on land. He soon realized, however, that the natives meant no harm. Although they did not speak any language that the shipwrecked men understood, they tried to communicate and be helpful. They began to prepare a fire to warm the shivering survivors.

Then Silas noticed Paul, once more a missionary, but a prisoner and no longer the one in charge, trying to make himself useful by picking up a pile of brush to add to the fire. As he reached over to drop the sticks in the flames, a deadly viper hidden inside the bundle was driven out by the heat and seized his hand and clung to it. Horrified, Silas offered a prayer for Paul's life. Then when he glanced at the natives he could tell by their reaction that their superstitious beliefs had led them to conclude that Paul was being punished for some horrible sin.

Paul's instantaneous reaction was only to shake the viper off. Silas found it difficult to believe that Paul had apparently suffered no ill effect, and the natives could not understand why the visitor to their island had not succumbed to the deadly poison. Silas realized from the sudden change of expression on the natives' faces that they now were sure they had witnessed a miracle. They probably believed that Paul was a god and had been sent to them for some reason they did not yet understand. Silas's memory took him back to a similar situation at Lystra where the inhabitants thought Paul was a heathen god.

When news of the castaways' arrival on the isolated shore reached the interior, the Roman governor of the island came to the coast to welcome his unexpected visitors. Publius proved to be a friendly and hospitable host. He confirmed that they were indeed on the island of Malta. During a conversation with him, the missionaries learned that his father was very ill. They offered their help and Publius accepted.

The governor led the four men and Julius to his estate, where his father laid suffering from fever and dysentery. While Luke administered medical treatment the others, except Julius, offered prayer and the laying on of hands. After a few similar sessions the sick man was cured.

Word of the patient's recovery became known to everyone on that part of the island and the missionaries were soon besieged by requests from the sick for help. Most of those treated were cured just as the governor's father had been. Although the healing mission was very successful, unfortunately the language barrier prevented the missionaries from bringing the full meaning of the Gospel to the natives.

Three months passed. The governor told Julius that another corn ship from Alexandria and bound for Rome had wintered in Malta just a short distance up the coast, and was being prepared to leave its berth.

The captain told Julius that he had space for him, his men, the prisoners, and the missionaries. Julius assured Silas and Paul that he would arrange for a ship to come to Malta to pick up the others. The natives of Malta were so grateful for the gift of healing brought by the missionaries that they stocked the ship with sufficient provisions for the last part of their voyage.[3]

Silas's fear of the sea, which had returned with the violent stormy weather encountered on the sail to Malta, left him again on the peaceful voyage to Italy. After a pleasant day on calm water, the ship arrived at the island of Sicily and put in at Syracuse, where it remained for three days. The next stop was at Rhegium at the southwestern tip of Italy. After a brief stay there the missionaries were carried further up the west coast.

As the ship came closer to Rome, Julius became even friendlier and one day he came to Silas and began to talk to him about the city where he had been born.

"You will soon be in the political capital and the biggest city of the world, Silas."

"Julius, I can't wait to get there. For some time now I have believed that my destiny waits for me in Rome and that I will fulfill it by bringing the message of salvation through belief in Jesus Christ to many of the people living there."

"But you must take time to see my great city. The theaters, libraries, temples, baths and basilicas are magnificent creations of mankind."

"My interest is in God's magnificent creation—the people of the city—and they need to hear about his Son."

"Silas, you will think differently when you arrive at my beautiful Rome. It is built on seven hills nestled up against the Tiber River on the west. For the comfort of its people there are two huge aqueducts that bring water into the city and a recently installed sewage system."

"I'm sure that I will see some of Rome as I move around serving its people. You are very proud of your home city, Julius. Do you have a family living there?"

"I will find the only family I need at the barracks. I have devoted my life to Caesar."

Two days after the ship left Rhegium, a favorable south wind brought it within sight of a populated area,

"Silas," Julius said, "that's Puteoli you can see in the distance. Our sea voyage will end there. Although it's the closest good port to Rome, it is almost two hundred miles south of the city. We will have to walk the remaining distance."

"Walking will not bother any of us. We have spent most of our lives walking and preaching."

"Although Puteoli is important because it receives all sea shipments bound for Rome, it is also a playground for the wealthy of the capital. Members of the nobility come to enjoy the mineral baths and the sea breeze."

"People like them will probably not listen to us now, but I'm sure someday the wealthy will realize that there is something more important than money."

"Silas, look over there at the beach. It's crowded with people from the city, and beyond them you can see their pleasure crafts anchored off shore. Then, if you look a little further along the coast, you will see the huge fleet of Roman warships berthed at Misenum, which is the naval harbor in Puteoli Bay."

"That's a terrifying display of military might. Rome will be a very different city from any we have visited previously."

Before long the ship docked. Silas felt somewhat fearful when the missionaries and prisoners began to disembark, but his uncomfortable feeling disappeared shortly after they stepped onto dry land. They were greeted by a small group of believers who had returned to Rome after Claudius's death and had been told that missionaries had just landed. They were a few of the Christians who had read Paul's letter written to the Romans from Corinth three years previously and were now living at Puteoli. They were excited about being able to talk to the very man who had done so much to increase their knowledge of Jesus Christ and to enrich their lives, by giving them a better understanding of his message.

When the group urged the missionaries to stay with them, they were surprised to discover that Paul was a prisoner and at the mercy of the officer who was escorting him to Rome. Silas heard their plea and approached his friend Julius to beg him to allow Paul to remain at Puteoli even if it was just for a day or two.

He knew that Julius had come very close to all of the missionaries during their terrible sea experience and later at Malta, and Silas hoped for a favorable response. Sometimes he even thought that the centurion was beginning to accept their message. He recalled Peter's experience fifteen years before with Cornelius, another Roman centurion. Perhaps one more officer of Rome would become a believer. Whether Julius believed or not, he agreed to allow the group to stay at Puteoli temporarily so the missionaries could meet with the Christians there.

Seven days later he announced that it was time to move on. As soon as the soldiers freed the prisoners enough so that they could walk, they led the way. Julius and the missionaries followed a short distance behind. When they reached the Appian Way at Capua, Julius said they would be at the outskirts of Rome in a week's time.

The missionaries were still a good two day's walk from the city when they were met at the market town known as Forum of Appius by a small group of Christians who had come from Rome to greet them and walk the rest of the distance with them.

A day later, at the Three Taverns, a rest area for travelers on the Appian Way, a second Christian party from Rome arrived to meet and escort the missionaries. Silas and Paul were cheered by this warm welcome and the knowledge that there were more believers in the city than they had thought.[4]

The next day, when Silas took his first step into the city, he was reminded once more of his father's vision and his own feeling that he was being drawn to Rome. He was sure now that he was where his destiny waited for him and where he would complete the fulfillment of the pledge made to his grandfather.

Chapter 25

Rome

SILAS DID NOT see much of what Julius had described as a spectacular city as he entered Rome through the Appian Gate. A huge pagan temple in front of him blocked his view completely. Then he found out Julius had ordered one soldier to stay with him and sent the others into the city to place the prisoners in the Mammertime prison. Julius and the single soldier walked off with Paul and his friends as they wound their way around the outskirts of the city to the remote Jewish quarter.

Paul, because of his Roman citizenship, would be allowed to live in a private home under house arrest. When Julius located the place that had been assigned to Paul, he left the soldier to stand guard over him and then said good-bye.

Paul soon became comfortable in his prison home where he lived with Silas. He was allowed to earn a living by his trade and was given the freedom to receive visitors. Silas, Timothy, and Luke were with him when they were neither working nor meeting with the believers, and Aquila, Priscilla, Titus and Aristarchus came often.

Silas found out that although many living in the Jewish quarter of the city were Christians, the majority were not. Many of them refused to listen to him because he was a friend of Paul, who they thought must have committed some serious crime. Silas told Paul that he should make the truth known about what had happened to him and why it had happened. Paul agreed and invited some of the Jewish leaders to his prison home, hoping they would listen and believe him.

The leaders accepted the invitation, and when they arrived, Paul described his arrest in the Temple at Jerusalem, explaining that he had done absolutely nothing against his people, their ancestral customs, or Rome. He emphasized that he was a true and loyal Jew. Then he told them about his trial before Felix and Festus and that he was only under arrest in Rome because he had demanded to appear before Caesar.

Next he confessed that the real reason he had invited them to meet with him was to tell them about his belief that the Messiah they had been waiting for had already come to them. The visitors became agitated. They said that although they had received no report about him from their friends at Jerusalem, they had heard that he had not been well received by Jews elsewhere. Nevertheless, after some urging by Paul they agreed to meet with him again to learn more about what he believed.

A much larger group came to hear Paul a few days later. He talked to them all day long, emphasizing that Jesus was the Messiah who had come to fulfill the Law and the word of the prophets. As often happened, a few believed but most did not, and the arguments among them did not end until the majority who disagreed decided to leave.

As they began to walk out, Paul reminded them that the Holy Spirit had predicted through Isaiah that the Jews would not accept God's word. He finished by saying that because of their denial of the truth, the Christian missionaries would take their message outside the Jewish quarter to the Gentiles, and he knew that they would listen.[1]

Silas was devastated by the outcome of the day-long session. He no longer shared Paul's belief that all Israel would eventually become Christian. Jesus had come to his people as their Messiah, but they would not listen and believe. Silas feared more than ever that Christianity would become the religion of the Gentiles, and Judaism would remain the religion of the Jews, and the best they could hope for would be a peaceful coexistence.

After the last of the Jews had left, Paul told Silas it was now clear their goal would be to serve the Gentiles of Rome along with those few Jews who believed and who would meet with them. He told Silas again that he loved him as a blood brother and knew that if his trial went badly and he would no longer be able to minister, Silas would carry on alone to spread the word.

Silas learned that Paul would have more time than he had expected to devote to their mission in Rome. Someone who had a good connection to the court told him that the docket of cases waiting to be tried grew longer daily, and the order in which they were heard changed with the whim of the authorities. Because Paul was earning his keep, his imprisonment was of no cost to the government, so they would be in no hurry to get rid of him.

Both Silas and Paul were surprised, but comforted, by the number of visitors who came to the prison home where Paul lived with Silas and the guard. Of course, most of them lived in Rome, but Christians occasionally came from Jerusalem or one of the numerous places the two men had served to meet with them.

One visitor who lived in the city was not a Christian when he first arrived to talk with Silas and Paul. His name was Onesimus. He had heard about the missionaries and had come to see them because he was troubled. Little by little he told them what was bothering him.

First of all he said that he had been a slave. They could not understand why this would concern him. One out of three persons in Italy was a slave. They tried to assure Onesimus that slaves and free men were the same in their eyes and in the eyes of God.

Silas and Paul had often discussed slavery. Almost everyone recognized it as a necessary part of life and realized that the economy of the world was dependent on it. Any attempt to abolish slavery would result in massive violence and bloodshed, so it would probably always exist. They could not understand why the Essenes opposed slavery.

As Onesimus's visits continued, he gradually became not only a believer but a most helpful worker. Paul became very close to him and soon thought of him as a son.

One day he and Silas were shocked when Onesimus admitted that he was not a freed slave but a runaway slave. This created a serious problem for the two missionaries. To complicate matters even more, Onesimus confessed that he had robbed his master before he fled.

Silas and Paul now knew why he was troubled, and they knew what they must do. They valued Onesimus so much that they would like to have kept his services for the rest of his life, but they had no alternative except to return him to the rightful owner he had sinned against. Then they discovered the rightful owner was Philemon, a native of Colosse, a town near Ephesus. The missionaries had converted Philemon when they were serving at Ephesus, and he had become a very good friend.

Silas and Paul were puzzled by what Onesimus had done. They knew that in most families slaves were treated well. Often they were better off than free persons. The fact that Onesimus had run away made Silas and Paul wonder if he had been abused, but they could not believe that Philemon would have mistreated him. They both knew that runaway slaves were usually punished when they were returned to their owner, and the two men did not want Onesimus to be harmed. But they knew they must send him back to Philemon. Silas suggested that they send a letter to Philemon with Onesimus, and that he thought Paul should write it because of his special relationship with the slave.

"Yes, Silas, you are right. I will write as a devoted friend in Christ and not as an apostle. I will appeal to Philemon to make a decision about what should happen to Onesimus based on his love for God and his fellow man and not on his sense of duty to either you or me.

"I will acknowledge all that Onesimus has done for the church at Rome and tell him that we are thankful for the joy he has brought us. I will talk about Onesimus, whom I love as a son, and who has been a special blessing to me while I have been in prison. I will tell him we would have preferred to keep him here with us, but we knew that we had to send him back.

"I will explain that when he was a slave he was useful only as a slave, but now that he is a Christian he is useful to all of us as a servant not to man, but to God. I will tell him that when I send him back I am sending a part of me, and ask him to receive him as he would receive me. I will tell Philemon that I will compensate him for anything Onesimus stole from him and for any damage he caused."[2]

The letter was written and sent to Philemon with Onesimus, but Silas continued to think about the fact that a few slaves were mistreated by their masters because they were considered to be different in some way. Then he began to wonder about the possibility that both Christian Jews and Christian Gentiles might someday be mistreated by Rome because they were considered to be different from most others.

Although Christians in Rome had no reason to fear the government at the present time, Silas was concerned that in the future they might have reason to fear. Roman leaders were inclined to be fickle. When Nero Claudius Caesar had come into power six years before, he had proclaimed the arrival of a golden age and pledged to cooperate with the Senate. Then, however, Agrippina II, Nero's own mother, attempted to gain power and influence in the government. Nero did not hesitate to have her murdered, so he could rule unrestrained. This knowledge was enough for Silas to realize that the emperor would not hesitate to get rid of the Christians also, if it became expedient for him to do so.

One of the missionaries' special friends who came to Rome to pay his respects was Tychicus, a Christian from Ephesus whom Silas and Paul had not seen for a very long time. Tychicus brought some very welcome news with him. On a recent visit to Colosse he had met Onesimus. The slave had returned to Philemon. He had been treated well and accepted as a Christian.

Suspecting that their guest had a particular reason for coming to Rome, Silas asked how matters were at the Ephesian church. After a brief hesitation Tychicus said, "When you and Paul first started your ministry at Ephesus seven years ago you soon discovered that you were beginning a very difficult assignment. You had to confront superstitious pagans, non-believing Jews, charlatan healers and worshippers of Artemis. In spite of these obstacles you were able to spread the Gospel.

"Then you left, and bit by bit the good you had done began to be overcome by the bad that was still there. The opposing religious and philosophical forces in Ephesus have weakened the faith of some of the Christians, regardless of whether they were Gentiles or Jews.

"Paul, after you are tried before Caesar and declared innocent, as I know you will be, you and Silas must return to Ephesus to strengthen the belief of the Christians there before it is too late."

Paul replied that he hoped they would be able to do so, but added that in the meantime he and Silas would write a letter to the church at Ephesus before their guest left Rome and ask him to take it and circulate it among the church members when he returned.

Silas and Paul met the next morning to discuss what they should say to the Ephesians to comfort and encourage them. A week later the message the two missionaries had written was on its way to Ephesus.[3]

Some weeks after the letter had been sent off to the Ephesians, Silas told Paul about gossip he had heard on the streets of the Jewish quarter. "Apparently there have been rumors for some time about trouble in Jerusalem and speculation that if it continues, harsh measures will be taken to prevent it from escalating. The unrest is the result of the Jews becoming increasingly resentful of the Roman rule.

"A group of terrorists known as Zealots have become the chief troublemakers. Some say that they came from our party, the Pharisees, but that's difficult for me to believe. They are said to have the lofty but unattainable goal of the destruction of the Roman Empire and the restoration of Jewish independence. Some claim that the Zealots have murdered Jews who were suspected of collaborating with Rome. I wonder if any of the victims were Sadducees. They have always collaborated with Rome.

"The Zealot's method of disposing of a collaborator is to follow him into a large crowd where the deed will be easily concealed. Then at the proper moment, the Zealot pulls a dagger out from his robe and stabs the targeted suspect. Once the mission is accomplished, the Zealot disappears into the crowd. I fear that as time goes by the Zealots will receive more support from the people, and their misdeeds will then become easier to achieve and more prevalent. I worry that the wrong approach to justice that their zeal has taken them on will bring the heavy hand of Rome against them, and we Jews will be worse off than ever. The Zealots' way is not the Christian way."

A few days later Epaphras, a leader in the Colossian church, came to the door with a letter from Philemon that was a message of gratitude not only for returning Onesimus, but also for sending him a new friend in Christ.

Epaphras had come to report a problem at Colosse. Silas and Paul had never visited that small town, but they felt close to it because it was the home of Epaphras, Philemon, and Onesimus. Many other Christians lived at Colosse as well, and they had joined the missionaries' three special friends on a weeklong trek to Ephesus when Silas and Paul were teaching there. They had learned a great deal about the new faith during the several weeks they stayed with the missionaries, and when they returned to Colosse they established a mostly gentile church there.

Now, almost ten years later, Epaphras had come to report that although the church at Colosse had continued to grow long after the missionaries left Ephesus, it had recently run into trouble. Some very strange pagan beliefs had begun to be accepted by a few of the believers.

Epaphras said that he and many others felt that the missionaries' presence at Colosse was necessary to prevent the situation from getting out of control. Paul explained that his imprisonment would keep him from going to Colosse and that Silas's help was sorely needed at Rome.

He said that he and Silas had achieved a great deal of success sending letters to other churches that had had difficulties, and that writing to Colosse was the best solution to the problem. Tychicus left with the letter the next day.[4]

The steady stream of visitors who came to Rome to visit Silas and Paul continued month after month. Of all those who came from near or far, none was more welcome than their friend of long ago, John Mark.

The three men had been separated for fifteen years after John Mark had withdrawn from the mission and Paul had refused to forgive him. Now John Mark had come to Rome to be reconciled with Paul. They once more became true friends in Christ, and Silas renewed the close friendship he thought he had lost forever.

The men joyfully greeted one another, and then John Mark turned to Silas, telling him he had been in Alexandria.

"You have my full attention now, John Mark," Silas said.

"And I'm very happy to report that after some time I began to enjoy success with bringing the Gospel to that city."

"That's wonderful news. I'm most happy to hear that you brought the Word to the city of my birth."

"But the best part of the story is still to come. I met a grand eighty-five-year-old gentleman when we were both studying at the library of Alexandria. As time went by the wise old Pharisee and I had many serious discussions together, and a congenial relationship soon developed.

"Then one day my new friend came to me with a letter which he said had been written by his son and grandson many years before. He explained that for the first time since he had received the letter, he now understood the message in it, and he went on to say his understanding was the result of what I had told him about my belief. This of course made me feel very happy.

"A few days later I found out something else about the Pharisee. I was overjoyed to discover that my good new friend Matthew was the grandfather of my good old friend Silas. As we became even better friends because of our new bond of common belief, I learned the story of your life in Alexandria, Silas, and I told Matthew about the wonderful success you had achieved as a Christian leader.

"Silas, your grandfather died soon after he was baptized, but before he died he made it known that he was extremely happy, not only because he had become a Christian, but also because he had learned that you were fulfilling the promise made to him by redirecting your search for the truth, then finding it, and sharing it with others."

Silas thanked John Mark for what he had done for him and his grandfather and urged him to stay and work with the Christians. John Mark replied that was the very reason he had come to Rome, and he soon became a dedicated member of the group.

One of the next visitors who came to Paul's prison home was Epaphroditus, an old friend from Philippi. When Silas greeted him at the door, the memory of their mission to Macedonia so many years before suddenly rushed back to him. He recalled the meeting place on the river bank, Lydia, and the insane slave girl who was being used by unscrupulous men as a fortune teller.

He remembered with a shudder how he and Paul were flogged, thrown into prison, and miraculously freed. The Philippians showed their love for Paul by sending him a gift, and he showed his love for them by accepting it, the only gift he ever did accept. He always insisted on earning his keep by using his trade.

Silas was suddenly awakened from his reverie by the sound of Epaphroditus's voice as he handed Paul another gift from the thankful Philippians. Then he told Paul that he had come not only to present the gift, but to offer himself as a personal servant.

Epaphroditus worked faithfully for Paul until he became so sick that the missionaries feared his death was imminent, but his life was spared and eventually he recovered. As much as Paul would have liked to have kept Epaphroditus at his side, he decided to send him back to Philippi so he could spend his last days there with his friends.

Paul asked Silas to help him write to the Philippians to thank them for the gift they had sent, and for Epaphroditus's help, and to let them know that he would be returning to them. He also wanted to ask the Philippian church to give Epaphroditus the royal welcome he deserved for risking his life to the point of death working for the Lord. Paul wrote to them not as an apostle with authority, but as a friend in Christ, with special love for them.

He lamented the fact that some were spreading Good News only because they were jealous of him or to win fame for themselves and added he was happy that others were working in the church only because of their love for God. He urged them to keep up the good work even though they might suffer for it, and told them that Silas had endured the pain of separation from his wife and family to be with him spreading the Good News.

Paul talked to the Philippians about some of their problems, thanked them for their gift, and sent a special greeting from government officials who had become Christians.[5]

Shortly after Epaphroditus left for Philippi with the letter, Silas greeted a young couple at his door. When he saw who it was, he experienced great joy, but at the same time overwhelming grief.

He did not know the woman, but he knew that the man with her was his twenty-year-old son, Joseph, and at once Silas knew they were in Rome to tell him of the death of Rebekah, his beloved wife. The silence that followed their initial greeting confirmed this fear.

Silas was the first to speak. "Has your mother . . . ?"

Joseph nodded silently. He introduced Ruth, his young wife. "My mother was the victim of a deadly illness that spread rapidly through Antioch," he said. "She incurred the disease of high fever and dysentery for which there seems to be no cure."

At that the heart-broken Silas began to lament the years apart from his wife that his devotion to the work of the church had made necessary.

Joseph spoke again. "My mother often said that as painful as her separation from you was, she understood that it was necessary to spread the Word and that gave her much happiness. Like you, she gave her life to the work of the Lord and became one of the very few women leaders in the church. She also raised both Martha and me to be good Christian Jews."

Joseph's last remark prompted Silas to turn his thoughts from his wife's death to the life of his daughter. When he was able to ask about her, Joseph assured his father that she was well, living with good friends, and very active in the church. "As for us," he continued, "we have decided to join you here and do whatever we can to help the Christian church in Rome." Silas was overwhelmed to hear that Joseph and Ruth were ready to dedicate the rest of their lives to the church, but he was also curious about their decision to leave Antioch and work in Rome, so he asked his son for an explanation.

Joseph did not hesitate before replying. "We first considered going to Jerusalem because that is where our church was born, but we could see that the opposition of non-believing Jews was preventing any Christian growth there. We knew, from our own experience at Antioch and your success in countless foreign places, that many Gentiles were accepting Christianity. That led us to believe that the major growth of our religion would probably occur in gentile areas.

"With that conclusion, we began to consider the three greatest gentile cities of the world. The first of these, of course, was our home city of Antioch. This would have seemed to be the most logical choice for us to make because we were already established there, but it did not seem to offer the greatest challenge. I'm happy to say that we believe half the people in Antioch are Christians and the number continues to grow. So we decided to look elsewhere.

"Next we thought about Alexandria, the adopted city of our forefathers, but we learned that the church John Mark had started there was well organized and growing. The third city we considered was Rome, and it appealed to us for two reasons. One is the great challenge for growth that the capital of the civilized world offered. The other is that we could work with my beloved father."

Silas agreed with his son's analysis, and added one more advantage for choosing Rome. He told Joseph that unlike the hostile Jews in Jerusalem and elsewhere, the non-believing Jews in Rome no longer bothered the Christians. "And," he added, "the Romans do not interfere with us either, and as long as we do not antagonize Nero all should be well."

Silas was very excited about having his son and daughter-in-law working with the church and anxious to get them started, so he took them into the next room to meet Paul. Paul welcomed the young couple and told them he was delighted to have two youthful and energetic new workers join the mission at Rome. He explained to Joseph and Ruth that each member of the group contributed according to his or her own specific skill, and that they would soon find the right place in the church for themselves.

After they left Paul, Silas outlined the organization of the church and named several disciples Joseph and Ruth would be working with and explained what they had accomplished. He talked about Timothy, who was just a few years older than Joseph, and whom he said Paul loved like a son; John Mark who had helped Joseph's great-grandfather find the truth; the physician Luke who had taken care of Paul since he joined the mission at Thessalonica; Tychicus who had been very helpful as a messenger; Epaphras who had just arrived; Silvanus who had worked with Peter at one time; Linus, one of the most enthusiastic and capable members of the church at Rome; Aristarchus, who joined the mission at Ephesus; and many others whom he said Joseph and Ruth would soon meet.

"Now that you know something about our organization," Silas said, "I will give you a tour of the city. Of course, most of our work is outside the Jewish quarter, so I have grown familiar with much of Rome. I soon discovered that Rome lacks much of the culture, pagan though it is, of Greece, and I've heard of no group that can compare with the philosophers of Athens.

"Rome is a large city, and you will have to know your way around to do your work safely. There are some areas where you might be beaten and robbed."

As they left the house where Paul had been kept in chains as a prisoner for two years, under the watchful eyes of the guard, Silas told Joseph and Ruth that they could live there with him and Paul until they found more suitable living quarters.

"Paul's prison home is a typical family dwelling, although it is one of the simpler ones," Silas told Joseph and Ruth as they walked along. "But instead of the two small rooms off the main room, as you have just seen, other family homes might have several rooms arranged around a courtyard. Of course your work will take you to homes that are smaller even than Paul's. Some will be tiny wooden houses that are frightening fire traps. Others, that you will probably never see the interior of, are quite luxurious.

"That tall building just ahead of us is a new kind of housing that is developing because of the scarcity of land in the city. It is a multiple-story building constructed with separate living quarters for several families on each level. Those who can afford to live there pay rent to the owner.

"The two-room *insula*, as it is called, has accommodation for sleeping only. The occupants need nothing more because they are away during most of their waking hours earning a living. They do not return for meals, but eat at local taverns. Cooking is not allowed in the building because of the fire hazard. The structure would be easily destroyed if a fire should break out, because no water is available at the site. The occupants follow the pagan practice of using public baths. The street side of the bottom floor of this tall building houses brothels, shops, and taverns where the less wealthy eat, drink, and spend what little money they have.

"One of the first things I learned about Rome is that it is situated on seven hills. One of the next things I learned was that the rich of the city prefer to live on these hills so they can be above the teeming crowds and noisy animals roaming on the streets of central Rome far below them.

"I once heard the description of the hilltop home of a wealthy Roman. I was told that the front door opened into a large atrium. An opening in the ceiling let the light in, and a depression in the floor beneath it collected the rain water that ran through it. Water flowed into the home also through a lead pipe, and the owner's tax was based on the diameter of his water pipe. The rich occupants of this atrium house were kept comfortable in cool weather by central under-the-floor heating. For entertainment they hosted lavish dinner parties with hired performers."

"Father, I can barely hear you, now. The noise of the chariots squeezing by around us makes it almost impossible for us to carry on a conversation."

"I know it's a problem, Joseph, but at least the noise will not interfere with your sleep, because chariot traffic is prohibited during the night. That's one of the good things that Nero has done for the people of Rome. Like previous emperors, he takes great pains to satisfy the basic needs of the huge population of the city.

"He fears that serious discontent might endanger his reign, so he provides free food to hundreds of thousands annually at many different kinds of entertainment provided without charge. Some events are attended by as many as fifty thousand people.

"The crowds are amused by such things as chariot races, wild beast hunts, public executions, gladiators in combat, and theatrical and musical performances. Although I do not approve of most forms of entertainment provided by the government, I do admire the ability of the Romans to acquire, ship, store, and distribute the food required for such a huge number of people at the games, as well as at their homes.

"Another quite different type of entertainment is enjoyed by heathens of every class. It is found at the huge public baths where many gather to bathe, socialize, exercise, read, and even shop. The sin of it all, of course, is that entertainment and leisure take the place of appropriate religious activity.

"Now we are at the outskirts of the central part of Rome. This is where the senate building, numerous temples, open forums for public meetings, and basilicas for court proceedings have been built. This section of Rome is located in a valley between the Palatine Hill and the Capitoline Hill, which had been a marsh before it was drained to permit construction of the great buildings. It is the business district and civic center, the heart of social and political activity. There is no need for us to venture into this area, because your work will not take you here, unless of course you are forced to appear in one of the law courts."

On the days following the tour, Joseph and Ruth joined the Christian leaders as they continued their good work.

After remaining in prison for two years, seemingly forgotten by the authorities, Paul was summoned to appear before a magistrate. The charge against his name had made it to the top of the list.

When the day came for Paul to go under guard to the forum where the court was located, Silas suggested that Timothy, Luke, and Joseph accompany him. Silas expressed hope that the worst that could result from the hearing would be a sentence of continued house arrest.

The trial began, and the magistrate was shocked to hear that the accusers had not been located and so could not appear to present their case. Silas was sure that they were still in Jerusalem, but not concerned about Paul because he was in prison where they thought he would spend the last days of his life.

The magistrate could not make any sense at all out of the charge against the accused. He asked Paul to explain it and then allowed him to defend himself. Paul obliged the magistrate by giving a lengthy recitation of all that had happened to him. When he was finished, the magistrate said that he saw no reason to keep Paul under arrest any longer and ordered him to be released at once.

Chapter 26

After the Trial

PAUL WAS ABLE to enjoy freedom for the first time in two years. After he had visited his many friends around the city, he joined the other leaders to talk about their future plans. They met in the same house where Paul had been kept in chains for such a long time. As long as the rent was paid the missionaries could continue to work there.

Now that Paul had been declared innocent and released from house arrest, neither he nor any of the other leaders would have to remain in Rome. They decided to disperse and go out to those churches needing help.

Paul outlined a program that the others readily agreed to. "I feel compelled to go to Macedonia, Achaia, and then Spain. Silas's future awaits him in Rome. He should stay here and shepherd the Christians of the city. Timothy should go to Ephesus and Titus to Crete." These four short sentences gave new momentum to the spread of Christianity.

Timothy left Rome first, followed by Titus a few days later. Some time after Timothy had left, Paul told Silas that he was worried about Timothy's assignment because they had heard nothing from the Ephesians since they had written to them. Silas suggested that the best thing to do would be to send Timothy a letter.

Paul wrote to Timothy to give him some good advice. He urged him to cling to his faith, doing only what he knew was right and teaching only sound doctrine.[1]

After writing the letter, Silas and Paul felt more comfortable about Timothy and his responsibility at Ephesus, but now they began to worry about Titus. Paul said that he would be leaving for Philippi soon, and after staying there for some time, he could go to Crete and visit Titus.

The following day Paul left for his destination alone, insisting that Luke remain in Rome to minister to the sick. After an enjoyable visit with the Philippians he headed for Crete. Paul soon found out after his arrival on the island that Titus had accomplished a great deal. The church was well organized and enjoying good growth. When Paul left Crete, he was certain that the church there was in good hands.

After returning to Philippi, Paul went to Corinth where he found that conditions were much improved. Paul knew that this was because Titus had not only delivered his harshly critical letter to the Corinthians, but had remained with them for several weeks helping to remedy many of the church's problems.

In Corinth Paul wrote Titus a letter to reinforce the effect of his visit, sending it with his friend Apollos. Much of what he told Titus was the same message he had sent to Timothy, but in closing, Paul asked Titus to meet him at Nicopolis in the fall. Paul told him that he expected to spend the winter there before returning to Rome, after which he would leave for Spain.[2]

Silas, in Rome, was separated from Paul for the first time in years. One day a messenger brought him horrible news that an earthquake had destroyed Colosse. The chief town of the Colossians no longer existed, and Silas feared that all of the Christians there had perished.

Then word came from Jerusalem that James, the brother of Jesus and head of the mother church, had been murdered in the Temple by an angry mob. The rumor was that his attackers had been urged on by the high priest. James had led the Christians in Jerusalem for more than twenty years. He had succeeded Peter when he felt his efforts were needed elsewhere.

In Rome, however, all was going well. The leaders were free to speak to groups of assembled people anywhere in Rome, except in any of the ten synagogues. When Peter arrived to offer his leadership, and renew his friendship with Silas after twenty-five years, the future of the Christian church in Rome looked brighter than ever before.

Two years after starting his mission, Paul was rolling up a scroll as he prepared to leave Corinth for Nicopolis to meet Titus, when he heard someone at the door. Opening it, he was shocked to see Aristarchus standing there. He had not seen his faithful friend since he left Rome.

Aristarchus offered Paul the reassuring Christian greeting of peace, and then he spoke, "I'm so glad that I found you. Silas told me you would be here."

"A day later, and you would not have found me. I will be leaving for Nicopolis before the day is over. After spending the winter there I will return to Rome."

"No, you must not," Aristarchus said. "Silas told me to inform you that you must not return to Rome, at least for the foreseeable future. There has been a terrible tragedy. Much of the city has been destroyed by fire. You and I have lost many good friends, but, thanks be to God, Silas, Joseph, and Ruth survived the holocaust uninjured and were alive when I left.

"The Christians are now being blamed for the fire and a desperate search is being made to find and kill every last one of us. Informants have told us that the Romans are especially anxious to find you because of a recent declaration made by Nero. I am exhausted. Let us sit down and I will explain everything.

"As you well know, Rome is a tinder box, and there are fires in the city every day, but most are extinguished quickly. Almost all of the fires in the past were in the poorest districts where the houses were built of dry wood, but this one was different. According to all reports, it began among the shops that lined the Circus Maximus, and spread rapidly from there.

"While the fire raged, many stories began to circulate. One early rumor was that gangs of unidentified youths were seen attacking citizens who were trying to extinguish the blaze. Another one was that you were responsible because you preached against the sinful life of that part of the city where the fire started. Then some began to wonder if Nero himself ignited the blaze to resolve an argument he was having with the Senate. They speculated that because the Senate had objected to his plan to tear down a major portion of the city and build elaborate palaces there, Nero chose to settle the issue his way.

"Nero, of course, had an alibi that prevented any official accusation of him. He said that when the fire started he was out of the city, and that could well be true. He was probably enjoying life at the coastal resort of Antium to escape the oppressive summer heat of Rome.

"Regardless of the cause, the fire was disastrous. It had no sooner started when most of the city erupted in flames. For six nights Rome was bright as day. Then the fire subsided briefly before blazing up again for another three days. When it was all over, at least two thirds of the city was in ashes. Nero's palace, the senators' stone homes, and that part of the forum where the senators worked were all destroyed.

"But what the conflagration did to human lives was the real tragedy. As the flames roared down street after street, terrified, shrieking men, women, and children did not know which way to run to escape the angry fire. Many times they did not escape, but perished trying to run away.

"Families who left their burning homes and scrambled toward an untouched building saw it burst into flames just as they arrived. Men and women struggling to survive and take a few possessions with them stumbled and fell over debris and were crushed by the masses stampeding close behind them. Many, exhausted from fleeing from one area to another for hours, finally chose to stay where they were and die. Others lost their lives trying to deliver the injured from the holocaust.

"Then, as the last embers disappeared, the desperate need to cast blame flared, and accusations that Nero was responsible for the tragedy were heard again. To put an end to this speculation, he announced it had been determined that the Christians had caused the catastrophe. Nero claimed that you, Paul, because your prison sentence had made you angry, had urged the Christians to start the fire just to fulfill a prophecy that Rome would be destroyed by flames.

"Nero ordered troops to take to the streets and arrest every Christian who had survived the fire until they were all gone and you were found. If anyone they interrogate confesses to being a Christian, he is either fed to the lions or crucified. It has been said that Nero illuminates the garden parties in his temporary home by soaking condemned Christians in flammable pitch and igniting them as torches.

"Those of us who by the grace of God did not perish in the fire were forced to remain hidden and there were very few places left to hide. We have heard that only four of the fourteen districts of Rome were left undamaged by the fire. We are barely existing in a reign of terror. Silas sent me to tell you to stay here and work from Corinth to keep the faith alive. If you did go back to Rome you would probably find that you were the only Christian in the city by that time, and you, too, would soon come to a violent end."

Chapter 27

After the Fire

PAUL'S RESPONSE TO Aristarchus was immediate and brusque. "After hearing your frightening story, I know what I should do. I agree with Silas that I should not go to Nicopolis as I had intended, but I will not remain in Corinth as he advised. I will leave at once for Lechaion, the city's port on the west side of the peninsula. Then as soon as I can arrange passage to Rome, you and I will be on our way. We are needed there more than ever now.

"Silas need not be concerned. There are many others besides me outside the city who will keep the faith alive for us. Nero is certainly an evil person and should be avoided if at all possible, but we have God on our side, and I must give my help."

Two days later Paul arranged accommodation on a ship, and early the following morning the two men were on their way to Rome. During the long voyage that followed, Aristarchus's story repeated itself over and over in Paul's mind. The feeling of helplessness that it brought him was almost unbearable. Paul was desperate to get to Rome and face the challenge waiting for him. In the meantime, all he could do was pray for guidance, and this he did constantly.

After what seemed like a never-ending voyage, the ship docked at Puteoli, and Paul set out with Aristarchus to enter Rome for the second time.

This time Paul was a free man. This time there would be no grand receptions for him along the way. This time his fear was not of an impending trial but of persecution without a trial. This time the magnificence of Rome would be gone. This time the city he was about to enter would be a very dangerous place for a Christian to be seen.

Ten days later, as the two men walked along the Appian Way, they passed fields where hordes of destitute people were huddled together in goatskin tents, or crude shacks constructed of pieces of scrap of all kinds. Others just sat motionless, as if in a trance, out in the open without any protection from sun or rain.

Aristarchus commented that although Nero had provided emergency shelter in Rome for many of the destitute survivors of the fire, he obviously had not been able to help all of them. "But these poor souls out here are lucky just to be alive," he said, "and we will stay here near them until it becomes dark enough for us to enter the city with some degree of safety."

When the daylight began to fade, the two men started out once more. As depressing as the long walk to Rome had been, it could not compare with the desolation that greeted Paul when he and Aristarchus entered the city. When Paul had last stood at a spot where they now paused, he could not have seen beyond the pagan temple, but now, even in the early darkness, he could see countless unobstructed acres of charred wood and ashes.

Aristarchus did not allow him to stop and stare. Without explaining where he was going, he led Paul along a circuitous path among the rubble. Stopping at a pile of debris he exclaimed, "Thanks be to God it is still here. I was afraid that it would be gone and we would be left without a place to hide. There will be a safe haven for us hidden among this litter. Follow me"

Paul felt secure once he entered a small wretched hovel with Aristarchus. He did not think the Romans would expect to find a human being living in such a place. As soon as his eyes adjusted to the semidarkness, the depression he had been enduring began to fade away because there, standing in front of him, illuminated by a single candle, was no one other than the apostle Peter. He had arrived in Rome shortly before the fire started and had become active in the leadership of the church.

Paul's first words to Peter were an anxious inquiry about the fate of the many Christians he had left behind. Although Aristarchus had assured him that Silas, Joseph, and Ruth had been fine when he left Rome, neither one knew what might have happened to them since that time, so they were both relieved when Peter told him that they were well and living nearby. The news about many others, however, was not good. Paul knew that most of the Christians lived among the impoverished of the city in homes constructed of wood, so he was not surprised to learn that many had either perished in the fire, or by the lions in the arena, and others had just disappeared.

Although Nero's edict condemning Christians and ordering them to be killed was still in effect, Paul soon found out from Peter that the special police were no longer concerned with those they referred to as the *common ones*. Nero's policy had changed. Christians who on arrest took an oath to give up their faith and recognize Nero as their god were no longer persecuted.

More interested in saving their lives than their faith, many of the common ones were easily swayed to confess their faith and then renounce Christianity. This meant that the police were deprived of the joy of killing innocent, defenseless people. They were now targeting their efforts at the leaders because they would be more of a challenge. Peter informed Paul that they would have to be very careful, because they were the two most wanted ones in Rome.

Silas was not surprised that Paul had paid no attention to him and returned to the hotbed of trouble. He understood, when he was told that Paul had said he was needed more in Rome than in the outside world.

Silas had realized soon after the fire that their decision to send Timothy to Ephesus and Titus to Crete was a very wise one. It assured them that Christianity would live on in those places, but he was disturbed that John Mark had recently returned to Alexandria, and that Luke was planning to leave for Greece very soon. He thought both those men should have remained in Rome and given their help there.

When Silas was able to meet with Paul, he ventured to tell him how he felt about John Mark and Luke. Paul explained that those two men were needed more outside Rome and that there was adequate support in the city without them. Paul had just found out that Eubulus, Linus, Pudens, and Claudia had escaped the fire and were still in Rome working for the church.[1]

In the long months following his return, Paul joined Silas, Peter, and others in an attempt to reassure the terrified Christians. Their efforts took them outside of their tumbledown shacks onto the debris-covered streets of the city to carefully selected secret meeting places. They soon discovered that much of the remnant Christian population had been reduced to groups of homeless and hopeless wretches, their faith severely weakened.

The leaders worked tirelessly attempting to restore the belief of the destitute, ignoring the danger to which they were exposing themselves. Roman soldiers patrolled the streets looking for them.

The church leaders met with the believers at the same time each week, at various secret meeting places. One day when Silas had other duties, Paul and Peter started out by themselves for one of these prearranged sessions. When they went up to the door of the secluded ramshackle building where the meeting was to be held, they were met, not by one of their own, but by a Roman centurion who questioned them. Neither one could deny his true identity. Soldiers appeared out of nowhere, and the two apostles were led away in irons.

Paul and Peter were marched through the rubble-covered streets and up the steep Capitoline Hill to the Mamertime Prison. The formidable construction of this prison had prevented its destruction by fire.

The two men were taken inside and turned over to prison guards. "These men will make you famous," one of the soldiers said to the guards. "You now have custody of two of the infamous leaders of the sect that destroyed our city. They are the most wanted criminals in all of the empire. Don't handle them with care."

The two guards, full of pride, led the prisoners away in different directions. The guard assigned to Paul took him through a maze of corridors until he reached his own quarters. Once inside his small room he pointed to a square hole in the floor and instructed Paul to grab the edge and lower himself through it.

Paul did as he was told, and found himself dangling in space. His only support was his grip on the rim of the hole. Paul did not know how long he could hold on, how far he would drop or what waited for him below when he did let go, but the guard grew impatient, and to hurry things along he gave Paul's knuckles a hard rap, causing him to lose his grip and drop a few feet into the dark cell below.

When Paul recovered from the shock of his fall, he realized that the cell was a damp, dirty, and foul-smelling dungeon. This imprisonment would be much different from his previous one, and Paul began to wonder how long he could survive in it because of his poor health.

When news of the arrest of the two apostles reached Silas, he feared that their end was near. He thought that in only a matter of days they would be slaughtered in the arena or crucified on crosses. As the days passed, however, and then the weeks went by, no signs appeared that either apostle had been martyred.

At first Silas could not understand why the Romans were delaying the executions. Then he realized they were hoping to use cruel treatment to force the apostles to renounce Christianity.

Silas knew the authorities would believe that if this happened it would put an end to the *troublesome sect* once and for all, but he also knew that they would not be successful. They had no concept of the strength and courage of the apostles. They did not know that the two Christian leaders would be faithful through every torture administered to them, even unto death.

Silas was helpless to do anything for either Paul or Peter. The imprisonment of the two apostles elevated his status in the eyes of the authorities, and he was now the most wanted criminal in Rome.

He had moved in with Joseph and Ruth, who had found a shelter, and they took great pains to keep him hidden and to make their shack look nothing like a hideout. Other believers were kept unaware of Silas's location, and he avoided going to homes that he felt the authorities suspected housed Christians.

Joseph went about only at night when he was reasonably sure no troops were prowling the streets. If all seemed clear, he made arrangements with a few church members who had survived the fire to meet with his father in some secluded spot for a worship service. They never gathered in the same place twice.

A full year elapsed since the two apostles were imprisoned. Throughout this period, Silas and others continued their secret meetings at night without drawing attention.

During this time the city was being rebuilt. Removing the debris took many weeks, and when this task was completed, the bigger task of replacing Rome's shanty town with a more fire-resistant city began. Construction projects forced the Christians to change their hiding places several times.

Occasionally, Silas heard about the plans Nero had for rebuilding Rome, and when he walked at night he could see some of the improvements that were already under way. The streets were being made broader, and narrow, winding alleys were being eliminated.

A new regulation limited the height of new houses, and another one specified that buildings must be constructed of material that was more fire resistant than wood, such as mud brick, stone, or a recently developed concrete made from volcanic ash and lime. This new concrete was widely used for pillars and arches in public buildings. When covered with colorful tiles, the volcanic concrete was preferred by the rich to marble for decorating walls and floors.

Nero and many wealthy citizens used their personal resources to finance the rebuilding process in the beginning, but when the construction cost began to escalate, an alternate source of funds had to be found. Nero did not hesitate to solve the problem by ransacking the provinces. Then he made a serious mistake which turned the people against him.

They learned that much of the money he took in would be used to build for himself what the citizens were calling the Golden Palace. The edifice was to be situated on an immense tract of land with meadows, groves, woodlands, and a lake. The palace itself would be adorned by gold, precious stones, and masterpieces of art from Greece. Near the entrance to the estate, a statue of Nero over one-hundred feet high was already being erected.

The immensity of that project, to be built on the site where the fire originated, made the citizens suspicious once more that Nero had started the conflagration to obtain the property for his personal use.

Paul continued to hold onto life in prison. He was allowed two buckets down and two buckets up each day. In the dark dungeon he had nothing to do but to pray and think. His greatest desire, of course, was to spread the Good News, but he could not do this while he was trapped in the bad-smelling subterranean cell.

The only person within hearing distance of his voice was the guard whose quarters were above him. Paul knew that many Romans, both ordinary citizens and members of the government, had become believers to one extent or another before the fire, but he had no idea whether his guard had ever listened to the message of the Gospel.

Paul also knew that many Romans who had been believers rejected Christianity after the fire. He did not think that he could influence the guard if he were a non-believer because of the lingering danger to all Christians. But if only the guard had the tiniest bit of belief, Paul thought he might be able to reach out to him, so he began to preach the Word in a loud voice. He could not tell what the guard's reaction was, but the fact that he was not told to keep quiet was encouraging, so he continued his effort day after day.

One evening, just before Silas was ready to venture out, he heard a knock at the door. It was the secret rap that only a few of the leaders knew, so he opened the door without fear. Even in the darkness he could distinguish the uniform of a centurion of the Roman army. The fact that the officer was there told him that he was not the first one to be arrested on that evening. Another Christian leader had apparently been caught and tortured until he divulged the location of the hideaway and the secret knock.

Silas was resigned to his fate. He had no intention of denying that he was a Christian, and he knew that resistance was impossible. The centurion would not have come without a detachment. He gave thanks that Joseph and Ruth were not at home and prayed that he would be gone before they returned.

Silas took a step outside, anxious to be led away. Then after what seemed like an eternity the centurion spoke his first words. "Let me in," he said gruffly. Silas opened the door and followed the centurion inside. Seeing the oil lamp on a table across the room, the centurion ordered Silas to bring it to him. When Silas handed the lamp to the officer he lifted it up in front of his face.

When Silas saw who it was he was dumbfounded. "Julius," he cried. "I never expected to be taken to prison by you!"

"Put the lamp back on the table, sit down, and listen to what I have to say."

Once more Silas did as he was told, and Julius spoke. "Two years after we survived that perilous voyage together, I was put in charge of the Mamertime Prison. Naturally I was informed when Paul and Peter were brought in. As you know, I felt a special kinship with both you and Paul because of the terrible time the three of us shared fighting the wild sea, and then you and I became very close in our final days together.

"What you may not know is the effect your Christian message had on me. By the time we parted, I was beginning to wonder if there might be some truth in it. When I left you and Paul, I did not think I would ever see either of you again. My connection to the Christian world was broken and I thought that it would never be restored.

"Then Paul and Peter were arrested and taken to Mamertime. Unfortunately there was nothing I could do to help either man in any way, let alone set them free. I grieved when I passed the guard's room above Paul's cell on my daily rounds to know that he was suffering in a hell hole below.

"Then one day as I was walking by his location, I could hear him preaching in Greek in a loud clear voice. I was amazed that a human being barely allowed to exist could carry on the mission he was devoted to. I thought there must be much more to his belief than I ever thought possible. After this revelation, I began to look forward to my rounds, hoping to hear him as I passed his cell.

"Before long I realized that I was hearing very little of his message just passing by, so I began to stop outside the guard's quarters to listen, making sure that I was not seen. I repeated this daily until I knew without any doubt that I was a believer.

"Now I long to be baptized and become a real Christian. I hope you will do this for me tonight after you hear the rest of my story.

"A great deal happened during the past year. One day as I neared the guard's quarters I could hear two voices conversing in Greek. One was Paul's, but the other one I had not heard before. This time I did not stop to listen, but continued to walk on so I could look inside the guard's room as I passed by. The second voice was that of the guard. Fascinated by the little bit that I saw and heard, I decided to stop and listen to what the two men were talking about. I crept back closer to the open door so I could hear more clearly.

"The guard was telling Paul that he had spent countless lonely hours in his quarters above the prison cell. He had listened to his almost endless preaching ever since it began, and although he had many questions, fear prevented him from asking for the answers. Now he could wait no longer, and while I stood outside, I heard him ask question after question.

"I listened to each one, and to Paul's replies, and my belief grew stronger with all that I heard. Just before I left that section, I heard the guard confess that he had been curious about the strange belief of the Christians and had marveled at their faith for some time, but had been afraid to do anything about it. Then he said that after he saw that Paul's imprisonment in a dungeon was doing nothing to destroy his faith or devotion to the cause, he was given the courage to speak up.

"Of course the guard's testimony affected me, but I did not think that I should ignore his violation of the prison rules. I did not know what to do. He had broken the law by fraternizing with a prisoner and should be severely punished for that. Then I realized that I had much to gain if I ignored the guard's transgression and so I developed a plan. I realized that if I told him I was aware of what he had done, but would not punish him because I too believed, I would be free to go into his quarters and visit Paul along with him.

"The next day, when I reached the area and heard the two voices I walked into the guard's quarters. When the guard saw me and knew that I must have heard him talking to Paul, he turned white and began to shake with fright. I tried to convince him that all was well, and that in spite of our difference in rank we were one under God, because, like him, I was a believer. Of course Paul could hear our conversation, but he had no idea who I was, and I was not able to tell him until I could convince the guard that he had nothing to worry about.

"When he calmed down and began to believe what I was telling him, I told Paul who I was and why I was there. Paul was thrilled to be with me again and to know that I had become a believer. He gave thanks that his imprisonment had not been in vain. The next day Lepidus the guard, Paul, and I had the first of many rewarding sessions together.

"Some time after that first meeting, Lepidus confessed to us that he had confided in his cousin what he had learned about the Gospel, who was teaching him, and with whom he was learning. I asked Lepidus how he could communicate with an outsider, because he lived in his tiny room and could not leave the prison. He said his cousin was also a guard at Mamertime and was in charge of Paul's friend Peter. I realized we could establish a line of communication between the two apostles, even though both were in solitary confinement.

"The five of us have shared many wonderful hours together over the past several months. Paul told us his imprisonment had become much easier to endure since the guards and I became believers, but he longed to visit with the many friends he had outside the prison and he regretted not being able to work with you, Silas.

"He said that he loved you as a brother, and that it had been very difficult to go on without you. Then I suggested that if I could find out where you lived, I could come to your home during the darkest hours and bring you into the prison under disguise. I would arrange for Lepidus's cousin to be assigned to guard duty at the entrance for that night so we could pass in unchallenged. Then you could visit with both Paul and Peter.

"The problem was that I didn't know where to find you, but fortunately Paul knew where you lived. He told me how to locate the place and explained about the secret knock that I would need for identification. Here, I have brought you the clothes of a Roman citizen, which you will wear tomorrow night."

"This has been a most amazing evening for me," Silas replied. "I'm ready to go with you tomorrow night if you can make the necessary arrangements. Now, let's make it a perfect evening with your baptism."

During the dark hours of the following night, Silas heard the secret knock. Julius slipped in as soon as the door opened. He held the lamp up to Silas's face and gave his approval of the disguise. "I would not recognize you and I see no reason why anyone else would, especially those on patrol who have never seen you before and have only heard a description of you. You do look like a Roman citizen who would be out with an officer for a good time after the last hours of the day.

"But I must warn you no disguise will save you if you are challenged inside the prison. No outsider has the right to be there, and any intruder will be arrested if discovered. If this visit works well and you decide to attempt it on a regular basis, I will not accompany you in the future. I do not intend to expose myself any more than is necessary.

"Let me know when you leave the prison tonight if you plan to make daily visits. If you do, I will arrange for Lepidus's cousin, Aristus, to be permanently scheduled for guard duty at the entrance gate for the third watch. Now, let's be on our way."

The two men walked along the less popular streets toward the prison. As they began the climb up the Capitoline Hill, Julius explained that for his own protection he would leave Silas once he was with Lepidus. At the prison entrance, Julius shouted the password to Aristus, and the two men walked in without stopping.

"Pay close attention to the route we will follow, because if you decide to return, you will be on your own coming in and going out," Julius whispered as he began to lead Silas down a series of corridors. When they reached the guard's quarters Julius said, "I will be back in one hour to lead you out." He left and Silas walked over to the nervous guard.

"I am Silas," he said. "I know that you are expecting me. Where is Paul?"

"You will not be able to see him, but you can talk to him if you go over to that square hole in the floor," was the reply.

Silas was horrified. Julius had referred to Paul's cell as a *hell hole below*, but Silas did not expect it to be that literally. Overwhelmed by the cruel reality of Paul's inhumane isolation, but anxious to talk to his friend, Silas went over to the hole in the floor and peered down into the darkness.

He could see nothing in the pit below, so he was surprised to hear Paul's greeting, but then Silas realized that even though the guard's room was only dimly lit by a single oil lamp, enough light shone on him so he was visible to Paul.

Conversation started at once and didn't stop until Julius appeared an hour later to escort Silas to the outside world. Silas told Paul he would come back the next night, and on many nights thereafter.

On Silas's third trip, Lepidus told him how to find Peter's cell, and Silas made his first call on him. Aristus, of course, was on guard duty at the gate, so Silas was unable to meet the man in charge of Peter.

Silas was able to come to the prison quite often, and after he gained sufficient confidence he frequently brought Luke or John Mark, and occasionally Onesiphorus, a disciple from Ephesus.

Paul began to worry about Timothy when he found out that Silas had not heard from him since Onesiphorus had arrived, so he and

Silas agreed to send him another letter. Over the next three nights Paul voiced his thoughts and Silas committed them to papyrus.

Lepidus was able to hear every word that went into the letter. The very personal message told Timothy how he should lead his life and minister to his church. Lepidus regretted that his cousin could not hear what Paul told his young friend, the leader of the Christians at Ephesus in Asia Minor.[2]

Not long after the letter to Timothy had started on its way to Ephesus, when Silas was in Lepidus's quarters talking to Paul, Julius appeared to advise them that he had been transferred, and to warn Silas not to trust his successor. The five Christians of Mamertime prison were saddened, but the nightly meetings continued for some time without problems of any kind.

Peter decided that he would like to send a letter to his friends in the outside world as Paul had done, so he, too, dictated to Silas. When the letter was finished Silas gave it to Peter's friend Silvanus. He had agreed to take it to Asia Minor and see that it was circulated among the churches there.[3]

A few nights later when it was time for Silas to leave Paul, he stepped out of Lepidus's quarters into the corridor. Looking both ways, as he always did before he went farther, he thought he saw the silhouette of a man in the dim light at the far end. His initial fear was soon replaced by a prayer of thanks when he realized that his route to safety was away from the distant shadow. Walking a little faster than usual, but not fast enough to make it look as if he was trying to outdistance someone, he was soon in the protection of the open air. Then he quickened his pace, and soon he was back enjoying the security of the modest home he shared with Joseph and Ruth.

By the time he returned to the prison he had almost forgotten the previous night's fright. As he always did, he approached the entrance to the prison carefully, coming out from cover only after he could identify the ever-faithful Aristus. He relaxed at the familiar sight of the man he owed so much to but had never met, but then he hesitated. Something was different about Aristus. The white band he had always worn before on his left arm was not there.

Silas remained hidden, but watched for some time, not sure what he should do. Then he decided to leave.

When Silas returned again and repeated his usual cautious approach, he knew that he had made the right decision the night before. He could see now that the guard on duty was shorter and fatter than Aristus. The absence of the white arm band had been a life-saving warning. Silas came back night after night until he was certain that Julius's replacement had made a permanent change of guard and that he could no longer visit Paul and Peter.

Some time after Silas's last visit, two soldiers came to Lepidus's quarters to take him to court for questioning by the magistrate. He had feared this day ever since it became obvious that Silas would never come to the prison again, but he was sure that Silas would not implicate him no matter how long they tortured him. The authorities must have discovered what had been going on some other way.

He began to wonder if Aristus had been arrested and had betrayed him. He had not seen him for two or three days. Perhaps he had been taken and tortured to divulge his cousin's name.

The march to the court was a long and tormenting one for Lepidus. Then he remembered that Paul had told Timothy that his suffering on earth would soon be forgotten when he achieved eternal life in heaven, and he began to calm down.

Finally Lepidus was paraded into court and the interrogation began. He was shocked when the magistrate made no mention of illegal visits to his quarters and when he was not asked if Paul continued to preach heresy from his prison cell. Instead he was questioned about Paul's reaction to life in a dungeon. He was asked if he had noticed any sign that Paul was ready to give up his belief.

This question Lepidus could reply to without any fear for himself, but the answer he had to make, that Paul would never give up his beliefs, created a new and even greater fear. If Paul was to be of no further use to the authorities he knew they would get rid of him quickly.

Lepidus's answer was all that the magistrate needed. He was dismissed, and the soldiers led him back to the prison and into his quarters.

When the soldiers had departed and all was quiet, Lepidus told Paul what had happened. Paul said he had expected this outcome for some time. "I only regret that I did not get to Spain, but I give thanks for all that I was able to accomplish. Have no fear, Lepidus! I know that my time has come, and I am ready for it. I have fought long and hard, even with poor health, for what I believe, and I have always been true to the Lord. The time has come for me to meet my Maker in heaven. I leave here thankful that this foul place made it possible to bring you, Aristus, and Julius to the Lord."

The next day four soldiers came for Paul. They brought a harness attached to a strong rope, lowered it through the hole in the floor into the cell below, and ordered Paul to put it on. Anticipating that Paul might not cooperate, one of the soldiers picked up a long pole with a sharp end to prod him if necessary, but it was not needed. They hoisted Paul out of the dungeon, battered and bruised as he was forced up through the small hole in the floor.

As Paul was led away, Lepidus remembered that he had said he was a Roman citizen. This meant that he could not be crucified without a direct edict from Nero, and Lepidus did not think this would be forthcoming. Nero was already suffering from more criticism than he wanted.

Of course, this was no consolation; the Romans had many other ways of killing innocent people. Lepidus wept silently above the empty cell. He was glad that without a prisoner he would be reassigned. He could not bear to be over the dungeon where such a great Christian had suffered for so long. Later when he went to his new post, he heard that an important Christian leader had been beheaded along the Ostien Way outside the city.

Although the news of Paul's fate was no surprise to Silas, it was devastating nevertheless. He and Paul had been very close during thirty years of working together, in good times and in bad times, in prison and out of prison, always fighting for their cause. Paul had told Silas often just as he loved Timothy as a son he loved him as a brother.

Silas had no idea when his time would come, but until it did he had to carry on without Paul. He knew that neither he nor Paul was indispensable, and each of them would be replaced by a worthy Christian.

Silas received a second blow soon after Paul's execution and, of course, it was to be expected also. They had no reason to let Peter live any longer than Paul. The rumor that circulated in Rome was that Peter, because his life had been given to Christ, insisted on being crucified upside down, refusing to mock the death of his Savior by being crucified in the same way.

Chapter 28

A Different World

WHEN SEVERAL OF the leaders of the Christian church in Rome had dispersed after Paul's release from house arrest, Silas had been left with a daunting task. He had been given the sole responsibility for guiding and advising the remaining leaders who were struggling to maintain the growth of the church in the capital city of the world and make it ever stronger. He saw his assignment as an opportunity also, not only to confirm that he was the right choice to oversee the administration of the church, but to take what he saw was the final step to fulfill the pledge made to his grandfather many years before.

Of course Silas had many able assistants. Although he valued the help he received from other members of what had become the church council, his favorite working partner was Joseph. The father-and-son team was kept busy day and night taking care of the daily needs of the Christians of the city. When Peter arrived, the workload of the two men was reduced, but then it was increased again by the fire and imprisonment and deaths of Paul and Peter. Although this demanded greater effort, it brought the father and son closer together, and as the years passed their relationship in the church became much the same as that of Silas and Paul had been, and their accomplishments were many.

Silas's associates called on him frequently to report on their problems and achievements. One day, several months after the death of Paul and Peter, John Mark (or Mark, as he was known since his recent return from Alexandria) came to the door. He was obviously excited and began speaking as soon as he was welcomed.

The words that came out of his mouth completely astounded both Silas and Joseph. "I just finished something I have been working on for some time, and here it is. It's my account of the life of Jesus, and it is a gift for you two in appreciation of all that you have done for the Christians of Rome. Hopefully it will make your job easier.

"This is how it came about," Mark explained to the speechless father and son. "While I was away, I was given a copy of a collection of Jesus' sayings written in the Hebrew tongue. I was positive that they were authentic and thought they might have been written by Matthew, the apostle. I was intrigued by what I read and decided to use it along with my own experience to preserve on papyrus at least a part of Jesus' ministry. I added what I remembered from the many sermons of Peter that I had listened to. I also made use of everything I had seen and heard in the home of Mary, my mother, when the apostles met there in the very early days of the church. Silas, now it is finished, and here is a copy of what I have written for your use in the church at Rome."

Shaking with excitement, Silas unrolled the precious papyrus with care. When he read those first few words, "The Gospel about Jesus Christ, the Son of God," he knew Mark's work would have a tremendous impact on everybody who would be exposed to it. At last teachers of the Gospel would have the use of Jesus' words instead of just their own. Mark left no doubt that he knew Jesus was the Son of God and that what he had written was the message Jesus had left for his followers.

Silas realized that Mark had explained Jewish customs in a way that gentile readers would understand, and he discovered that Mark did not hesitate to address persecution and give encouragement to the persecuted Christians of Rome. The host of stories Mark had gathered together gave a meaningful account of the life of Jesus.

Mark had emphasized the acts of Jesus more than his words. At last the church would have the true story. What some others had written about Jesus earlier was based on hearsay and legend.[1]

Silas thanked Mark profusely for his great work, which he said was really a gift for the entire Christian world. When Silas turned Mark's document over to Joseph for him to read he said, "This first appearance of an authentic record of the life and teachings of Jesus may soon be followed by other similar documents that may not be truthful like this one. We have to be careful about which ones we accept and use in our teaching. Stories written by those who had actual contact with the apostles or with Jesus himself are going to be the most reliable."

Shortly after Mark left, Luke paid Silas a visit to report on the sick in the church, but before he could say anything Silas spoke. "Luke, here is something Mark has written. I want you to read it. You will see immediately what it is and realize how important it is." He handed the scroll to Luke and then remained quiet while he read it. When Luke finished, he gave thanks for Mark's contribution to the Christian faith and high praise for the content of his work. He said that those who wrote about the life of Christ should be highly qualified to do so, and without any doubt Mark was that.

Later, as Luke continued to think about what his friend had written, he realized that he, too, was qualified to write about Jesus. Although he had never served with him or the apostles, he had acquired a mass of knowledge about many of the same events Mark had described and knew of others that Mark had not mentioned. He not only had Mark's great work as a reference, he had his own experience traveling with Paul and would be able to use all that he had heard from both Peter and James, the brother of Jesus when he was in Jerusalem.

The more he thought about it, the closer he came to deciding to write his own version of Jesus' life. He realized that because he was not a Jew, what he wrote might be particularly meaningful for Gentiles, and the church was becoming increasingly gentile. He would do all that he could to make the Jewish role in Christianity understandable to the Gentiles. He resolved not to dwell on the life of Jesus as the fulfillment of Jewish prophecy. He was very excited as he began to write.

The writings of Mark helped to restore the faith of the Christians of Rome when they needed help to face emerging hostility from non-believers, as well as a shortage of food, but the church in many places outside Rome did not seem to have these problems. Reports from Timothy in Ephesus, Titus in Crete, and Ignatius, a new leader in the church in Antioch, were encouraging.

In spite of the growing hostility toward Christians the situation in Rome began to improve. As details of the heroic defense of the Christian faith by Paul and Peter became more widely known, new believers came into the church. To accommodate the larger membership, Silas turned his attention to organization. Rome was divided into several areas, each with its own church administration, and this led to the development of capable leaders. Among those rising to the top, the most notable one was Linus, who had been one of Paul's closest friends.

Luke worked night and day on his Gospel. Of course, Silas was the first one to read it, and he was very excited by what Luke had written. In deference to the Gentiles, Luke had portrayed Jesus as the servant of God rather than as the promised Messiah of the Jews. To stress the fact that the Gentiles were truly part of the Christian church, Luke wrote about Jesus removing the barriers between them and the Jews. Luke showed that Christianity was not a threat to Rome, and he emphasized prayer by describing the many occasions when Jesus prayed. Silas was particularly interested in Luke's references to the role of women in the church and society.

Silas gave thanks for one more contribution to the true story of Christianity,[2] and he made sure that the churches used the writings of Mark and Luke as well as the letters he and Paul had written. Copies of the writings of Mark and Luke were needed for church services and teaching, which meant that Joseph and others began to devote more of their time to copying manuscripts, being very careful to avoid errors.

Soon after Mark finished his book, word arrived that fighting between Jews and Romans had been going on in Judea for about two years. Silas was surprised that the Roman authorities had made no announcement of the problem during such a lengthy period. He could only surmise that the fighting had not gone as well as they would have liked. Then a new arrival to Rome reported that the Jews had achieved a great deal of success, which Silas realized was why no official announcement of the action in Judea had been made in Rome.

One story that began to circulate on the streets of Rome was that Jewish rebels had massacred the Roman garrison quartered in Jerusalem, with the result that the Roman army stationed in Syria had been called in to attack the city. Later Silas heard that the rebels had held the Roman forces off for eight days, after which they withdrew and retreated to a location where they were soundly defeated by the Judeans. Silas had no way of knowing how true these favorable reports were, but he was certain that in the end Rome would be victorious.

Silas, like many others, was not surprised by the rebellion. Inevitably the mistreatment of the Jews by the Romans for more than one hundred years would lead to serious trouble. Tax collectors were allowed to collect more than the legal amount and keep the excess funds for their own personal use, and this dishonest custom had put a great financial burden on the Jews. Then, when Rome took over the responsibility for appointing priests, the spiritual leaders of the Jews became puppets of Rome.

These and other exasperating actions by the Roman government had taken place against a background of expectation by the Jews that a Messiah would come and bring them relief. Of course they anticipated a warrior Messiah who would defeat the Romans on the battle field, not the Messiah of love who did come and was not recognized by them. Silas suspected that the radical Zealots, weary of waiting for a military leader sent by God, had led the rebellion.

When Silas first heard about the trouble in Judea, he realized that the fighting had started while Nero was attending the Olympic Games in Greece. The gossip making the rounds at that time was that the inept emperor had entered the competition and embarrassed his attendants when he fell out of his chariot during a race. Instead of being disqualified, he was declared the winner, because of course he was the emperor.

Then Silas learned from a later report that, instead of returning to Rome, Nero had remained at the games and ordered Vespasian to lead an army as big as was needed to defeat the rebels once and for all. The result of this action was that all of Judea, except Jerusalem, had been subdued. Silas thought now that the criticism of the emperor that he had heard was the result of his absence from Rome during the time of the rebellion in Judea.

When Nero suddenly appeared back in Rome, he was not greeted as a victorious Olympian, but as a criminal. He was hastily tried (for some crime), found guilty and sentenced to death, but he took matters in his own hands and in his last act of defiance committed suicide. Nero's death came less than two years after the execution of Paul and Peter. Vespasian, recalled from Judea, was made emperor to succeed Nero and he was replaced in Judea by his son Titus.

By the beginning of Vespasian's reign, Silas was beginning to feel uncomfortable as a Jewish leader of what had become a gentile organization. He had served in a leadership role in Rome for seven years and had worked long and difficult hours to keep the church healthy and growing.

Silas had assumed responsibility just after Paul was released from prison, when the leaders who were in Rome before Peter's arrival had met to discuss their strategy for the future. The group had unanimously decided that Silas was the one to remain in the city and nourish the growth of Christianity. The other leaders were sent away from Rome to serve the churches where it was felt that help was needed, and the plan had worked well.

Now, however, Silas believed the time had come for the Christians to have a gentile bishop to lead their gentile church, and he knew the right man for the job was his friend Linus. Silas called the council together for a meeting, and proposed Linus as their bishop. The vote by the leaders was unanimous in favor of Linus.

With the deaths of Paul and Peter the special police became less interested in capturing Silas and the other leaders, and then with the death of Nero they turned their attention elsewhere. With the streets of Rome much safer for the leaders their chief concern was for the mother church in Jerusalem. Reports from there were few and far between. All they knew was that Vespasian was back in Rome, and that Titus was preparing to storm Jerusalem.

Eventually, Silas found out just how serious the situation in Judea had become, and what the consequences had already been when Titus made his triumphal entry into Rome. Carrying the golden Menorah stolen from the Temple in his right hand, he marched in front of hundreds of Jewish prisoners who looked half-starved and too weak to walk. Silas feared none of them had the will to live. He assumed that those who still had some strength left would be made slaves, and because Christians were not being persecuted for their belief at the time, the remaining Jewish prisoners would take their place and be fed to the lions to entertain the Romans.

Silas heard more about the tragedy weeks later, when one of Titus's prisoners, a Jewish Christian, managed to escape. Somehow he found his way to Silas's home where he told his story. "The last straw," he said, "was when Florus, the Roman procurator, stole vast quantities of silver from Herod's Temple. Rumor had it that the loot was sent to Rome to be used for Nero's palace. What made this sacrilegious theft unbearable was that the Temple had just been completed after more than one hundred years of construction. We Christian Jews were as horrified as the Judaists.

"Only the Zealots, however, thought that an armed attack was the proper response. Because they were well armed, they were able to wipe out the only small Roman garrison stationed in Jerusalem. Roman reinforcements were then rushed in from Syria.

"When the assault began, the Zealots announced that anyone who tried to surrender would be executed. Their threat was successful, and the attackers were defeated. This threat and their early successes did much to persuade the weaker pacifists to join the ranks of the Zealots, and the number of armed rebels continued to increase.

"The defeat of the Roman troops got Nero's attention, and he responded by sending out a huge force, but he ordered the army to Galilee, not Jerusalem. We believe he wanted to take Galilee first because it had been the seat of insurgency in the past, and Nero feared that many sympathizers would come from there to the defense of Jerusalem and make that city more difficult to take. Word of the invasion came down to us, but the city leaders refused to send help to Galilee and it fell.

"Somehow a large contingent of Galileans escaped and came south to Jerusalem. They brought stories of horror and estimates of thousands of dead Jews. But their anger was not only directed at the Romans. They despised the leaders of the Jews in Jerusalem who had refused to send aid north to Galilee, and they expressed their anger by murdering a few of the decision makers. Then they attacked the Zealot leaders and a short civil war broke out. This eliminated any hope for a united front against the Romans.

"The Galileans and the Zealots defended the city against attack without a common commander. The Galileans knew that Vespasian was a very successful but cruel general, and they busied themselves preparing for the attack of the Roman army that was approaching under his leadership. The Zealots' preparation, however, was limited to burning the entire reserve supply of food. They believed that the lack of provisions would give the defenders no alternative but to fight desperately to survive.

"When Vespasian's troops reached the city, they surrounded it, sealing us inside the walls, but they did not launch an attack. We did not understand the reason for this for some time. Then we learned from one of our spies that after a rapid succession of emperors had come and gone following Nero's suicide, Vespasian himself had been appointed emperor. His top priority had changed from taking Jerusalem to rushing off to Rome to receive his title.

"Some weeks later, we noticed renewed activity. This time it was on the Mount of Olives. Heavy equipment was being assembled, and before long catapults were hurling huge rocks down upon our city. The siege had begun in earnest. After three weeks of bombarding Jerusalem, the Roman army marched through the shattered walls led by Vespasian's son, Titus.

"Victory was not to come easily for the invaders, however. Although some Christians had refused to take part in the rebellion and had fled to the city of Pella east of the Jordan River and southeast of the Sea of Galilee, every able-bodied man remaining in Jerusalem, regardless of his religious beliefs, had joined the resistance to the attack. Fighting continued door to door and we had the advantage of knowing the crooked streets.

"Before long, however, the shortage of food and the spread of disease gave the Romans the advantage they needed. Soon the Temple was burned and the city leveled. Thousands and thousands of Jews were killed, among them most of the leaders of the mother church. Others were taken prisoner and brought to Rome, as you have seen. A few Christians managed to escape the beleaguered city. I have heard that among them were two church leaders, John, the son of Zebedee, who was said to be bound for Ephesus, and Philip, the evangelist, who hoped to reach one of the cities of Phrygia, a sub-region of Galatia."

The defeat of the Jews, the slaughter of so many of them, and the cruel persecution of survivors were events horrible almost beyond imagination to Silas. The destruction of Jerusalem and the fall of the Temple would put an end to the power of the Sanhedrin and the existence of the high priesthood. The priests had come from the party of the Sadducees, the collaborators with Rome. Silas could not believe that either they or their party would find favor with the few Jews who were left in the city. He thought that the disaster would bring prominence to the Pharisees.

He recalled being told about his ancestors' separation from the Temple during the Babylonian exile. At that time the Pharisees had established the synagogue, not to replace the Temple but to provide a place for study and worship. Because the Jews would be separated from the Temple again, this time by its total destruction, Silas believed that the synagogue would once more hold his people together. It had always been the domain of the Pharisees and it would now continue to be that.

Silas visualized the learned Pharisees dedicating themselves to become rabbis and to spend their lives teaching in the synagogues.

He feared though, because Jewish Christians had been murdered along with everyone else in Galilee and at Jerusalem, that Jewish Christianity had taken one step closer to extinction.

Not long after the full story of Jerusalem's demise had been heard, more bad news arrived. This time it came from Alexandria. A dispute between the Jews and the Greeks of the city had grown into a riot. To prevent further escalation, and the risk of his dismissal from office, the governor ordered the army to do whatever was necessary to drive the Jews back into their districts. The troops responded by killing and plundering mercilessly. When the massacre was over, fifty thousand Jews had lost their lives and the enclave of the Jewish Christians had been completely destroyed.

Silas mourned for the dead of his race, Judaists and Christians both, in the city of his birth, and he also mourned for the city itself and the terrible damage the carnage must have done to it. He found some comfort knowing that many Egyptians had become Christians. Now his prayer would be that they would make Alexandria a Christian city and that the day would come when believers who strolled down to the Pharos lighthouse to watch the ships on the Great Sea would not be molested because of their religion.

Although the tragic destruction of Jerusalem and the massacre at Alexandria were crushing blows, Silas realized that the Christians in Rome must carry on. How difficult this would be would depend on how Vespasian would treat them. He had been a cruel general. Would he be a cruel emperor also? He had become very popular with the Roman citizens as a general early in his career when he conquered Britain, but even they would not venture to guess what kind of emperor he might turn out to be.

After Vespasian had been in power just a short time, however, he distanced himself from the unscrupulous Nero in every way possible. The Christians were relieved when he left them alone. Silas, however, worried he was ignoring them only because he was very busy with a huge construction program and feared his attitude might change when he had more time for frivolity.

His plans included erecting buildings on vacant property and restoring the capital that had been destroyed in the fire so that it would once more become the seat of government. He destroyed Nero's villa and began construction of the Coliseum on the same site near an artificial lake. The people on the street claimed that it would have a seating capacity of fifty thousand when it was completed. Eventually, he realized his projects would be more costly than projected, so he responded by increasing taxes. The higher tax rate was endured by all without protest because Vespasian's reign had become one of tranquility.

In spite of the peaceful administration, the believers knew that they must be careful not to antagonize the authorities. Conditions could change with little warning, as they had in the recent past. Before the reign of Nero very little persecution of Christians took place in the Roman Empire. In fact, attacks on Christians were usually made by non-believing Jews, and often the Roman government came to their rescue.

In the early days of the church, most of the Christians were Jews, and the Romans did not distinguish between them and the Judaists, so they were not singled out for any reason. Then later, when the Jewish Christians were recognized as being somewhat different, they were just considered to be an insignificant sect of the Jews and were ignored by the authorities. Even when they were identified as a separate entity, the Christians were still left alone because they were considered to be harmless to the empire.

Then came the fire. At first the Roman citizenry believed Nero had started the conflagration to clear enough property to accommodate his building program. Of course he did not want to accept the blame, so he looked for a scapegoat, and he found it in the tiny Christian community. When he recalled hearing that they had talked about a world-ending fire, he wasted no time before accusing the Christians of trying to destroy Rome.

Nero got the support he needed from both Jews and Gentiles who were not believers, because widespread criticism of the Christians had developed when certain of their practices, which were misunderstood, became known. One of them that many had heard about was what was called the Lord's Supper, and because only Christians were allowed to participate in it, the perception was that it was a mysterious secret ceremony. Then when the people heard that references to *body and blood* were being made during the church service, accusations of cannibalism began to circulate.

When outsiders learned that the Lord's Supper was referred to as a *love feast* and the *kiss of peace* was practiced during it, rumors of sexual orgies resulted. Because some families contained both believers and non-believers, incessant arguments took place about their beliefs, which outsiders interpreted as a breakup of the home.

Destroying family relationships was sinful in the eyes of the Romans. Gradually, at first, and then by leaps and bounds any support the Christians had enjoyed was replaced by antagonism.

Once Nero had realized that the public would be receptive to his action, he began to persecute the Christians in large numbers, much to the enjoyment of the hostile non-believers. That horrible era had come to an end, but caution was still the word. The Christians continued to meet in small groups in members' homes, or in caves outside the city.

The Christians met at least once a week for worship and fellowship, remembering the commandment, "Love each other as I have loved you." Over time the custom of the early Christians of worshipping on the Sabbath had been replaced by meeting in a home church on Lord's Day, the first day of the week, the day of Christ's resurrection. On that day the Lord's Supper was celebrated as part of a common meal to which all those attending contributed.

The belief of many that Jesus' return was imminent, served to strengthen the commitment of the early Christians. Silas was encouraged by the steady stream of new believers entering the church through baptism. The order of worship now made good use of the writings of Mark and Luke. One great contribution that Luke had made was the introduction of a special prayer that Jesus had taught his disciples. They sometimes called it the Lord's Prayer.

Silas was beginning to use this prayer in the service, which now conformed to what had become a common theme. It began by proclaiming that the prophecies of the scripture had been fulfilled through the life, crucifixion, and resurrection of Jesus Christ. The resurrection of Jesus Christ was the proof that he was the promised Messiah. The return of Jesus Christ was said to be inevitable and imminent. Finally the congregation was told that Christians are those who believe these things, repent, ask for forgiveness, and, if they have the faith, will be forgiven and receive the gift of eternal life from the Holy Spirit.

One day Luke told Silas that he was so pleased by the reception of his book about the Good News that he had decided to write the story of the infant church, relating the events after Jesus' ascension up to Paul's and Peter's executions. Although, as he said, he had not been an eyewitness to Jesus' ministry, he had been intimately associated with much of the missionaries' work, and he did have access to the few church records that were in existence.

He told Silas that he wanted to emphasize the role of the Holy Spirit in the Christian faith, and he wanted to show that Christianity was for everyone. He also wanted to continue his attempt to convince the Roman government that the Christians were no threat to them, and he was anxious to show the great spread of Christianity. His story would cover a thirty-year span and extend from Jerusalem to Rome. During this time the number of Christians had increased from just a few to several thousand.

When Luke finished giving some of the highlights of what he wanted to include in his book, Silas told him that he had one request to make. He said that because Paul and Peter had been martyred for Christianity, Luke's book should be their story alone. He wanted them to have the recognition and honor they deserved.[3]

One of the happiest events for Silas during Vespasian's reign was the birth of his grandson. Joseph and Ruth named him Thomas after his great-grandfather, the first Christian in the family. Silas knew how happy his father would have been to know that there were now five generations of Christians in Matthew's family.

His father would also have experienced great sorrow because of some of the changes that had occurred in Christianity as it developed. He would have seen that the number of Jewish families in the church had continued to decrease, and he would have known that some Gentile Christians interpreted the destruction of Jerusalem and the Temple as fulfillment of scriptural prophecy, which widened the gap between them and the Jews even more. Silas also thought how happy his grandfather would have been that a new generation would carry on the family tradition of seeking, finding, and disseminating the truth.

One day a stranger came to the door of the home where Silas lived with his son, daughter-in-law, and baby grandson. After introducing himself as a Christian from Ethiopia, he asked if he was speaking to the leader of the church at Rome. Silas gave his name and replied that he was one of the leaders.

The visitor said he recognized the name, and began to talk as he walked through the open door, a rolled-up scroll under his arm.

"I arrived in Rome earlier today. I was sent here to find you and give you one of the very few copies of a new book that presents the message of Jesus Christ in a special way.

"I know that you are familiar with two earlier accounts of the life of Jesus, but this one is different, and I think you will find it interesting and helpful. It has been directed to the Jews in an attempt to keep believers faithful to Christianity and to bring in additional converts.

"I can assure you that this work is true to the faith, because the author is Matthew, who as you know was one of the original twelve apostles. He finished his book shortly before he died. When you read what he has written, you will see that Matthew either had the same source as Mark or used his work along with Luke's to bolster his own memories.

"Matthew has attempted to show to the Jews that Jesus fulfilled the prophecies they had always believed in, and that therefore he must be the Messiah they have been waiting for. Also, Matthew has stressed the fact that Jesus said he did not come to destroy the Law, as some would like to believe, but to fulfill it.

"Matthew has traced Jesus' genealogy to prove to the Jews that he was a descendent of King David. Although I don't believe it, there has been some talk that Matthew took on the task to make reparation for the hurt he had caused the Jews by over-assessing them when he was a tax collector. Now, with Matthew's compliments, here is your copy of his document."[4]

When the visitor left Silas, after several hours of discussion of Matthew's work, the two men had agreed that what Matthew had written would become a great teaching tool for both Jews and Gentiles.

With Matthew's work, as well as those of Mark and Luke, added to the ancient Scriptures, the church was well prepared to serve the believers, and Christianity in Rome enjoyed ten peaceful years of growth during Vespasian's reign. Nero's excess spending and a civil war that raged after his death had put the empire in serious financial trouble, but Vespasian was able to return Rome to a sound monetary basis with a stable government.

Of course, what the emperor accomplished, the people paid for through heavy taxation. Silas, however, was convinced that Vespasian spent the people's money wisely, so he counseled the church members to accept the burden without protest. One well-recognized achievement of Vespasian that Silas found interesting was his reduction of the backlog of court cases. This eliminated another troublesome practice of Nero's time but the very one that had prolonged Paul's life and service to the church.

The more Silas read Matthew's document, the more he appreciated it. Encouraged by what Matthew had done for the Jews, he decided that he, too, would make what might be one last effort to bring a few more of them into the church. He would prepare a sermon designed for his Hebrew brothers and somehow get them to listen to it. He thought he might be able to convince them that any religion that could force a Pharisee to abandon his heritage for a new belief must be the true one. He would tell them that he was a third-generation Pharisaic Christian and describe the journey he had taken, along with his father and grandfather, to abandon the thousands of meaningless rules that had governed their lives and find the simple message that was the truth.

He could see an insurmountable problem, however. He could only speak to a Jewish group in a synagogue, and he had been banned from all ten of Rome's. Silas was afraid that he would have to abandon his idea.

Then one day he remembered Manasseh, a Jewish Christian who attended church regularly on the Lord's Day but also went to the synagogue on the Sabbath. Manasseh had told Silas once that his synagogue had a few members who had been Christians for a short while, but then had reverted to Judaism. He had said, though, that all of the members of the synagogue were very tolerant of him and his Christian belief. This would be an ideal place to experiment with his idea, and if by some miracle it worked, he might be able to get in the door somewhere else.

After the service on the next Lord's Day, Silas spoke to Manasseh, explained his plan, and asked him what he thought about the possibility of carrying it out in his synagogue. Manasseh said he had yearned for more Jews to become Christians, but he had long ago given up hope of converting any of his friends. He told Silas that he would do what he could, but he thought he already knew the answer his congregation would give him. He could see little possibility that the members of his synagogue, as tolerant as they were, would allow Silas to come in with his message.

Nevertheless, well before the next Sabbath, Manasseh spoke to the men of his congregation and explained his Christian friend's plan. This started a great deal of heated discussion, and then one wise old man made a proposal.

"Our belief is so strong and so true," he said, "that we should not fear the presence of an infidel. In deference to Manasseh, I suggest that we allow his friend a few minutes to have his say. I will volunteer to cut him off when I feel that he has had a fair chance to deliver his message. Nothing he says will change our belief, and we can hope that Manasseh will realize how wrong his new religion is, as some of us here have done before."

The other men agreed to this. Manasseh thanked them and instead of waiting until the Lord's Day, he left at once to give Silas the news.

Silas arrived at the synagogue in time for the service on the next Sabbath. Although he participated in the worship, just as all the others did that day and just as he always had in the past, he knew that every eye must be focused on him. Then it was his turn to speak.

"First of all, I would like to thank all of you for the opportunity to tell you about my belief and the belief of my family. My grandfather, my father, my son, and I have all become Christians, and I expect that my young grandson will become one in due time. Although this represents four generations of my family, I consider that we are just entering the second generation of Christianity, so in that sense I am a second-generation Christian. My family and I have a much better life because all of us are committed Christians.

"The past history of my family is much like that of yours. We are all Israelites. Yet it is different also. We are entering our second generation as Christians and leaving behind countless generations of Pharisees. You try to follow the Law. We not only followed the Law, we interpreted it and formulated thousands of rules and regulations to explain it. Now we understand that all we did was meaningless.

"My ancestors well knew that the Law said that no work was to be done on the Sabbath, but they also knew the Law could not be adhered to unless work was defined. The Pharisees recognized that countless activities could be considered work, so they began to list them.

"One of many such activities they tallied was *carrying a burden*. Then they asked themselves, 'What is a burden?' The Pharisees knew that many things could be classified as a burden, and they began to enumerate them. One such definition I recall. A burden was said to be a bit of food as big as a dried fig.

"I hope that you will agree that we Pharisees were overzealous and blind to the truth. Now at last we know that loving God and loving others is the true interpretation of the Law and much more important than ensuring that we carry nothing larger than a dried fig on the Sabbath. I'm sure you understand that my family's journey from the rigid culture of a Pharisaic life to the freedom of the Christian belief was much more difficult than the one any of you here would have to take to receive the truth.

"My message today will be for those who have been Christians for a brief time and then returned to their old way, as well as for those who have never been of the new faith. As you know, God first revealed himself through the prophets that you hold sacred, but then he revealed himself again, this time through his Son as your prophets had foretold.

"God's Son, Jesus Christ, is the Messiah you have waited for. He was born as a Jew in the form of a human. He is greater than angels, Moses, Joshua, and Aaron your first high priest. Many of you are grieving because with the destruction of the Temple, you are suffering from the loss of your high priest, the sacrifices he offered, and his intercession with God on your behalf. But there is no loss, only gain.

"The gain will come to you if you believe in Jesus Christ, your heavenly high priest. He was your perfect sacrificial lamb without a single blemish, who has made your animal sacrifices unnecessary. Unlike the earthly high priest who made sacrifices time after time, the heavenly high priest only had to make one sacrifice, and that was the sacrifice of his life. That single sacrifice guarantees the redemption of all of you who believe in him.

"Do not refuse to accept this opportunity to receive forgiveness. Some of you have had an introduction to the Christian message. Now is the time to expand what you already know and reap the benefit of salvation. When your understanding becomes complete, you will know that you cannot earn your way into heaven.

"I will admit that acceptance of Christianity may bring persecution, but strong faith will see you through difficult times. Faith is believing in God through Jesus Christ, and surviving harsh treatment with the help of faith will lead toward perfection and righteousness. Jesus was tempted as you are, but he did not sin, and even though he was horribly abused, he remained faithful to God. He was obedient to God in spite of the suffering, and you should be also. If your faith is strong you will be. Do not deny being Christians to avoid persecution. Stay with Christianity. It is superior to your old faith.

"You must listen to God through Jesus and not fail to pay attention as your ancestors did. Some of you were believers before and have slipped back. There is nothing for you in the past, as great as it was, but everything for you in the present and future if only you will believe. God has prepared a place of peace and rest for you, and it is not Israel but heaven. He knows what we do and what we think. None of our secrets are hidden from him. He wants you to live a life of pure love."

Silas saw the leader of the synagogue rise and make a signal. He did not know whether his time was up or whether the leader did not like what he was hearing. In any case Silas knew that his talk was over so he said, "Now as I leave you, may the God of peace, who through the blood of the eternal covenant brought back from the dead our Lord Jesus, that great Shepherd of the sheep, equip you with everything good for doing his will, and may he work in us what is pleasing to him, through Jesus Christ, to whom be glory for ever and ever. Amen."[5]

The total silence that greeted Silas as he walked across the front of the candle-lit synagogue and out into the bright light of the street told him more than words that his mission had failed. He did not need the confirmation and apology that Manasseh brought the next day. He was disappointed and hurt, of course, but he was not discouraged. Strangely it was words from the old belief that gave him solace, "Be strong and courageous, for the Lord your God goes with you; he will never leave you nor forsake you."[6]

Notes

Chapter 2

1. Exodus 11:1-14:31
2. Deuteronomy 6:4, 5

Chapter 3

1. 2 Kings 9:13
2. Mathew 21:1-11
3. Lamentations 2:15
4. Matthew 9:10
5. John 4:7-30
6. Luke 14:1-6
7. 1 Kings 6:19; 8:1, 6

Chapter 4

1. Matthew 21:12, 13
2. Matthew 21:23
3. Matthew 8:1-5
4. John 6:1-14
5. Matthew 23:13-15
6. John 3:2-5

Chapter 5

1. Exodus 12:5
2. Genesis 4:2-5
3. Leviticus 17:11
4. Exodus 6:6
5. Psalm 112:1
6. Exodus 6:6
7. Exodus 6:7
8. Exodus 6:7

Chapter 6

1. Mark 14:10, 11
2. Mark 14:41-50
3. Leviticus 24:16
4. Mark 14:53-65
5. Matthew 27:11-26
6. Mark 15:21

Chapter 7

1. Matthew 27:33-50, Mark 15:22-41, Luke 23:27-44
2. Matthew 27:51
3. Matthew 27:54
4. John 19:38-42

Chapter 8

1. Luke 24:1-3
2. Matthew 27:62-66; 28:11-15
3. Matthew 20:17-19
4. Mark 16:1-8
5. John 11:1
6. Matthew 28:7, 16
7. Matthew 16:15-17
8. Matthew 17:1-9
9. Luke 24:36-40
10. Matthew 28:19

Chapter 9

1. Acts 1:12, 13
2. Acts 1:15
3. Luke 24:44-49
4. Acts 1:8
5. Acts 1:9-11
6. Acts 1:15-26

Chapter 10

1. Acts 2:1
2. Matthew 26:26-29
3. Hebrews 10:16, 17
4. Acts 2:2-4
5. Mark 16:15
6. Acts 2:9-11
7. Acts 2:13-15
8. Acts 2:6
9. Joel 2:28
10. Acts 2:29-32
11. Acts 2:37-39
12. Acts 2:41

Chapter 11

1. Acts 2:46
2. Luke 22:19, 20
3. Mark 12:28-31
4. Acts 2:44, 45; 4:32-35
5. Acts 2:46
6. Acts 3:1-10
7. Acts 3:12-16
8. Acts 3:17, 18
9. Acts 4:1, 2, 7
10. Acts 4:3
11. Acts 4:23

12. Acts 4:13-21
13. Acts 5:16
14. Luke 3:1
15. Acts 5:17, 18
16. Acts 5:25
17. Acts 5:21-26
18. Acts 5:27-40
19. Acts 5:19, 20

Chapter 12

1. Acts 9:31
2. Acts 6:1
3. Acts 6:2-4
4. Acts 6:5, 6
5. Acts 6:8
6. Acts 6:9-15
7. Acts 7:1-60

Chapter 13

1. Acts 8:1, 2
2. Deuteronomy 13:10
3. Acts 8:5
4. John 4:6-26
5. John 4:39-43
6. Acts 8:15-17
7. Acts 1:8
8. Luke 6:27
9. Acts 4:36, 37
10. Acts 9:10-12
11. Acts 9:16
12. Acts 9:13, 14
13. Acts 8:9
14. Acts 9:18-20
15. Acts 9:1-17

16. Acts 9:19-22
17. Acts 9:24, 25

Chapter 14

1. Acts 9:32
2. Acts 9:36-43
3. Acts 10:1-23, 30-32
4. Acts 10:23-29
5. Acts 11:2-18
6. Matthew 27:55, 56
7. Luke 23:49
8. Matthew 28:1-7
9. Acts 9:26
10. Acts 9:27
11. Acts 9:28, 29
12. Acts 11:20-22

Chapter 15

1. Matthew 25:6
2. Genesis 29:21-25
3. Acts 11:26
4. Acts 11:25, 26
5. Acts 11:27-30
6. Acts 12:25
7. Acts 12:1-6
8. Acts 12:8-19

Chapter 16

1. Matthew 28:19, 20
2. Acts 13:4
3. Acts 13:5
4. Acts 13:6
5. Acts 13:6-12
6. Acts 13:13

7. Acts 13:46
8. Acts 13:14-51
9. Acts 14:1-6
10. Acts 14:8-18
11. Acts 14:19, 20
12. Acts 14:21-25

Chapter 17

1. Proverbs 11:1
2. Acts 14:27
3. Acts 15:1
4. Acts 15:2
5. Acts 15:4-11
6. Acts 15:13-35

Chapter 18

1. Acts 15:36
2. Acts 15:37-39
3. Acts 15:39
4. Acts 15:41
5. Acts 16:1
6. John 11:25
7. Acts 16:1
8. Acts 16:1-3
9. Acts 16:6-10
10. Acts 16:11, 12
11. Acts 16:13-15
12. Acts 16:16
13. Acts 16:17-19
14. Acts 16:19-24
15. Acts 16:25
16. Acts 16:26-34
17. Acts 16:35-40
18. Acts 17:1

19. Acts 17:1-5
20. Acts 17:4-10
21. Acts 17:10-13
22. Acts 17:14, 15

Chapter 19

1. Acts 17:17
2. Acts 17:16-21
3. Acts 17:22-34
4. Acts 18:1-4
5. Philippians 4:10-20
6. 1 Thessalonians 1:1-5:28, 2 Thessalonians 1:1-3:18
7. Acts 18:5, 6
8. Acts 18:7
9. Acts 18:12-17
10. Galatians 1:6-6:18
11. Acts 18:18-21

Chapter 20

1. Acts 18:24-26; 19:1-7
2. Acts 18:27, 28
3. Acts 19:8-10
4. 1 Corinthians 1:1-16:24
5. Acts 19:13 20
6. Acts 19:23-41
7. Acts 19:22
8. Act 19:21
9. 1 Corinthians 16:1, 2 Corinthians 9:1, Romans 15:25, 26
10. 2 Corinthians 7:8
11. 2 Corinthians 1:1-13:14
12. Romans 16:23
13. Romans 1:1-16:27

Chapter 21

1. Acts 20:2, 3, 6
2. Acts 20:7-12
3. Acts 20:13
4. Acts 20:17-38
5. Acts 21:1-3
6. Acts 21:4-14

Chapter 22

1. Acts 21:16
2. Acts 21:17-23:35

Chapter 23

1. 1 Kings 18:1-29
2. Acts 24; 25; 26

Chapter 24

1. Acts 27:3-6
2. Acts 27:7-28:1
3. Acts 28:2-10
4. Acts 28:11-15

Chapter 25

1. Acts 28:16-31
2. Philemon 1:8-20
3. Ephesians 1:1-6:24
4. Colossians 1:1-4:18
5. Philippians 1:1-4:23

Chapter 26

1. 1 Timothy 1:1-6:21
2. Titus 1:1-3:15

Notes

Chapter 27

1. 2 Timothy 1:1-4:22, Philemon 1:1-25
2. 2 Timothy 1:1-4:22
3. 1 Peter 1:1-5:14, 2 Peter 1:1-3:18

Chapter 28

1. Mark 1:1-16:20
2. Luke 1:1-24:53
3. Acts 1:1-28:31
4. Matthew 1:1-28:20
5. Hebrews 1:1-13:25
6. Deuteronomy 31:6

LaVergne, TN USA
27 August 2009
155946LV00002B/10/P

9 781414 112275